JESUS OT

The Compelling Portrait of Christ
in the Old Testament

VOLUME I

The Pentateuch
Genesis through Deuteronomy

RONNIE CARTER

WESTBOW
PRESS®
A DIVISION OF THOMAS NELSON
& ZONDERVAN

WestBow Press books may be ordered through booksellers or by contacting:

WestBow Press
A Division of Thomas Nelson & Zondervan
1663 Liberty Drive
Bloomington, IN 47403
www.westbowpress.com
844-714-3454

ISBN: 979-8-3850-3562-5 (sc)
ISBN: 979-8-3850-3563-2 (e)

Library of Congress Control Number: 2024921107

Print information available on the last page.

WestBow Press rev. date: 12/03/2024

CONTENTS

PREFACE

In reading the Bible over the years, one of my greatest pleasures in reading through the Old Testament has been discovering the many and various ways that Jesus Christ is portrayed. As far back as I can remember, I have known that there are prophecies about Christ in the Old Testament, many we hear around Christmas. One day I remember being shocked when a friend told me that there were whole chapters in the Old Testament that are about Jesus. Some of the better-known ones are Psalm 2, Psalm 22, 23, and Isaiah 53. In Psalm 2, Jesus is alternately referred to as "God's Anointed," "His King", and "His Son." Psalm 22 foretells the crucifixion from Christ's perspective on the cross! The first verse opens with "My God, my God, why hast Thou forsaken me." Later, we read that he was scorned: "He trusted on the Lord … let Him deliver Him," and "they pierced My hands and My feet," and "They part My garments among them, and cast lots upon My vesture." All these verses clearly point to the crucifixion as told in the gospels. In Isaiah 53, Jesus is spoken of as a suffering servant, and Isaiah reveals that His death is atoning—"Surely He hath borne our griefs and carried our sorrows … He was wounded for our transgressions, He was bruised for our iniquities. The chastisement of our peace was upon Him, and with His stripes we are healed … All we like sheep have gone astray; we have turned every one to his own way; and the Lord hath laid on Him the iniquity of us all."

Prophecies are the most familiar messianic references in the Old Testament. I have read books that compiled these prophecies and grouped them under specific headings. However, there are also other ways that Christ is portrayed in the Old Testament. In addition to prophecy, this book examines scriptures that utilize these other prophetic devices, such as types and shadows, dreams and visions, theophanies, Christophanies, the messianic prophetic genealogy, and the Old Testament language and culture. My personal favorite is *types*. These are persons, events, or actions in the Old Testament that depict Christ. This volume looks at passages in the Pentateuch (Genesis—Deuteronomy) that contain these various devices including prophecy. Paul writes of "Christ our Passover" in his letter to the Corinthian Church (1 Corinthians 5:7), identifying the Passover as one *type* of Christ, which will be examined in the chapter on Exodus. It has long been my belief that anyone who has not explored these OT messianic references has an incomplete picture of Christ. When we turn on a light, we see its white rays, but when we look at light through a prism, we see a rainbow of colors. The various OT depictions of Christ show us various aspects of who He is, and how magnificent He is. They give us a rainbow perspective of His various roles, including high priest, kinsman redeemer, prophet, and king. When the book of Hebrews declares Him to be our high priest, that would have little meaning without an OT understanding of the office of high priest.

My reason for writing this book is to point out these various references as evidence of God's *fingerprints* on the scriptures. The Bible was written by approximately forty authors. How can anyone look hundreds of years into the future and tell what will happen there? Yet this is exactly what the Bible does with stunning clarity! There is a unity in both testaments in the various authors' writings, with Christ being the central figure. My hope for this book is that God will be glorified, and my hope for you as a reader is that you will find a new love for reading the Old Testament and that your faith will be strengthened and that you will have an increased appreciation for the sovereignty, omniscience, and majesty of God.

SUMMARY OF FIGURES AND TABLES

PART 1
OVERVIEW OF THE BIBLE

CHAPTERS

1

THE UNIQUENESS OF THE BIBLE

ANYONE WHO HAS EVER READ AND STUDIED THE BIBLE FOR ANY LENGTH OF TIME HAS COME to realize through the internal evidence of the scriptures that it is truly a remarkable book. The study of how we came to have the Bible is also fascinating and will only serve to increase our appreciation and reverence for this special book. People have given their lives for this book throughout history, for possessing copies of it, attempting to preserve it, translating it into other languages, and taking its message to people around the world. It is a book that bears up well under the most intense scrutiny and indeed has had to throughout its existence. The Bible is truly the most unique book in the annals of human history. There is not even a close second. Among all the writings that are regarded as sacred among the various religions of the world, the Bible stands alone in so many ways. In this chapter, we will look at some of the ways that the Bible is unique.

a) **Unique in the Time Span of Its Writing:** In fulfillment of His covenant with Abraham, God called Israel through Moses to become His nation while they were in slavery in Egypt. Moses led Israel's exodus from Egypt around 1447 BC, where they then wandered in the wilderness for forty years. For a timeline of the Old Testament showing this event, see figure 1.1, Timeline of Old Testament Period, at the end of this chapter. It is commonly held that Moses is the author of the Pentateuch, the first five books of the Bible—Genesis, Exodus, Leviticus, Numbers, and Deuteronomy. The New Testament books are believed by most conservative scholars to have been completed by the end of the first century AD. Thus, the time span for the writing of the scriptures is believed to be over 1,500 years.

b) **Unique in Its Window of Divine Revelation:** Given the period of time covered in the scriptures, we can discern that the *window of divine revelation* was over 4,000 years! That is, the period of time during which God inspired and even spoke directly to the Bible's human authors and others He had called on various occasions. Perhaps this is at least a partial explanation for the timeless message of the scriptures, which appeals to people of every generation and has the remarkable ability to transform their lives!

c) **Unique in Its Historicity:** The Bible's numerous and meticulous genealogies and other time-span information make it possible to anchor the Bible to secular history. From the Bible's own time information, which overlaps secular history, we are able to determine that God created Adam, the first man, around 4000 BC, as established in the timeline noted above, which is supported by the spreadsheets in table 1.1, Creation Date, and table 1.2, Historical Dates of Biblical Lineage and Benchmark Dates, located at the end of this chapter. The geographic information contained in the early chapters of Genesis identifies the Garden of Eden, the seat of God's creation, as the area of earth known as the Fertile Crescent, also known as the cradle of civilization. Jesus's genealogy alone, recorded in the gospel of Luke, spans 4,000 years! Also, from the book of Genesis, we have the origins of several of the ancient nations and tribes, which are noted in figure 1.2, Table of Nations, located at the end of this chapter. It is also noted that the people groups descended from these genealogies established three of the world's religions: Judaism, Christianity, and Islam. From the Bible's meticulous records in the books of 1 and 2 Kings and 1 and 2 Chronicles, we have the lengths of the successive reigns of the kings of Israel and Judah that can also be tied to historical dates, as shown in table 1.4, The Kings of Israel and Judah, located at the end of this chapter. The book of Judges also recorded the lengths of the reigns of the various judges of Israel, which was the time between Joshua's leadership and the kings, as noted in table 1.3, The Judges of Israel, located at the end of this chapter. However, the time information in Judges is not as straightforward as it is in the books of Kings and Chronicles, as noted in the table.

d) **Unique in Its Circulation:** "The Bible has been read by more people and published in more languages than any other book. There have been more copies produced of its entirety and more portions and selections than any other book in history. Some will argue that in a designated month or year more of a certain book was sold. However, over all there is absolutely no book that reaches or even begins to compare to the circulation of the Scriptures. The first major book printed was the Latin Vulgate. It was printed on Gutenberg's press."[1] Missionaries risk their lives daily to bring the Bible's gospel message to remote and uncivilized parts of the world, as well as dangerous areas like the Middle East and communist countries. There are ongoing efforts to translate it into every language of the world in order to preach the gospel to every nation, as commanded by our Lord in the Great Commission (Matthew 28:18–20).

e) **Unique in the Diversity of Its Literature:** The Bible is a veritable treasure trove of various types of literature and is unparalleled in the quality of its writings. These types are outlined below.

OLD TESTAMENT

- **Pentateuch:** This unique section of scripture, as noted earlier, includes the first five books of the Bible, Genesis through Deuteronomy, and is a combination of history and law. It spans the period of time from approximately 4000 to 1400 BC and includes the creation account, the fall of man, the global flood, the origin of the Jewish nation, Israel's 400-year slavery and exodus from Egypt, the wilderness wanderings, and the receiving of God's law and provisions for tabernacle worship.

- **History:** This section includes the books of Joshua through Esther and spans a period of time from approximately 1400 to 400 BC. It includes the periods of time where Israel followed Moses's successor Joshua, the Canaan conquests, the periods of the judges and the kings, and the captivity of Judah and Israel after the kingdom split. It also includes their return to and rebuilding of Jerusalem.

- **Wisdom/Poetry:** This section includes the books of Job through Song of Solomon. These are books of deep thought, poetry, lament, and celebration. The books of Job and Ecclesiastes consider many of the hard questions of life. The Psalms express worship in all its varied emotions. The Proverbs are collections of wise sayings.

- **Prophets:** This section includes the major prophets, Isaiah to Daniel, and the minor prophets, Hosea to Malachi. The distinction of major and minor is based on the lengths of the books rather than their importance. These writings were messages of warning and comfort and were predictive of future events. The ministries of these prophets overlapped the period of the kings and the captivity, approximately 900–400 BC.

NEW TESTAMENT

The New Testament in its entirety is believed to have been written in the last half of the first century. The New Testament declares and explains the coming of Jesus Christ as Israel's promised Messiah. It reaches back to the Old Testament prophecies of Messiah and the new covenant through Him and affirms that they are fulfilled in Christ.

- **Gospels:** The four gospels, Matthew, Mark, Luke, and John were biographies of Jesus's life, which recorded His miraculous virgin birth, His teachings and claim of messiahship, His many miracles, and His atoning death, resurrection, and ascension.

- **History:** The book of Acts chronicles the birth of the early church through the ministries of the apostles in the midst of persecution as well as the birth pangs of applying the new covenant in Christ to the old culture of Judaism.

- **Epistles:** The Pauline Epistles, Romans through Philemon, were letters written by Paul, some to churches and some to pastors he had helped establish and continued to mentor. The book of Philemon is a letter to a friend urging him to receive his runaway slave Onesimus back as a Christian brother. The General Epistles, Hebrews through Jude, were letters written by James, Peter, John, and Jude. The author of Hebrews is unknown, though some attribute its authorship to Paul. These letters were extremely important to the infant church. They established theology, provided directions for Christian living, and answered specific questions of various churches, and addressed errors of understanding and conduct in these churches.

- **Prophecy:** The book of Revelation records the apostle John's vision of the end times, given to him by the risen Christ while he was exiled on the Isle of Patmos. It also gives Jesus's message to seven churches. This book is a specific category of prophecy referred to as apocalyptic and is characterized by symbolism and its subject matter, end-time events. There is also apocalyptic material in the Old Testament, particularly in the prophetic books.

f) **Unique in Its Authorship:** The credibility of the Bible is enhanced by the fact that its many authors, who were each inspired by God, lived over a 1,500-year period, in very diverse conditions, with very diverse backgrounds, yet wrote a unified message that is both compelling and transforming.

- **Multiple Authors:** The Bible was written by many human authors who were guided by one divine author. The apostle Peter, referring to the Old Testament scriptures, writes, "But know this first of all, that no prophecy of Scripture is a matter of one's own interpretation, for no prophecy was ever made by an act of human will, but men moved by the Holy Spirit spoke from God" (2 Peter 1:20–21 NASB). It is believed that the Bible was "written by 40 plus authors from every walk of life including kings, peasants, philosophers, fishermen, poets, statesmen, scholars, etc."[2] Just a casual inspection of the Bible will show that thirty authors can be identified simply from book and chapter subtitles and verses identifying authorship.

- **Diversity of the Authors' Lives:** Consider the ramifications of the diverse lives of the authors below spanning a 1,500-year period. This gives further insight into the Bible's ability to speak to people of all ages and stations in life, from the simple to the most sophisticated. The information in the following paragraphs is taken from the scriptures.

1) **Diversity of Occupations:** Many of the human authors of scripture were not men with religious backgrounds. Rather, they were fishermen, tentmakers, shepherds, fruit pickers, cupbearers, tax collectors, physicians, soldiers, government officials, and kings. What a diverse group of people! Would you not say that this covers the gamut of human experience? These authors

from all walks of life poured out their lives to express the messages that God placed on each of their hearts.

2) **Diversity of Spiritual Roles:** Also, many of these authors fulfilled invaluable roles in the accounts they wrote. They were called of God as prophets, judges, rulers, military commanders, priests, scribes, governors, kings, songwriters, choir directors, apostles, missionaries, and church leaders for a newborn faith. How fortunate we are to have a God who is so fluent in communicating with and guiding His people. His work in our hearts covers such a diversity of roles! This was no sedate group of men whose primary occupation in life was authorship. They were men empowered by God to accomplish great things for Him. Consider how God used these human authors for His divine purpose:

- *Prophets* like Isaiah, Jeremiah, and Daniel proclaimed God's message of repentance, warned of impending judgment, and spoke of deliverance through a future Messiah.

- *Judges* like Moses, Joshua, and Samuel maintained justice, law and order, and encouraged the people.

- *Rulers* like Moses and Joshua led the people of God.

- *Military commanders* like Moses, Joshua, and David led the people of God in battle to protect them from their enemies.

- *Priests* like Ezra served as mediators between God and man until the great high priest, Jesus Christ, paid the ultimate atonement and now sits at the right hand of God making intercession for us!

- *Scribes* like Ezra kept the meticulous records necessary for portions of the Bible to be written and preserved.

- *Governors* like Nehemiah governed the people of God and kept them on track to accomplish great things, like rebuilding the walls of Jerusalem.

- *Kings* like David and Solomon ruled the people of God.

- *Musicians, singers, and songwriters* like David, Moses, Deborah, and others inspired the people of God to praise and worship!

- *Apostles* like Matthew, John, Peter, and Paul, who had walked with Jesus firsthand or, in Paul's case, had met the resurrected Christ, established and encouraged the church of God.

- *Missionaries* like Luke and Paul continued to plant new churches.

- *Church leaders*, like James the half brother of Jesus, provided needed authority and direction when handling complex new issues confronting the church.

3) **Authors Were Eyewitnesses of Things They Wrote:** Many of the things written about by several of the biblical writers were witnessed firsthand by them. For example, the apostles walked with Jesus daily for three years! James[3] and Jude,[4] who wrote the epistles by the same names, are believed to be the half brothers of Jesus. The scriptures themselves testify to the gospel being seen and experienced firsthand by the writers:

Simon Peter writes in his second epistle, "For we have not followed cunningly devised fables, when we made known unto you the power and coming of our Lord Jesus Christ, but were eyewitnesses of his majesty" (2 Peter 1:16).

Paul, in his defense before King Agrippa, told him, "Whereupon as I went to Damascus with authority and commission from the chief priests, At midday, O king, I saw in the way a light from heaven, above the brightness of the sun, shining round about me and them which journeyed with me. And when we were all fallen to the earth, I heard a voice speaking unto me, and saying in the Hebrew tongue, Saul, Saul, why persecutest thou me? *it is* hard for thee to kick against the pricks. And I said, Who art thou, Lord? And he said, I am Jesus whom thou persecutest. But rise, and stand upon thy feet: for I have appeared unto thee for this purpose, to make thee a minister and a witness both of these things which thou hast seen, and of those things in the which I will appear unto thee … for the king knoweth of these things, before whom also I speak freely: for I am persuaded that none of these things are hidden from him; for this thing was not done in a corner" (Acts 26:12–16, 26:26).

John wrote, "That which was from the beginning, which we have heard, which we have seen with our eyes, which we have looked upon, and our hands have handled, of the Word of life; (for the life was manifested, and we have seen *it*, and bear witness, and shew unto you that eternal life, which was with the Father, and was manifested unto us;) that which we have seen and heard declare we unto you, that ye also may have fellowship with us: and truly our fellowship *is* with the Father, and with his Son Jesus Christ" (1 John 1:1–3). He further wrote, "And the Word [Jesus] was made flesh, and dwelt among us, (and we beheld his glory, the glory as of the only begotten of the Father,) full of grace and truth" (John 1:14).

The Old Testament was also written by those who saw and experienced firsthand what God was doing among His people. *Moses* not only recorded the direct revelations he received from God like the Ten Commandments and instructions for the tabernacle, but he also chronicled events like the mysterious unconsumed burning bush whereby God called him, the experiences of the wilderness wanderings and the grumblings of the children of Israel, various miracles, etc. These are just a few of many examples that could be cited. These eyewitness accounts make the Bible read like a story, which makes it so interesting and intriguing to read.

4) **Written Under Diverse Conditions:** Moses wrote during his wilderness wanderings. Joshua probably wrote between military campaigns. Nehemiah may have written as he was leading the rebuilding of the Jerusalem wall, possibly in the midst of having to fend off enemies. Solomon most likely wrote from a king's palace. David wrote both on the run as a fugitive from Saul, and at rest as king of Israel. Jeremiah wrote as a Hebrew citizen in Jerusalem as Judah and Jerusalem were racing toward judgment, and later as a lamenting captive. Luke likely wrote the book of Acts during his missionary travels with Paul. Paul wrote both during his missionary journeys and within prison walls. John likely wrote the Revelation during his exile on the isle of Patmos as he saw the revelatory vision.

g) **Miracles and Signs:** Another incredible aspect of the Bible is the extraordinary number of miracles recorded by those who saw them firsthand. The fact that many of these miracles like the *Passover* and the *manna* in the wilderness are *foreshadows* of Christ further enhances their credibility and intrigue, which will be the subject matter in parts 2 and 3 of this book. John in his gospel referred to some of Jesus's miracles as signs, that is, miracles attesting to the fact that He was God's Son and the promised Messiah. Among Jesus's many miracles, the disciples saw Him change water into wine, feed multitudes with a sack lunch, walk on water, calm a stormy sea, transfigure into a bright radiant glory, raise people from the dead, and finally, they saw Him after He arose from the dead on the third day, and they saw Him ascend into the sky.

h) **Unique in Its Scope:** The scope and detail of the Bible are unparalleled. First, in scope the Bible reaches back to the creation of the universe and the first people on earth, Adam and Eve. In fact, the Bible reaches back even *before* creation, to the foreordained redemptive plan of God. Note the following words in Jesus's high-priestly prayer, "Father, I will that they also, whom thou hast given me, be with me where I am; that they may behold my glory, which thou hast given me: *for thou lovedst me before the foundation of the world*" (John 17:24, emphasis added). Also note Paul's words in his letter to the Ephesians, "According as *he hath chosen us in him before the foundation of the world*, that we should be holy and without blame before him in love" (Ephesians

1:4), and note Peter's words in his first epistle, "*Who verily was foreordained before the foundation of the world*, but was manifest in these last times for you …" (1 Peter 1:20).

The Bible defines the problem of mankind, which is his rebellion against God, and then gives the solution, Christ the Savior as the atoning mediator between God and man.

Then the Bible reaches forward to tell us of the end times and the final resolution of all of history. This includes detailed information on the final period of history, the Great Tribulation prophesied in both the Old and New Testament, the rapture of the saints and the second coming of Christ, God's final judgment of the unsaved, the destruction and recreation of the earth, Christ's millennial reign on earth, Satan's final rebellion and banishment to the lake of fire, and God's eternal reign in heaven on His recreated earth. It is worth noting that there is some debate as to the order of these events, and it is not the purpose of this author to discuss the various views. The Bible even gives signs that can be observed that will enable those alive at that time to recognize the approach of Christ's second coming. Below are scriptures on these events:

- **The Great Tribulation Period:** "For then shall be great tribulation, such as was not since the beginning of the world to this time, no, nor ever shall be. And except those days should be shortened, there should no flesh be saved: but for the elect's sake those days shall be shortened. Then if any man shall say unto you, Lo, here *is* Christ, or there; believe *it* not. For there shall arise false Christs, and false prophets, and shall shew great signs and wonders; insomuch that, if *it were* possible, they shall deceive the very elect. Behold, I have told you before. Wherefore if they shall say unto you, Behold, he is in the desert; go not forth: behold, *he is* in the secret chambers; believe *it* not. For as the lightning cometh out of the east, and shineth even unto the west; so shall also the coming of the Son of man be" (Matthew 24:21–27).

- **The Rapture:** "For the Lord himself shall descend from heaven with a shout, with the voice of the archangel, and with the trump of God: and the dead in Christ shall rise first: *Then we which are alive and remain shall be caught up together with them in the clouds, to meet the Lord in the air:* and so shall we ever be with the Lord" (1 Thessalonians 4:16–17).

- **The Second Coming of Christ:** "And then shall appear *the sign of the Son of man in heaven:* and then shall all the tribes of the earth mourn, and *they shall see the Son of man coming in the clouds of heaven with power and great glory.* And he shall send his angels with a great sound of a trumpet, and *they shall gather together his elect from the four winds,* from one end of heaven to the other" (Matthew 24:30–31).

- **The Destruction and Remaking of Earth:** "But the day of the Lord will come as a thief in the night; in the which *the heavens shall pass away with a great noise, and the elements shall melt with fervent heat, the earth also and the works that are therein shall be burned up.* Seeing then that all these things shall be dissolved, what manner of persons ought ye to be in all holy conversation and godliness, Looking for and hasting unto *the coming of the day of God, wherein the heavens being on fire shall be dissolved, and the elements shall melt with fervent heat?* Nevertheless we, according to his promise, *look for new heavens and a new earth, wherein dwelleth righteousness*" (2 Peter 3:10–13).

- **The Millennial Reign of Christ:** "And he *laid hold on the dragon,* that old serpent, which is the *Devil,* and *Satan,* and *bound him a thousand years,* And cast him into the bottomless pit, and shut him up, and set a seal upon him, that he should deceive the nations no more, till the thousand years should be fulfilled: and after that he must be loosed a little season. And I saw thrones, and they sat upon them, and judgment was given unto them: and *I saw the souls of them that were beheaded for the witness of Jesus, and for the word of God, and which had not worshipped the beast, neither his image, neither had received his mark upon their foreheads, or in their hands; and they lived and reigned with Christ a thousand years*" (Revelation 20:2–4).

- **Satan's Final Rebellion and Banishment:** "And when the thousand years are expired, *Satan shall be loosed out of his prison, And shall go out to deceive the nations* which are in the four quarters of the earth, Gog and Magog, to gather them together to battle: the number of whom *is* as the sand of the sea. And they went up on the breadth of the earth, and compassed the camp of the saints about, and the beloved city: and fire came down from God out of heaven, and devoured them. And *the devil that deceived them was cast into the lake of fire and brimstone, where the beast and the false prophet are, and shall be tormented day and night for ever and ever*" (Revelation 20:7–10).

- **God's Final Judgment of the Unsaved:** "And I saw a great white throne, and him that sat on it, from whose face the earth and the heaven fled away; and there was found no place for them. And I saw the dead, small and great, stand before God; and the books were opened: and another book was opened, which is *the book* of life: and the dead were judged out of those things which were written in the books, according to their works. And the sea gave up the dead which were in it; and death and hell delivered up the dead which were in them: and they were judged every man according to their works. And death and hell were cast into the lake of fire. This is the second death. And whosoever was not found written in the book of life was cast into the lake of fire" (Revelation 20:11–15).

- **God's Eternal Reign in Heaven on the Newly Created Earth:** "And *I saw a new heaven and a new earth: for the first heaven and the first earth were passed away; and there was no more sea. And I John saw the holy city, new Jerusalem, coming down from God out of heaven*, prepared as a bride adorned for her husband. And I heard a great voice out of heaven saying, *Behold, the tabernacle of God is with men, and he will dwell with them, and they shall be his people, and God himself shall be with them*, and be their God. And *God shall wipe away all tears from their eyes; and there shall be no more death, neither sorrow, nor crying, neither shall there be any more pain: for the former things are passed away.* And he that sat upon the throne said, Behold, *I make all things new …*" (Revelation 21:1–5).

i) **Unique in Its Power to Transform Lives:** The Bible is a very powerful book! This is attested to by the Bible itself and by millions of believers all over the world who have had their lives radically changed by believing its message and trusting in its proclaimed Savior.

- "Blessed is the man that walketh not in the counsel of the ungodly, nor standeth in the way of sinners, nor sitteth in the seat of the scornful. But *his delight is in the law of the LORD; and in his law doth he meditate day and night. And he shall be like a tree planted by the rivers of water, that bringeth forth his fruit in his season; his leaf also shall not wither; and whatsoever he doeth shall prosper*" (Psalm 1:1–3, italics added).

- "So shall my word be that goeth forth out of my mouth: it shall not return unto me void, but it shall accomplish that which I please, and it shall prosper *in the thing* whereto I sent it" (Isaiah 55:11).

- "For the word of God *is* quick, and powerful, and sharper than any two-edged sword, piercing even to the dividing asunder of soul and spirit, and of the joints and marrow, and *is* a discerner of the thoughts and intents of the heart" (Hebrews 4:12).

- "For I am not ashamed of the gospel of Christ: for it is the power of God unto salvation to everyone that believeth; to the Jew first, and also to the Greek" (Romans 1:16)

- "*All scripture is given by inspiration of God, and is profitable* for doctrine, for reproof, for correction, for instruction in righteousness: *That the man of God may be perfect, thoroughly furnished unto all good works*" (2 Timothy 3:16–17, italics added).

j) **Unique in Its Prophecy and Fulfillment:** One of the most amazing attributes of the Bible is its recording of the historical fulfillment of many of its Old Testament prophecies in the life of Jesus Christ. Since this is the subject of parts 2 and 3 of this book, it will not be elaborated on here, except to say that the Bible stands alone of all the religions of the world in that it contains both the Old Testament predictions of the Messiah and the New Testament fulfillment of many of these same predictions hundreds of years later. It is noted that some of the Old Testament predictions about Christ are yet to be fulfilled.

k) **Unique in the Volume of Its Reference Works and Quotations by Others:** There is no book that is more often quoted, or for which more study materials and other books have been written. Consider Strong's exhaustive concordance, which lists *every* word that appears in the Bible in alphabetical order, and then lists *every place* the word occurs in the Bible. There are volumes and volumes of commentaries on the Bible, study Bibles, books containing Bible maps, charts, tables, and timelines, books about the Bible and archaeology, Bible dictionaries and lexicons, and books written about the Bible's principles, teachings, characters, and a plethora of other subjects. Cleland B. McAfee writes in *The Greatest English Classic*: "If every Bible in any considerable city were destroyed, the Book could be restored in all its essential parts from the quotations on the shelves of the city public library. There are works, covering almost all the great literary writers, devoted especially to showing how much the Bible has influenced them."[5]

IN CONCLUSION

After reading about this wonderful, unique, and compelling book, can you justify not applying yourself to reading it from beginning to end? It has a personal message to you from God. God is calling you to be in relationship with Him. This can be seen in Jesus's illustration about the Good Shepherd and the sheep in John 10, and in His high priestly prayer in John 17. If you've never applied yourself to reading the Bible, it can seem to be a daunting task, given the sheer volume of it. table 1.5, Do You Have a Plan to Read God's Word, located at the end of this chapter is a listing of Bible books and chapters and a spreadsheet that shows various plans for reading through the Bible. The table shows various numbers of chapters to be read daily and weekly with the corresponding time it would take to read either the New Testament alone or the entire Bible. This author recommends that you commit to the latter, but only after completing the New Testament first.

Summary of Figures and Tables		No. of Pages
Figure 1.1	**Timeline of Old Testament Period**	1
Figure 1.2	**Table of Nations**	1
Table 1.1	**Creation Date**	1
Table 1.2	**Historical Dates of Biblical Lineage and Benchmark Events**	1
Table 1.3	**The Judges of Israel**	1
Table 1.4	**The Kings of Israel and Judah**	2
Table 1.5	**Read through the Bible** (spreadsheet)	1
		————
		8

Timeline of Old Testament Period

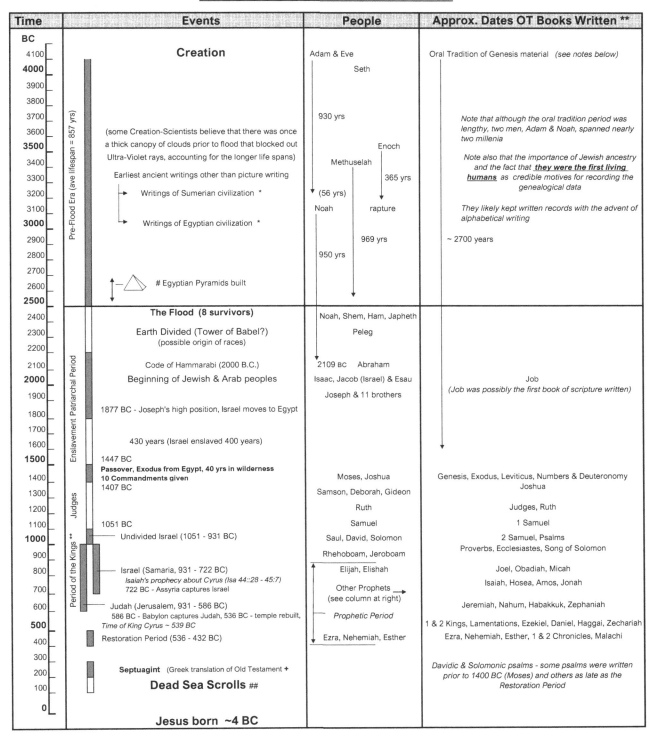

Time	Events	People	Approx. Dates OT Books Written **
BC			
4100	**Creation**	Adam & Eve	Oral Tradition of Genesis material *(see notes below)*
4000		Seth	
3900			
3800			
3700		930 yrs	*Note that although the oral tradition period was lengthy, two men, Adam & Noah, spanned nearly two millenia*
3600	(some Creation-Scientists believe that there was once		
3500	a thick canopy of clouds prior to flood that blocked out	Enoch	
3400	Ultra-Violet rays, accounting for the longer life spans)	Methuselah	*Note also that the importance of Jewish ancestry and the fact that **they were the first living humans** as credible motives for recording the genealogical data*
3300	Earliest ancient writings other than picture writing	365 yrs	
3200	Writings of Sumerian civilization *	(56 yrs)	
3100		Noah rapture	*They likely kept written records with the advent of alphabetical writing*
3000	Writings of Egyptian civilization *		
2900		969 yrs	~ 2700 years
2800		950 yrs	
2700			
2600	# Egyptian Pyramids built		
2500			
2400	**The Flood (8 survivors)**	Noah, Shem, Ham, Japheth	
2300	Earth Divided (Tower of Babel?)	Peleg	
2200	(possible origin of races)		
2100	Code of Hammarabi (2000 B.C.)	2109 BC Abraham	
2000	Beginning of Jewish & Arab peoples	Isaac, Jacob (Israel) & Esau	Job
1900		Joseph & 11 brothers	*(Job was possibly the first book of scripture written)*
1800	1877 BC - Joseph's high position, Israel moves to Egypt		
1700			
1600	430 years (Israel enslaved 400 years)		
1500	1447 BC		
1400	**Passover, Exodus from Egypt, 40 yrs in wilderness** **10 Commandments given** 1407 BC	Moses, Joshua	Genesis, Exodus, Leviticus, Numbers & Deuteronomy Joshua
1300		Samson, Deborah, Gideon	
1200		Ruth	Judges, Ruth
1100	1051 BC	Samuel	1 Samuel
1000	Undivided Israel (1051 - 931 BC)	Saul, David, Solomon	2 Samuel, Psalms
900		Rhehoboam, Jeroboam	Proverbs, Ecclesiastes, Song of Solomon
800	Israel (Samaria, 931 - 722 BC)	Elijah, Elishah	Joel, Obadiah, Micah
700	*Isaiah's prophecy about Cyrus (Isa 44::28 - 45:7)* 722 BC - Assyria captures Israel	Other Prophets (see column at right)	Isaiah, Hosea, Amos, Jonah
600	Judah (Jerusalem, 931 - 586 BC)		Jeremiah, Nahum, Habakkuk, Zephaniah
500	586 BC - Babylon captures Judah, 536 BC - temple rebuilt, *Time of King Cyrus ~ 539 BC*	*Prophetic Period*	1 & 2 Kings, Lamentations, Ezekiel, Daniel, Haggai, Zechariah
400	Restoration Period (536 - 432 BC)	Ezra, Nehemiah, Esther	Ezra, Nehemiah, Esther, 1 & 2 Chronicles, Malachi
300			
200	**Septuagint** (Greek translation of Old Testament +		*Davidic & Solomonic psalms - some psalms were written prior to 1400 BC (Moses) and others as late as the Restoration Period*
100	**Dead Sea Scrolls** ##		
0			
	Jesus born ~4 BC		

Side labels (left column): Pre-Flood Era (ave lifespan = 857 yrs); Enslavement Patriarchal Period; Judges; Period of the Kings **

* dates obtained from www.worldhistory.org/timeline/writing/
** Approximate dates of Old Testament Books & the period of the Kings taken from "The Bible Knowledge Commentary" by Walvoord & Zuck
+ date of Septuagint translation (285 - 247 BC) taken from en.wikipedia.org/wiki/Septuagint
# approximate date obtained from www.history.com/topics/ancient-egypt/the-egyptian-pyramids
approximate date of Dead Sea Scrolls obtained from en.wikipedia.org/wiki/Dead_Sea_Scrolls

Figure 1.1

13

Table of Nations

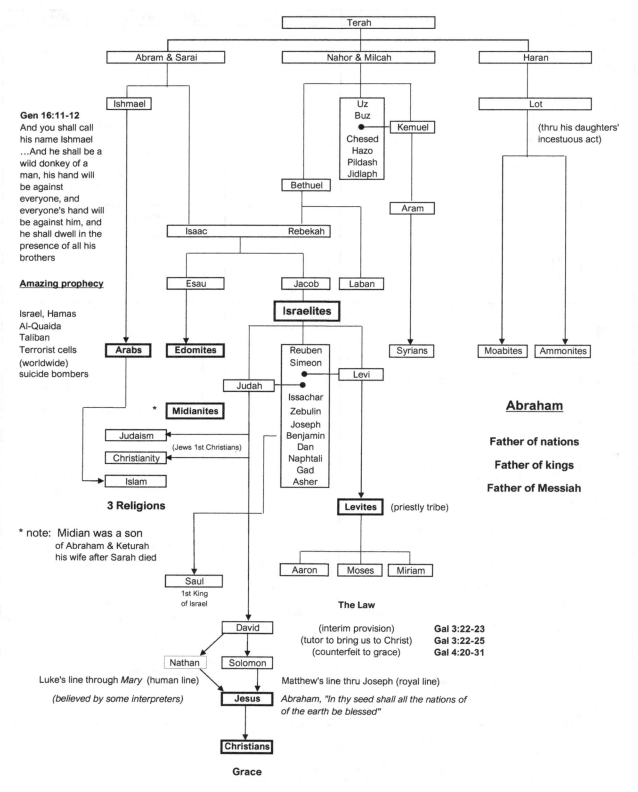

Gen 16:11-12
And you shall call his name Ishmael …And he shall be a wild donkey of a man, his hand will be against everyone, and everyone's hand will be against him, and he shall dwell in the presence of all his brothers

Amazing prophecy

Israel, Hamas
Al-Quaida
Taliban
Terrorist cells
(worldwide)
suicide bombers

3 Religions

* note: Midian was a son
of Abraham & Keturah
his wife after Sarah died

Terah

Abram & Sarai | Nahor & Milcah | Haran

Ishmael

Uz
Buz
●
Chesed
Hazo
Pildash
Jidlaph

Kemuel

Lot

(thru his daughters' incestuous act)

Bethuel

Aram

Isaac — Rebekah

Esau | Jacob | Laban

Israelites

Syrians

Moabites | Ammonites

Arabs | **Edomites** | Reuben
Simeon
● Levi
Issachar
Zebulin
Joseph
Benjamin
Dan
Naphtali
Gad
Asher

Judah

* **Midianites**

Judaism
(Jews 1st Christians)
Christianity
Islam

Abraham

Father of nations

Father of kings

Father of Messiah

Levites (priestly tribe)

Aaron | Moses | Miriam

The Law

Saul
1st King
of Israel

David

Nathan | Solomon

(interim provision)　**Gal 3:22-23**
(tutor to bring us to Christ)　**Gal 3:22-25**
(counterfeit to grace)　**Gal 4:20-31**

Luke's line through *Mary* (human line)

(believed by some interpreters)

Matthew's line thru Joseph (royal line)

Jesus　*Abraham, "In thy seed shall all the nations of of the earth be blessed"*

Christians

Grace

Figure 1.2

Creation Date

Spreadsheet Computing the Approximate Historical Date of Creation Based on the Bible

Scripture Reference	Person Event	Son	Years Lived				Historical Date	
			Before Son	Subtotals	After Son	Total		
Gen 5:	**Creation**		0				**4115**	BC
3	**Adam**	Seth	130		800	930	3985	BC
6	Seth	Enos	105		807	912	3880	BC
9	Enos	Cainan	90		815	905	3790	BC
12	Cainan	Mahalaleel	70		840	910	3720	BC
15	Mahalaleel	Jared	65	1558	830	895	3655	BC
18	Jared	Enoch	162		800	962	3493	BC
21	**Enoch**	Methuselah	65		300	365	3428	BC
25	**Methuselah**	Lamech	187		782	969	3241	BC
28	Lamech	Noah	182		595	777	3059	BC
32 *	**Noah**	Shem	502		448	950	2557	BC

* 7:11, 11:10 (consider for possibly more accurate age)   Ave = 857

prior to flood

Gen 7:6	Flood begins	Noah 600 yrs old			Noah & fmly board ark		2459	BC
Gen 8:13	Flood ends	Noah 601 yrs old			departure from ark		2458	BC

Gen 11:								
10	Shem	Arphaxad	100		500	600	2457	BC
12	Arphaxad	Salah	35		403	438	2422	BC
14	Salah	Eber	30		403	433	2392	BC
16	Eber	Peleg	34		430	464	2358	BC
18	**Peleg**	Reu	30	390	209	239	2328	BC
20	Reu	Serug	32		207	239	2296	BC
22	Serug	Nahor	30		200	230	2266	BC
24	Nahor	Terah	29		119	148	2237	BC
26	Terah	Abram (Abraham)	70		135	205	2167	BC

Gen 21:5	**Abraham**	Isaac	100		75	175	2067	BC
Gen 25:26	**Isaac**	Jacob (Israel), Esau	60	290	120	180	2007	BC
Gen 47:28	**Jacob** moves to Egypt	Jacob & 12 sons (12 tribes of Israel)	130			147 / 130	1877	BC
Gen 50:22	**Joseph**		Genealogies			110		
			Time Spans					
Ex 12:40	**The Exodus**	Israelites leave Egypt	430	910			1447	BC
1 Kings 6:1	**Solomon** *	(4th yr of his reign)	480				967	BC

			3148			**Anchor Date**	**967**	BC
			Total Years					

* Note: His reign 971 - 931 BC, dates from "The Bible Knowledge Commentary" by Walvoord & Zuck

(There are some conservative Bible Scholars who believe that creation is older than this)

Table 1.1

Historical Dates of Biblical Lineage & Benchmark Events

Scripture Reference	Event	Person	Dates BC	Son	Years Lived — Before Son	After Son	Total	Historical Dates BC — Birth	Son's Birth	Death
Gen 5:										
3	Creation	**Adam**	4115	Seth	130	800	930	**4115**	3985	**3185**
6		Seth		Enos	105	807	912	**3985**	3880	**3073**
9		Enos		Cainan	90	815	905	**3880**	3790	**2975**
12		Cainan		Mahalaleel	70	840	910	**3790**	3720	**2880**
15		Mahalaleel		Jared	65	830	895	**3720**	3655	**2825**
18		Jared		Enoch	162	800	962	**3655**	3493	**2693**
21	Enoch raptured	**Enoch**	3128	Methuselah	65	300	365	**3493**	3428	**3128**
25	Methuselah, the oldest man (969), died (presumably before flood)	**Methuselah**	2459	Lamech	187	782	969	**3428**	3241	**2459**
28		Lamech		Noah	182	595	777	**3241**	3059	**2464**
Gen 11:10		Noah		Shem, Ham, Japheth	502	448	950	**3059**	2557	**2109**
Gen 7:6	Noah & family board ark, flood begins	Noah's age	2459		600		Ave = 857 (prior to flood)			
Gen 8:13	Water subsides, Noah & family leave ark (8 survivors)	Noah's age	2458		601					
Gen 11:										
10		Shem		Arphaxad	100	500	600	**2557**	2457	**1957**
12		Arphaxad		Salah	35	403	438	**2457**	2422	**2019**
14		Salah		Eber	30	403	433	**2422**	2392	**1989**
16		Eber		Peleg	34	430	464	**2392**	2358	**1928**
18	Earth divided (Tower of Babel, origin of races)	Peleg	2358 - 2119	Reu	30	209	239	**2358**	2328	**2119**
20		Reu		Serug	32	207	239	**2328**	2296	**2089**
22		Serug		Nahor	30	200	230	**2296**	2266	**2066**
24		Nahor		Terah	29	119	148	**2266**	2237	**2118**
26	Prophecy of 400-yr Egyptian slavery	Terah		Abram (Abraham)	70	135	205	**2237**	2167	**2032**
Gen 21:5	Birth of Arab & Jewish Nations (Isaac's birth, after Ishmael)	**Abraham**	2067	(Ishmael), Isaac	100	75	175	**2167**	2067	**1992**
Gen 25:26		**Isaac**		Jacob (Israel), Esau	60	120	180	**2067**	2007	**1887**
Gen 47:28	Jacob's 12 sons, the 12 tribes of Israel	**Jacob** age @ move	1877		130		147	**2007**		**1860**
Gen 47:1,9	Jacob & family join Joseph in Egypt							**1877**		
Gen 50:22		**Joseph**					110			
Ex 12:40	Exodus from Egypt	**Moses**	1447		430			**1447**		
1 Kings 6:1	Solomon's reign, 971 - 931 BC *; began temple 4th year (4th yr of his reign - 967 BC)	**Solomon**			480			**967**		
			967	**Anchor Date**	**Total Years**		**3148**			

Note: last 3 no's in column not birth dates

* Note: Dates of Solomon's reign obtained from "The Bible Knowledge Commentary" by Walvoord & Zuck

Table 1.2

16

The Judges of Israel

Judge	Scripture	Time Period (Years)	Noted for
Othniel	3:9-11	8	Israel enslaved to Cushan-Risathaim, King of Mesopotamia
	3:9-14	40	Driving out King of Mesopotamia
		18	Israel enslaved to Eglon, Moabite King
Ehud	3:15 - 4:1	80	"Lefty let Fatty have it" (Ehud stabbed Eglon in his chamber)
	4:2-3	20	Israel enslaved to Jabin, King of Canaan
Deborah	4:4 - 5:31	40	She & Barak Defeated Jabin & Sisera (King & Commander of Canaanite army)
	6:1-10	7	Israel enslaved to Midianites
Gideon	6:11 - 8:35	40	Sign of golden fleece, defeated Midianite army with 300 men
Abimelech	9:1-57	3	Slew 70 sons of Gideon to become King
Tola	10:1-2	23	Nothing notable
Jair	10:3-5	22	Nothing notable, his 30 sons rode 30 donkeys, ruling 30 cities
	10:6-18	18	Israel oppressed by Philistines & Ammonites
Jepthah	11:1 - 12:7	6	Destroyed altar of Baal, defeated Ammonites, vow, daughter sacrificed
Ibzan	12:8-10	7	Had 30 sons, 30 daughters, got foreigners to wed them, foreign gods
Elon	12:11-12	10	Nothing notable
Abdon	12:13-15	8	Had 40 sons, 30 grandsons who rode 70 donkeys
	13:1	40	Israel enslaved to Philistines
Samson	13:2 - 16:31	20	Strongest man in history, deceived by Delilah, killed 3000 at his death
	17:1 - 21:25	?	Story of Micah, the Levite's concubine, Benjamin wiped out except for 600 men

Total Period of Time (Years)

410

Table 1.3

Given that Israel entered the promised land around 1407 BC at the end of the 40-year wilderness wandering, and given that Saul's reign as king began around 1051 BC, the period of the Judges would have begun sometime after 1407 BC and ended sometime before 1051 BC. These two dates yield a time span of 356 years, and most likelly the period of the Judges did not begin until after Joshua's death, perhaps in the mid 13th century BC. Accordingly, the period of the judges could have been as short as 300 years. Some expositors think that the judgeships may have been regional and may have overlapped which would account for the shorter period.

The Kings of Israel & Judah

Kings (Judah)	Kings (Israel)	Son of	Began reign in ___ of ___'s Reign	Began Reign @ Age	Ended Reign @ Age	Length of Reign	Began Reign Year BC	Ended Reign Year BC	Good or Evil	Noted for...	Scripture Reference
Undivided Israel (Jerusalem)											
Saul		Kish	first king	40	80	40	1051	1011	Weak	First King	1 Sam 10 - 24
David		Jessie	year of Saul's death	30	70	40	1011	971	Good	Best King, Type of Christ, Standard by which all other kings judged	2 Sam 1 - 1 K 2:12
Solomon		David	year of David's death	?	?	40	971	931	Good	Wisest & Wealthiest King, Built Temple (5)	1 K 1 - 11
Divided Kingdom											
Judah (Jerusalem)	**Israel (Samaria)**										
Rehoboam		Solomon	year of Solomon's death	41	58	17	931	913	Evil	Caused Division of Judah & Israel	1 K 12:1 - 14:31
	Jeroboam	Nebat	year of Solomon's death			22	931	910	Evil	Built Golden Calf Altars @ Bethel & Dan	1 K 12:25 - 14:20
Abijah		Rhehoboam	18th of Jeroboam			3	913	911	Evil		1 K 15:1-8
Asa		Abijah	20th of Jeroboam			41	911	870	Good	Godly King	1 K 15:9-24
	Nadab	Jeroboam	2nd of Asa			2	910	909	Evil		1 K 15:25-28
	Baasha	Ahijah	3rd of Asa			24	909	886	Evil		1 K 15:29 - 1 K16:6
	Elah	Baasha	26th of Asa			2	886	885	Evil		1 K 16:8 - 9
	Zimri	?	27th of Asa			7 days	885	885	Evil	Killed Elah & rest of Baasha's household	1 K 16:11 - 20
	Omri	?	31st of Asa			12	885	874	Evil	6-yr reigns, Tirzah & established Samaria	1 K 16:21 - 28
	Ahab	Omri	38th of Asa			22	874	853	Evil	Most Wicked King, Married Jezebel	1 K 16:29 - 22:40
Jehoshaphat		Asa	4th of Ahab	35	60	25	873	848	Good	Godly King	1 K 22:41 - 50
	Ahaziah	Ahab	17th of Jehoshophat			2	853	852	Evil		1 K 22:40 - 2 K 2:18
Jehoram		Jehoshaphat	5th of Joram (Jehoram)	32	40	8	848	841	Evil	Married Ahab's daughter	2 K 8:16 - 24
	Joram (Jehoram)	Ahab	18th of Jehoshophat			12	853	841	Evil	Killed by Jehu, fulfilling Elijah's prophecy	2 K 3:1 - 9:29
Ahaziah		Jehoram	12th of Joram (Jehoram)	22	23	1	841	841	Evil	Son-in-law of Ahab	2 K 8:25 - 27, 9:29
	Jehu	Jehoshaphat 2				28	841	814	Evil	Carried out God's judgment on Ahab's seed	2 K 9:2 - 10:36
	Jehoahaz	Jehu	23rd of Jehoash (Judah)			17	814	798	Evil		2 K 10:35 - 13:1
Athalia (Queen)		Omri				6	841	835	Evil	Usurped throne, killed royal seed, but Joash	2 K 11:1 - 20
Jehoash (Joash)		Ahaziah	7th of Jehu	7	47	40	835	796	Good	Repaired the temple, stoned Jehoiada's son	2 K 11:21 - 12:21
	Joash (Jehoash)	Jehoahaz	37th of Jehoash (Judah)			16	798	782	Evil	Wept for Elisha, only struck arrows 3 times	2 K 13:9 - 25
Amaziah		Joash (Judah)	2nd of Joash (Israel)	25	54	29	796	767	Good		2 K 14:1 - 18
Azariah (Uzziah)		Amaziah	27th of Jeroboam II	16	68	52	790	739	Good	Good king, became proud, struck w/ leprosy	2 K 14:21 - 15:7

The Kings of Israel & Judah

Kings (Judah)	Kings (Israel)	Son of	Began reign in ___ yr of ___'s Reign	Began Reign @ Age	Ended Reign @ Age	Length of Reign	Began Reign Year BC	Ended Reign Year BC	Good or Evil	Noted for...	Scripture Reference
	Jeroboam II	Joash (Israel)	15th of Amaziah			41	793	753	Evil		2 K 14:23 - 29
	Zechariah	Jeroboam II	38th of Azariah (Uzziah)			6 mo's	753	752	Evil	4th descendant of Jehu	2 K 15:8 - 12
	Shallum	Jabesh	39th of Azariah (Uzziah)			1 mo	752	752	Evil	Slew Zecharia	2 K 15:13 - 14
	Menahem	Gadi	39th of Azariah (Uzziah)			10	752	742	Evil	Slew Shallum	2 K 15:14 - 23
	Pekahiah	Menahem	50th of Azariah (Uzziah)			2	742	740	Evil		2 K 15:23 - 25
	Pekah	Remaliah	52nd of Azariah (Uzziah)			20	752	732	Evil	Slew Pekahiah	2 K 15:25 - 31
Jotham		Uzziah	2nd of Pekah	25	41	16	750	735	**Good**	Built the upper gate of the temple	2 K 15:32 - 38
	Hoshea	Elah	20th of Jotham		36	9	732	**722**	Evil	Slew Peka, last king, fell to Assyria	2 K 15:30 - 17:6
Ahaz		Jotham	17th of Pekah	20	36	16	732	715	Evil	Made sons pass thru fire, heathen altar	2 K 16:1 - 20
Hezekiah		Ahaz	3rd of Hoshea	25	54	29	715	686	**Good**	delivered from Assyria, Passover, given 15 more yr	2 K 16:20 - 20:21
Manasseh		Hezekiah	co-reigned w/ Hezekiah	12	67	55	697	642	Evil	Rebuilt altars, made sons pass thru fire	2 K 21:1 - 18
Amon		Manasseh		22	24	2	642	640	Evil		2 K 21:19 - 23
Josiah		Amon		8	39	31	640	609	**Good**	Read Law to people, kept Passover	2 K 22:1 - 23:29
Jehoahaz		Josiah		23	23	3 mo's	609	609	Evil	Captured by Pharaoh Neco	2 K 23:30 - 34
Eliakim (Jehoiakim)		Josiah		25	36	11	609	598	Evil	Surrendered to king of Babylon	2 K 23:34 - 24:6
Jehoiachin		Jehoiakim		18	18	3 mo's	598	597	Evil	Reigned under Babylon	2 K 24:6 - 17
Mattaniah (Zedekiah)		Josiah		21	32	11	597	**586**	Evil		2 K 24:17 - 25:7

722 BC → Israel lost its national identity, and were assimilated into the other nations

586 BC
Babylonian Captivity
Babylon fell to Medo-Persia
(70 years)

Prophecies Foretelling Kings

Gen 17:6, 35:11, Deut 17:14-20, 28:36

Israel Requests a King

Judg 9:6, 1 Sam 8

Notes: 1. Messianic line shown in bold font
2. Not a single Israelite King was good (divided Israel)
3. Dates taken from "The Bible Knowledge Commentary" by Walvoord & Zuck [6]
4. Solomon began to build temple 480 yrs after the exodus (1 K 6:1), his 4th yr

Divided Kingdom Among the 12 Tribes of Israel

Judah (Southern Kingdom) (3 tribes) →	Israel (Northern Kingdom) (9 tribes) ←
Judah	Ephraim (tribe of Joseph)
Benjamin	1/2 tribe of Manasseh (tribe of Joseph)
Levi (priestly tribe, no inheritance)	1/2 tribe of Manasseh (tribe of Joseph) → Lived beyond Jordan River
	Reuben Gad
	Simeon Naphtali
	Zebulun Issachar
	Dan Asher

2 Chro 11:14

Table 1.4

19

Do You Have a Plan to Read God's Word?

O.T. Books	Chapters		N.T. Books	Chapters
1 Genesis	50		1 Matthew	28
2 Exodus	40		2 Mark	16
3 Leviticus	27		3 Luke	24
4 Numbers	36		4 John	21
5 Deuteronomy	34		5 Acts	28
6 Joshua	24		6 Romans	16
7 Judges	21		7 I Corinthians	16
8 Ruth	4		8 II Corinthians	13
9 I Samuel	31		9 Galations	6
10 II Samuel	24		10 Ephesians	6
11 I Kings	22		11 Philippians	4
12 II Kings	25		12 Colossians	4
13 I Chronicles	29		13 I Thessalonians	5
14 II Chronicles	36		14 II Thessalonians	3
15 Ezra	10		15 I Timothy	6
16 Nehemiah	13		16 II Timothy	4
17 Esther	10		17 Titus	3
18 Job	42		18 Philemon	1
19 Psalms	150		19 Hebrews	13
20 Proverbs	31		20 James	5
21 Ecclesiastes	12		21 I Peter	5
22 Song of Solomon	8		22 II Peter	3
23 Isaiah	66		23 I John	5
24 Jeremiah	52		24 II John	1
25 Lamentations	5		25 III John	1
26 Ezekiel	48		26 Jude	1
27 Daniel	12		27 Revelation	22
28 Hosea	14			**260**
29 Joel	3			
30 Amos	9			
31 Obadiah	1		Number of books =	66
32 Jonah	4		Number of chapters =	1189
33 Micah	7			
34 Nahum	3		% O.T. = 929/1189 =	78.1%
35 Habakkuk	3		% N.T. = 260/1189 =	21.9%
36 Zephaniah	3			
37 Haggai	2		Approximate Reading Ratio	
38 Zechariah	14		4 O.T. Chapters / 1 N.T. Chapter	
39 Malachi	4			
	929			

Bible Reading Plans

Plan	Average Time / Day (Min's)	Number of Chapters to Read per Day							Chapters per Week	Time to Complete		
		Weekday					Weekend			Weeks	Months	Years
		M	T	W	T	F	S	S				
		New Testament Only (260 chapters)										
1	5 - 15	1	1	1	1	1			5	52	12	1.0
2	10 - 25	2	2	2	2	2			10	26	6	0.5
3	15 - 25	3	3	3	3	3			15	17	4	0.3
		Entire Bible (1189 chapters)										
1a	5 - 15	1	1	1	1	1			5	238	55	4.6
1b	5 - 15	1	1	1	1	1	1	1	7	170	39	3.3
2a	10 - 25	2	2	2	2	2			10	119	27	2.3
2b	10 - 25	2	2	2	2	2	2	2	14	85	20	1.6
3a	15 - 25	3	3	3	3	3			15	79	18	1.5
3b	15 - 25	3	3	3	3	3	4	4	23	52	12	1.0

Table 1.5

NOTES (CHAPTER 1)

[1] Josh McDowell, *Evidence That Demands a Verdict* (Campus Crusade for Christ, Inc., 1972), 21

[2] Ibid., 18

[3] John F. Walvoord and Roy B. Zuck, eds., *The Bible Knowledge Commentary, New Testament* (Colorado Springs: David C Cook, 1983), 815

[4] Ibid., 917

[5] McDowell, op. cit., 26

[6] John F. Walvoord and Roy B. Zuck, eds., *The Bible Knowledge Commentary, Old Testament*, (Colorado Springs: David C Cook, 1985), 513

2

THE MESSAGE OF THE BIBLE

In the last chapter, we explored the uniqueness of the Bible. In this chapter, we will consider its message. Just what is the primary message that God is communicating to us through His Word? Given the volume of the Bible (1,189 chapters) and the fact that it is filled with so many compelling messages and themes, it could certainly seem like a daunting task to determine its primary message. There is probably no aspect of human life that the Bible does not have relevance to, and people throughout history have continually testified to its power to change their lives. This author is one who makes that claim. The Bible's pages are filled with principles for living a full and meaningful life, and it gives a plethora of human examples, both good and bad, that illustrate the inviolable nature of these principles.

So what is the Bible's primary message? The primary message of scripture is threefold. The three-strand chord that weaves its way throughout the scriptures is (1) the holiness of God, (2) the sinfulness of man, and (3) the coming judgment of man by God. This threefold message tends to create a sense of fear and dread in everyone who has taken the time to read it, as it speaks of our total inadequacy before God. Indeed, the ramifications of this message are literally terrifying! The consequences of God's judgment are eternal, and there are no do-overs, no second chance after death. Fortunately for us, there is also a mysterious fourth strand of the message that is interwoven with the other three. This fourth strand is often referred to as the scarlet thread of redemption—scarlet because the redemption was paid for by the very blood of Jesus Christ, the Son of God.

THE GOSPEL

The gospel is the revelation of this fourth strand. The word *gospel* means "good news" and is God's foreordained plan for salvation. It is the only escape from the horrible fate awaiting every person who must one day stand before a holy God to be judged. The gospel is the climactic moment in the scriptures that the Old Testament moves toward, and the New Testament fully reveals. The astounding mystery of scripture is that God prepared a way of redemption for mankind. This redemption enables us (1) to escape God's eternal wrath against sinners, (2) to be declared holy in His sight, and (3) to have eternal life and be empowered to live this life in harmony with His purpose.

This threefold message of scripture is neatly summarized in Jesus's own words, as he described the threefold ministry of the Holy Spirit who would come into the world after His death, resurrection, and ascension to continue the work that He so faithfully began.

> And when he is come, he will reprove the world of *sin*, and of *righteousness*, and of *judgment*: of sin, *because they believe not on me;* of righteousness, *because I go to my Father, and ye see me no more;* of judgment, *because the prince of this world is judged.* (John 16:8-11)

In this passage, Jesus was declaring that

- the Holy Spirit would reprove the world of sin, as Jesus had
- the Holy Spirit would convict the world of God's righteousness, as Jesus had
- the Holy Spirit would warn of God's judgment on Satan and his followers, as Jesus had

The scarlet thread of redemption (the gospel) is actually *hinted* at by the somewhat unexpected ending of this passage: "because the *prince of this world* is judged." We might well have expected it to read: "because *the unrighteous* of this world *are* judged."

The Gospel Defined: The shortest definition of the gospel in the scriptures is shown below.

> Moreover, brethren, I declare unto you *the gospel* which I preached unto you, which also ye have received, and wherein ye stand; *By which also ye are saved,* if ye keep in memory what I preached unto you, unless ye have believed in vain. For I delivered unto you first of all that which I also received, how that *Christ died for our sins* according to the scriptures; And that *he was buried*, and that *he rose again the third day* according to the scriptures. (1 Corinthians 15:1–4)

Paul makes an astounding claim regarding the gospel.

> For I am not ashamed of the gospel of Christ: for it is the power of God unto salvation to every one that believeth; to the Jew first, and also to the Greek. For therein is the righteousness of God revealed from faith to faith: as it is written, The just shall live by faith. (Romans 1:16–17)

The gospel is the *power of God* for *salvation* to *everyone* that believes it! What a statement that is, and who would know better than Paul? After all, his salvation experience took place on the road to Damascus—where Paul was preparing to capture the true disciples of God to bring them back to Jerusalem to be imprisoned or executed, when the resurrected Christ appeared to him. That experience changed his life in a way that few, if any, others have experienced. So why is the gospel so powerful? I see four very compelling points about the gospel that make it such a powerful message.

The gospel is compelling for …

1. **What was done:** What Jesus did was the most heroic act ever performed by a human. He had to endure the Garden of Gethsemane, where He sweated drops of blood, an illegal trial, examination by Pilate and Herod, the scourging that tore the flesh off His back, and six hours on the cross! How unfair that the only one who ever did God's will perfectly on earth, when He asked that the cup of suffering might pass from Him, was given God's silent answer of no. Thus, He had to endure the absence of fellowship with the Father that He had experienced from all eternity at the most crucial moment of His life, as He hung naked, despised, and abandoned on the cross. Not only did Jesus have to endure the passion, but He had to live with this knowledge, from the time He became cognizant of His mission, that He would have to die. We read His words in John 12:

   Now is my soul troubled; and what shall I say? Father, save me from this hour: but for this cause came I unto this hour … And I, if I be lifted up from the earth, will draw all men unto me. This he said, signifying what death he should die. (John 12:27, 12:32–33)

2. **Who did it:** This incredible feat of courage and suffering was accomplished by Jesus, the Eternal Son of God! How do you fathom the priceless sacrifice that God the Son, who was omnipotent and omniscient coming to earth to make Himself completely vulnerable! The author of Hebrews describes it like this.

   Who in the days of his flesh, when *he had offered up prayers and supplications* with *strong crying* and *tears* unto him that was able to save him from death, *and was heard* in that he feared; *Though he were a Son, yet learned he obedience by the things which he suffered*; And being *made perfect, he became the author of eternal salvation* unto all them that obey him. (Hebrews 5:7–9)

   The omnipotent God crying out for deliverance; the omniscient God learning obedience! I used to think to myself that Jesus's deity somehow *helped* Him to man up to the tortures of the cross. However, I became convicted that the total opposite was true—the one who was cosovereign with God the Father, completely shielded from even being touched by any form of pain, was now to endure the most torturous death known to man, and the most shameful as well.

3. **Its attestation to the reality of heaven and hell!** Considering points 1 and 2 above, *what was done* and *who did it*, can you conceive of the Eternal Son of God paying such a horrific price if both heaven and hell were not real? Jesus's mission was twofold in

24

the sense that He came to save those who would receive Him from a torturous, godless eternity of suffering and bring them into a glorious eternity with unimaginable beauty and harmony to live with Him and the Father forever! Think of all the beauties of this fallen world and then try to imagine a world with no pollution, no pain, no tears (unless there be tears of joy), no death, no goodbyes, and everyone loving one another perfectly! But the greatest joy of heaven will be to see Jesus our hero in all His glory and to live under His righteous reign—no more fake news and lies and wars and cruelty!

And *the glory which thou gavest me I have given them; that they may be one, even as we are one*: I in them, and thou in me, that they may be made perfect in one; and that the world may know that thou hast sent me, and hast loved them, as thou hast loved me. Father, *I will that they also*, whom thou hast given me, *be with me where I am; that they may behold my glory*, which thou hast given me: for thou lovedst me before the foundation of the world. (John 17:22–24)

I see heaven as being like retirement, but on an unimaginable scale—before retirement, we worked out of necessity to survive, to pay the mortgage and all our other bills, but after retirement, we still work, but we work for the joy of it. Our pension covers our bills. So back to the argument—if we just die and cease to exist, why would Almighty God allow His Holy Son to endure such horrific pain and shame? And yet the resurrection and the empty tomb still loudly proclaim today, the gospel is real! He lives! And He's coming back!

4. **Christ being the *only* means of salvation!** Can you imagine standing before God, who provided such a magnificent means of salvation that you rejected and then having the audacity to ask Him to accept you? How can an argument for your own righteousness possibly succeed, when throughout His Word, He repeatedly states that everyone is a sinner, and no one is acceptable to Him by any other means than faith—that salvation comes only through Him and the righteousness of His Son?

How shall we escape, if we neglect so great salvation; which at the first began to be spoken by the Lord, and was confirmed unto us by them that heard him. (Hebrews 2:3)

How, indeed!

In the passage below, Paul expresses his lament that his own kinsmen who had the scriptures and the Mosaic Law failed to recognize Christ as the promised Messiah and thus failed to understand God's plan of salvation. He noted the futility of any attempt to gain salvation by good works:

What shall we say then? That the *Gentiles, which followed not after righteousness,* have *attained to righteousness,* even the righteousness which is of faith. *But Israel, which followed after the law of righteousness, hath not attained to the law of righteousness.* Wherefore? Because *they sought it not by faith, but as it were by the works* of the law. For they stumbled at that stumblingstone. (Romans 9:30–32)

Brethren, my heart's desire and prayer to God for Israel is, that they might be saved. For I bear them record that they have a zeal of God, but not according to knowledge. For *they being ignorant of God's righteousness, and going about to establish their own righteousness, have not submitted themselves unto the righteousness of God.* For *Christ is the end of the law for righteousness to every one that believeth.* (Romans 10:1–4)

JESUS CHRIST, THE CENTRAL FIGURE OF SCRIPTURE

The Old Testament: The whole of scripture is literally centered on God's love for mankind, expressed through the giving of His Son Jesus Christ. There are literally hundreds of *snapshots* of Christ throughout the Old Testament that form a composite prophetic picture of God's sovereign plan of redemption through Him. This composite picture is woven through all thirty-nine books of the Old Testament and contains a wealth of information about Him, including His birthplace (Bethlehem); His lineage (through Abraham, Isaac, Jacob, Judah, and David, and that He is God's only begotten Son!); His hometown (Nazareth); His ministry (healing, teaching, miracles, and prophesying, which would amaze and unlock mysteries); His atoning death (crucifixion despite His innocence); His resurrection from the dead; the salvation (of all who trust in Him); His battle with and ultimate defeat of Satan; and His ushering in of heaven, where He will reign eternally. These Old Testament prophetic promises and pictures will be covered in part 3 of this book, which will cover the Pentateuch (Genesis through Deuteronomy).

The New Testament: The scarlet thread of redemption reaches its climax in the four gospels, which record Christ's incarnation and return to heaven. The book of Acts then continues Jesus's ministry by the Holy Spirit through the birth of the church and Christianity. Then the epistles provide (1) a doctrinal foundation for Christianity, tying Christ's ministry, death, and resurrection to the Old Testament prophecies; (2) a transition from the practice of Judaism to Christianity; and (3) the application of the gospel to daily life. Finally, the book of Revelation reveals the last chapter of earth, which will be marked by the return of Christ, the final judgment, and the establishment of the eternal heaven on the recreated earth.

JESUS CHRIST, THE MOST COMPELLING FIGURE OF HUMAN HISTORY

Of all the people who have ever walked the earth, there has never been another person like Jesus Christ. The world's calendar is even divided at the very point where Jesus Christ came into this world. Without a doubt, there is no more revered person in all of history than He. A well-known poem about Christ speaks of the irony of His uncanny impact on the world, despite His humble circumstances:

ONE SOLITARY LIFE

He was born in an obscure village, a child of a peasant woman. He grew up in another obscure village, where he worked in a carpenter shop until he was thirty. Then for three years he was an itinerant preacher. He never had a family or owned a home. He never set foot inside a big city. He never traveled two hundred miles from the place where he was born. He never wrote a book or held an office. He did none of the things that usually accompany greatness. While he was still a young man, the tide of popular opinion turned against him. His friends deserted him. He was turned over to his enemies. He went through the mockery of a trial. He was nailed to a cross between two thieves. While he was dying his executioners gambled for the only piece of property he had, his coat. When he was dead, he was taken down and laid in a borrowed grave.

Nineteen centuries have come and gone and today he is still the central figure for much of the human race. All the armies that ever marched, All the navies that ever sailed And all the parliaments that ever sat, And all the kings that ever reigned Put together have not affected the life of man Upon this earth As powerfully as this One Solitary Life[1].

The Jewish historian Flavius Josephus (born AD 37/38, Jerusalem—died AD 100, Rome[2]) wrote the following concerning Jesus and His followers:

Now there was about this time Jesus, a wise man, if it be lawful to call him a man, for he was a doer of wonderful works—a teacher of such men as receive the truth with pleasure. He drew over to him both many of the Jews, and many of the Gentiles. He was the Christ, and when Pilate, at the suggestion of the principal men amongst us, had condemned him to the cross, those that loved him at the first did not forsake him; for he appeared to them alive again the third day; as the divine prophets had foretold these and ten thousand other wonderful things concerning him. And the tribe of Christians, so named from him, are not extinct at this day.[3]

Jesus is compelling for a number of reasons:

1. The Old Testament's prophetic picture of Him
2. His miraculous birth (born of a virgin, in the town of Bethlehem, His pre-eternality)
3. His life (moral excellence—sinless perfection)
4. His miracles (pointed to His divine nature)
5. His teaching (He is the most revered religious teacher of all time)
6. His claim to be God and mankind's only redeemer
7. His death on a cross, which paid the penalty for our sin
8. His resurrection, ascension, and post-resurrection appearances (which proved His claims of messiahship and deity)

There are numerous illustrations in the scriptures of each of these aspects of Jesus's life. We will examine scriptural examples below:

1. **Old Testament Prophecies of Jesus:** The prophetic tapestry that is woven throughout the Old Testament scriptures paints a panoramic view of Jesus that is literally breathtaking. In this author's opinion, an in-depth understanding of the Old Testament is essential to properly understand who Jesus is. We will only look at two examples below, since this is the subject matter in part 3 of this book, where we will explore this in great detail in those chapters.

   Psalm 22 (Crucifixion Psalm): This psalm is a prophetic picture of the crucifixion of Jesus and what it accomplished. It is worth noting here that the psalm is attributed to David who lived from 1041 to 971 BC (see Kings table in chapter 1). This is significant when considering the details of Jesus's crucifixion mentioned in this psalm, noting that crucifixion was not used for several hundred years after that. Below are excerpts from the psalm and the New Testament references that fulfilled the prophetic details listed:

   His words from the cross
   My God, my God, why hast thou forsaken me? (Matthew 27:46)

   He was mocked
   All they that see me laugh me to scorn: they shoot out the lip, they shake the head, saying, He trusted on the LORD that he would deliver him: let him deliver him, seeing he delighted in him. (Matthew 27:39–43)

   The pangs and thirst of crucifixion
   I am poured out like water, and *all my bones are out of joint:* my heart is like wax; it is melted in the midst of my bowels. *My strength is dried up* like a potsherd; and *my tongue cleaveth to my jaws; and thou hast brought me into the dust of death.* (John 19:28–30)

Crucifixion wounds, dividing up and gambling for His garments

For dogs have compassed me: *the assembly of the wicked have inclosed me: they pierced my hands and my feet.* I may tell all my bones: they look *and* stare upon me. *They part my garments among them, and cast lots upon my vesture.* (Matthew 27:35, Luke 24:36–43)

His judgment of mankind and Gentile acceptance in the church

* *All those who go down to the dust will bow before Him,*
Even he who cannot keep his soul alive. A seed shall serve him; it shall be accounted to the Lord for a generation. They shall come, and *shall declare his righteousness unto a people that shall be born*, that he hath done *this*. (Philippians 2:9–11,** Ephesians 2:11–16, 1 Peter 2:10)

* Note: verse 29 only is NASB
** Note: verses 10–11 yet to be fulfilled

Isaiah 53 (The Suffering Servant): This prophecy of Isaiah was uttered approximately 700 years before Jesus was born and was written to foretell Christ's coming and to proclaim that His death would atone for our sins and bring healing to our souls. The passage is clear that Christ will not come with pomp and fanfare but as a lowly servant. His suffering would be on our behalf. He would literally become a human sacrifice! By means of this offering, He would later justify those who become His children through faith in Him.

Isaiah 53:

Who hath believed our report? and to whom is the arm of the LORD revealed? For he shall grow up before him as a tender plant, and as a root out of a dry ground: he hath no form nor comeliness; and when we shall see him, *there is* no beauty that we should desire him. *He is despised and rejected of men; a man of sorrows*, and acquainted with grief: and *we hid as it were our faces from him; he was despised, and we esteemed him not.*

Surely *he hath borne our griefs, and carried our sorrows*: yet we did esteem him stricken, smitten of God, and afflicted. But *he was wounded for our transgressions,* he was bruised for our iniquities: *the chastisement of our peace was upon him*; and *with his stripes we are healed.* All we like sheep have gone astray; we have turned everyone to his own way; and *the LORD hath laid on him the iniquity of us all.* He was oppressed, and he was afflicted, yet he opened not his mouth: *he is brought as a lamb to the slaughter,* and as a sheep before her shearers is dumb, so he openeth not his mouth. He was taken from prison and from judgment: and who shall declare his generation? for *he was cut off out of the land of the living: for the transgression of my people was he stricken.* And *he made his grave with the wicked, and with the rich in his death*; because he had done no violence, neither *was any* deceit in his mouth.

Yet *it pleased the* LORD *to bruise him*; he hath put *him* to grief: *when thou shalt make his soul an offering for sin, he shall see his seed*, he shall prolong *his* days, and the pleasure of the LORD shall prosper in his hand. He shall see of the travail of his soul, *and* shall be satisfied: *by his knowledge shall my righteous servant justify many; for he shall bear their iniquities*. Therefore will I divide him *a portion* with the great, and he shall divide the spoil with the strong; because *he hath poured out his soul unto death*: and *he was numbered with the transgressors*; and *he bare the sin of many, and made intercession for the transgressors*.

In this prophecy, Isaiah paints an incredibly detailed picture of Jesus's life as a servant and a human sacrifice. Below is a verse-by-verse explanation:

Verse		New Testament Fulfillment
3	Jesus was despised and rejected by His people	John 1:11
4	He bore our griefs and carried our sorrows	2 Cor. 5:21
5	His wounds were for *our* transgressions	1 Cor. 15:3
	His stripes spoke of His scourging	Matt. 27:26
6	His atoning death was God's plan	Rev. 13:8 (KJV)
7	As a (Passover) lamb to the slaughter	John 1:29, 1 Cor. 5:7
8	Cut off (unnatural death) for people's sins	Matt. 27:35
9	His grave … wicked … rich in his death	Mark 15:27, Matt. 27:57–60
10	It pleased the Lord to bruise Him	Rev. 13:8 (KJV)
	If you make His soul offering … He'll see His seed	John 1:12
11	By His knowledge (knowledge of Him) … justify	Rom. 1:16
	He shall bear their iniquities	1 Cor. 15:3, 2 Cor. 5:21
12	He poured out His soul unto death	Phil. 2:6–8
	He was numbered with the transgressors	Mark 15:27, Heb. 2:10–11
	He bare the sin of many	1 Cor. 15:3, Heb. 2:10
	He made intercession for the transgressors	Luke 23:24, Rom. 8:34

2. **Jesus's Miraculous Birth:** Jesus's birth is miraculous for at least three reasons: (1) He was born of a virgin; (2) His birthplace, Bethlehem, was foretold approximately 700 years prior by the prophet Micah; and (3) Jesus was God in the flesh! Note the scriptures below:

a) **His Virgin Birth**

Therefore the Lord himself shall give you a sign; Behold, *a virgin shall conceive, and bear a son*, and shall *call his name Immanuel*. (Isaiah 7:14)

And in the sixth month the angel Gabriel was sent from God unto a city of Galilee, named Nazareth, To *a virgin espoused to a man whose name was Joseph, of the house of David*; and the virgin's name *was* Mary ... (Luke 1:26–27)

And the angel said unto her, Fear not, Mary: for thou hast found favour with God. And, behold, *thou shalt conceive in thy womb, and bring forth a son, and shalt call his name JESUS. He shall be great, and shall be called the Son of the Highest: and the Lord God shall give unto him the throne of his father David: And he shall reign over the house of Jacob forever; and of his kingdom there shall be no end.* Then said Mary unto the angel, *How shall this be, seeing I know not a man?* And the angel answered and said unto her, *The Holy Ghost shall come upon thee, and the power of the Highest shall overshadow thee:* therefore also *that holy thing which shall be born of thee shall be called the Son of God.* (Luke 1:30–35)

b) Prophesied Birthplace, Bethlehem

But thou, Bethlehem Ephratah, though thou be little among the thousands of Judah, yet *out of thee shall he come forth* unto me *that is to be ruler in Israel; whose goings forth have been from of old, from everlasting.* (Micah 5:2)

Note that this powerful prophecy uttered approximately 700 years before Jesus's birth foretells that Jesus would (1) be born in Bethlehem, (2) be ruler in Israel, and (3) that He has existed from eternity! No other person's birth has ever been preceded with such a complete and astounding prophetic disclosure of his life. The second prophecy in this passage will be fulfilled at Jesus's Second Coming.

3. **Jesus's Life:** Jesus lived a morally perfect, sinless life. His life is the perfect model of love and self-sacrifice. His entire life was spent demonstrating God's love through His endless ministry as He traveled from town to town, healing the sick and teaching in the synagogues. Who among us would be able to say at the end of his life that he had not a single regret, not one thing that he would do differently if given the opportunity? Jesus could say that. Have you lived the kind of life where you could ask others, "Which of you convicts me of sin?" (John 8:46 NASB). Jesus asked that question of his very enemies! The apostle John closed his gospel with these words: "And there are also many other things which Jesus did, which if they were written in detail, I suppose that even the world itself would not contain the books that would be written" (John 21:25 NASB). Jesus's life was indeed a life well lived!

4. **Jesus's Miracles:** Jesus worked many miracles throughout His life both publicly and privately in the presence of the disciples. These miracles were supernatural signs of His deity and covered the gamut of the supernatural as noted below:

Nature—he calmed the sea (Matthew 14:22–33), walked on water (Mark 4:35–41)
Ministry—miraculously fed multitudes (John 6:1-14), turned water to wine (John 2:1–11)
Healing—paralytic, blind (Mark 2:1–12, 10:46–52), internal bleeding (Mark 9:25–34)
Death—raised people from the dead (John 11:1-46), His resurrection (John 20:19–29)
Demonic—cast out demons (Mark 5:1-20)
Divinity—spoken to by God (Mark 1:9–11), transfiguration (Luke 9:28–36)

5. **Jesus's Teaching:** Jesus was the consummate teacher. At the age of *twelve*, He amazed the teachers in the synagogue (John 2:41–52). There are so many things that made Jesus the most profound teacher in human history. He taught in parables, which were stories from everyday life that illustrated spiritual truths. He used hyperbole (speck/log in eye, Matthew 7:3); drama (feeding the 5,000/Bread of Life in John 6, washing the disciples' feet in John 13, the Lord's Supper in Matthew 26); riddles and enigmas ("What think ye of Christ—whose son is he?" in Matthew 22:42–46); object lessons (used a child to illustrate humility and servitude in Matthew 18:1–6, a widow's mite to illustrate sacrificial versus superficial giving in Mark 12:41–44); and His perfect knowledge and understanding of the scriptures, to name a few. Jesus had a remarkable way of asking rhetorical questions, often as part of His parables. The inescapable answers to these questions left His audience with no rational alternative but to accept the truth He was teaching.

6. **Jesus's Claim to be God and Mankind's Only Redeemer**

   a) **The Deity of Christ:** One of the tenets of Christianity that is clearly taught in scripture is the deity of Christ and that He is the sole redeemer of mankind. C. S. Lewis, in his book *Mere Christianity*, makes a very compelling argument about the implications of Jesus's claim to be God in the passages below:

   > Then comes the real shock. Among these Jews there suddenly turns up a man who goes about talking as if He was God. He claims to forgive sins. He says He has always existed. He says He is coming to judge the world at the end of time …

   > A man who was merely a man and said the sort of things Jesus said would not be a great moral teacher. He would either be a lunatic—on the level with the man who says he is a poached egg—or else he would

be the Devil of Hell. You must make your choice. Either this man was, and is, the Son of God, or else a madman or something worse.[4].

In this passage, C. S. Lewis, himself formerly an agnostic, so eloquently says that each of us who encounter the gospel record is pressed into deciding who Jesus is—Lord, liar, or lunatic. Those are the options.

There are numerous scripture references to Jesus's deity. The following are shown below:

1) John, in his gospel, claimed that Jesus was God

In the beginning was the Word, and the Word was with God, and *the Word was God*. He was in the beginning with God. *All things came into being through Him*, and apart from Him nothing came into being that has come into being. (John 1:1–3)

And *the Word became flesh, and dwelt among us*, and *we saw His glory, glory as of the only begotten from the Father, full of grace and truth*. (John 1:14)

2) A healed blind man's incredulity

In this passage, for the second time, the Pharisees are grilling the blind man whom Jesus had just healed. Having rejected Jesus from the beginning of His ministry, they certainly did not want to be confused by the inconvenient facts of the blind man's miraculous healing, so they searched in vain for an alternate reality.

Then again called they the man that was blind, and said unto him, Give God the praise: we know that this man is a sinner. He answered and said, Whether he be a sinner or no, I know not: *one thing I know, that, whereas I was blind, now I see*. Then they reviled him, and said, Thou art his disciple; but we are Moses' disciples … (John 9:24–25)

We know that God spake unto Moses: as for this fellow, we know not from whence he is. *The man answered and said unto them, Why herein is an amazing thing, that ye know not from whence he is, and yet he hath opened mine eyes.* Now we know that God heareth not sinners: but if any man be a worshipper of God, and doeth his will, him he heareth. *Since the world began was it not heard that any man opened the eyes of one that was born blind.* If this man were not of God, he could do nothing. (John 9:29–33) ["an amazing"—NASB word substitution v. 30]

3) Jesus claimed His own deity

Jesus said unto them, Verily, verily, I say unto you, *Before Abraham was, I Am.* Then took they up stones to cast at him: but Jesus hid himself, and went out of the temple, going through the midst of them, and so passed by. (John 8:58–59)

Jesus was pre-eternal—note that Abraham died nearly 2,000 years before Jesus was born. Also, Jesus used God's name I Am, which had its origin in the "burning bush" passage below:

When I come unto the children of Israel, and shall say … God … hath sent me unto you; and they shall say to me, *What is his name?* what shall I say unto them? And *God said* unto Moses, *I Am That I Am …* *Thus shalt thou say* unto the children of Israel, *I AM* hath sent me unto you … *The Lord God of your fathers* … hath sent me unto you: *this is my name for ever,* and *this is my memorial unto all generations.* (Exodus 3:13–15)

Interestingly, John's gospel contains seven "I Am" statements by Jesus, which many students of the Bible are familiar with. Each of these statements point to His deity:

I Am the Bread of Life

I Am the Light of the World

I Am the Door of the Sheep

I Am the Good Shepherd

I Am the Resurrection and the Life

I Am the Way, the Truth, and the Life

I Am the True Vine

As Jesus was preparing His disciples for His impending death, He made the sixth statement above, "I am the Way, the Truth, and the Life, no man cometh to the Father, but by Me." Shortly thereafter, Philip asked Him …

Philip saith unto him, Lord, *shew us the Father, and it sufficeth us.* Jesus saith unto him, *Have I been so long time with you, and yet hast thou not known me,* Philip? he that hath seen me hath seen the Father; and how sayest thou then, Shew us the Father? (John 14:8–9)

Jesus made the clear claim here that anyone who had seen Him had seen the Father.

4) Jesus's disciple Thomas worshipped Him after His resurrection

But Thomas, one of the twelve, called Didymus, was not with them when Jesus came. The other disciples therefore said unto him, We have seen the Lord. But he said unto them, *Except I shall see in his hands the print of the nails, and put my finger into the print of the nails, and thrust my hand into his side, I will not believe.*

And *after eight days* again *his disciples* were within, and *Thomas with them:* then came *Jesus,* the doors being shut, and stood in the midst, and said, *Peace be unto you. Then saith he to Thomas, Reach hither thy finger, and behold my hands; and reach hither thy hand, and thrust it into my side: and be not faithless, but believing.* And *Thomas answered and said unto him, My Lord and my God.* (John 20:24–28)

b) Jesus is the Only Redeemer: The Bible teaches that Jesus is mankind's redeemer and the only way to God. There are numerous passages that speak of Jesus as the only means of salvation. Note the passages below:

1) Jesus claimed to be the only way to God, as Savior, Redeemer

For God so loved the world, that *he gave his only begotten Son,* that *whosoever believeth in him should not perish, but have everlasting life.* (John 3:16)

Jesus saith unto him, *I am the way, the truth, and the life: no man cometh unto the Father, but by me.* (John 14:6)

2) The apostles claimed that Jesus was the Only Way to God

Neither is there salvation in any other: for *there is none other name under heaven given among men, whereby we must be saved.* (Acts 4:12)

For I am not ashamed of the *gospel of Christ*: for *it is the power of God unto salvation to everyone that believeth*; to the Jew first, and also to the Greek. (Romans 1:16)

Moreover, brethren, I declare unto you *the gospel* which I preached unto you, which also ye have received, and wherein ye stand; … For I delivered unto you first of all that which I also received, how that *Christ died for our sins* according to the scriptures; And that *he was buried,* and that *he rose again the third day* according to the scriptures. (1 Corinthians 15:1, 15:3–4)

3) He was made like us

Wherefore *in all things it behoved him to be made like unto his brethren,* that he might be a merciful and faithful high priest in things pertaining to God, to make reconciliation for the sins of the people. For *in that he himself hath suffered being tempted, he is able to succour them that are tempted.* (Hebrews 2:17–18)

For *we have not an high priest which can not be touched with the feeling of our infirmities*; but *was in all points tempted like as we are, yet without sin*. Let us therefore come boldly unto the throne of grace, that we may obtain mercy, and find grace to help in time of need. (Hebrews 4:15–16)

7. **His Resurrection and Post-Resurrection Appearances:** Jesus's resurrection was and is the ultimate proof of His deity and messiahship. The resurrection of Jesus was the historical pivot from Judaism to Christianity. The mystery is now completely revealed. Jesus is indeed the Messiah promised throughout the Old Testament and fulfilled in the New. After His resurrection, Jesus appeared at various times to women, to His disciples, to Saul of Tarsus, whose life was completely transformed into that of Paul the apostle, and on one occasion, to over 500 men at one time. He appeared over a period of forty days. During these appearances, He walked along a road and gave two men a crash course on the real meaning of the scriptures. On a separate occasion, He suddenly appeared in a room with closed doors; on another, he prepared a breakfast for and gave a fishing lesson to experienced fishermen. On His final appearance, He ascended into the clouds and vanished into heaven.

IN SUMMARY

Can you imagine being the Creator of heaven and earth, and then *volunteering* to go live on the planet that You created with the people that You created, and humbling yourself to become not only one of them, but a lowly servant? Then as if that were not enough, you are even willing to submit yourself as an act of love, as a human sacrifice, dying on a cross, nailed there and speared by hands that You created and mocked by mouths that You created?

Jesus walked this incredibly courageous walk to the point where He intentionally gave Himself into the hands of sinful men. During every part of His passion, He could have called 72,000 angels[5] at any point to rescue Him from His suffering, yet amazingly, He refused. This includes His agony of prayer in the garden, His cruel trial, His incarceration, His scourging, His long walk toward Calvary, carrying the very cross that He would die on, and the hours of agony in which He hung upon the cross, alternately gasping for breath, then pushing up with his cramped legs against the nails through His feet, in order to breathe. Can you think of any other heroic action by any person that even approaches that of Christ? Therefore, Jesus is the hero of all heroes. Consider the following passage:

Who, being in the form of God, thought it not robbery to be equal with God: But made himself of no reputation, and took upon him the form of a servant, and was made in the likeness of men: And being found in fashion as a man, he humbled himself, and became obedient unto death, even the death of the cross. Wherefore God also hath highly exalted him, and given him a name which is above every name: That at the name of Jesus every knee should bow, of *things* in heaven, and *things* in earth, and *things* under the earth; And *that* every tongue should confess that Jesus Christ *is* Lord, to the glory of God the Father. (Philippians 2:6–11)

As believers, we can certainly see that our salvation rests in the finished work of Christ. We place *all* our hope for being acceptable to God in His substitutionary death, which paid for every sin that we ever have or ever will commit. When we submit ourselves to Christ as our Lord and Savior, absolutely nothing will be able to separate us from God's love!

So, friend, in a nutshell, the message of the Bible is about the most pivotal person in human history—Jesus Christ.

What about you?

Has there been a time in your life where you (1) realized who Jesus is, (2) prayed for Him to save you from sin and its eternal penalty, and (3) began to follow Him as *your* Savior and Lord? If not, why not make that choice right now? The scriptural admonition is …

Now is the accepted time; behold, now is the day of salvation. (2 Corinthians 6:2)

Please don't put it off, dear friend.

NOTES (CHAPTER 2)

[1]   James Allen Francis, *The Real Jesus and Other Sermons* (Philadelphia: Judson Press, 1926, http://www.davidschrock.com/2013/12/16/one-solitary life/ (accessed 09/11/24)

[2]   Gary William Poole, *Flavius Josephus, Jewish Priest, Scholar, and Historian*, last updated: 09/10/24, http://www.britannica.com/biography/Flavius-Josephus

[3]   Flavius Josephus, *The Works of Flavius Josephus / Translated by William Whiston, Antiquities, 18.3.3,* (Nashville: Thomas Nelson, 1998), 576

[4]   C. S. Lewis, *Mere Christianity* (C. S. Lewis Pte. Ltd., 1952, Copyright renewed 1980 C.S. Lewis Pte. Ltd.), 51–52

[5]   *NASB Side-Column Reference Edition*, (Anaheim, The Lockman Foundation, 1996), footnote for Matthew 26:53, 48

3

THE HOLINESS OF GOD

The heavens declare the glory of God; and the firmament sheweth his handywork. Day unto day uttereth speech, and night unto night sheweth knowledge. There is no speech nor language, where their voice is not heard. (Psalm 19:1–3)

THIS PASSAGE SPEAKS OF THE *GLORY* OF GOD—THAT IS TO SAY, HIS MAGNIFICENCE OR HIS awesomeness.

Anyone who has seriously read and studied the Bible has come to understand that God is very different from us. The more that we read the scriptures and consider the vastness of this universe that He created, the more we come to realize His uniqueness, complexity, vastness, and superiority to us. As students of the Bible, our current thoughts about God have evolved from our earliest thoughts of Him. Our earliest thoughts of God were somewhat simplistic— perhaps we saw Him metaphorically as a benevolent old man or as a distant God who sees from afar. Some of this growth in our conception of God is due to our own growth in our ability to perceive deeper and more abstract thoughts through experience and education. Similarly, in my earlier years I saw righteousness and sin as being only external actions, but later came to realize that sin begins in the heart. I still remember my shock in discovering from scripture that God knows not only my thoughts, but even my innermost motives as we see clearly from Psalm 139, Jesus's teachings, and James 1:13–15, in which James describes the anatomy of sin. This discovery was just a small step in my journey toward understanding God's *otherness*, His complete superiority to us.

GOD'S TRANSCENDENCE

The theological word we use to explain God's superiority to us is *transcendence. Transcend* means "to go or *be* beyond the range of human experience or belief or powers of description etc." [1] Consider the following ways that God is transcendent according to the Bible:

1. **God is Creator, whereas we are creatures:** One of the foundational teachings of scripture is that God created the entire universe, including man. Although we have grown quite fond of our perceived autonomy, the truth is that we belong entirely to God and were created to love, honor, worship, and serve Him.

   Creator of the Universe
   In the beginning God created the heaven and the earth. (Genesis 1:1)

   Creator of Man
   And God said, Let us make man in our image, after our likeness: and let them have dominion over the fish of the sea, and over the fowl of the air, and over the cattle, and over all the earth, and over every creeping thing that creepeth upon the earth. So God created man in his own image, in the image of God created he him; male and female created he them. (Genesis 1:26–27)

   God the Son, Creator
   In the beginning was the Word, and the Word was with God, and the Word was God. The same was in the beginning with God. *All things were made by him; and without him was not anything made that was made* … And the Word was made flesh, and dwelt among us, (and we beheld his glory, the glory as of the only begotten of the Father,) full of grace and truth. (John 1:1–3, 14)

2. **God is Spirit and invisible, whereas we live in bodies:** This is significant, in that we cannot dialogue with God in the same way that we would with a person. On the one hand, He has spoken to us clearly by His Word, and through His Son, but on the other, it can be very difficult for us to connect with Him, which is where faith comes in, as we see in the scriptures below.

   God Exists as Spirit
   God is a Spirit: and they that worship him must worship him in spirit and in truth. (John 4:24)

   Faith Required to Experience God
   But without faith it is impossible to please him: for he that cometh to God must believe that he is, and that he is a rewarder of them that diligently seek him. (Hebrews 11:6)

   Two Different Worlds
   While we look not at the things which are seen, but at the things which are not seen: for the things which are seen are temporal; but the things which are not seen are eternal. (2 Corinthians 4:18)

3. **God is eternal and self-existent, whereas we had an origin:** This is a difficult concept to grasp, for us whose lives began at a point in time and considering that we see death all around us on a daily basis every time we see the evening news. The most familiar verse on the eternality of God is also the most familiar verse in scripture. Obviously, for God to promise eternal life to those who place their faith in His Son, He would necessarily have to be eternal Himself.

    God, Giver of Eternal Life
    For God so loved the world, that he gave his only begotten Son, that whosoever believeth in him should not perish, but have everlasting life. (John 3:16)

    God is eternal
    John to the seven churches which are in Asia: Grace be unto you, and peace, from him which is, and which was, and which is to come; and from the seven Spirits which are before his throne; and from Jesus Christ, who is the faithful witness, and the first begotten of the dead, and the prince of the kings of the earth. (Revelation 1:4–5)

    Christ is eternal
    I am Alpha and Omega, the beginning and the end, the first and the last. (Revelation 22:13)

    God's name signifies His eternality
    And Moses said unto God, Behold, when I come unto the children of Israel, and shall say unto them, The God of your fathers hath sent me unto you; and they shall say to me, What is his name? what shall I say unto them? And God said unto Moses, *I AM THAT I AM:* and he said, *Thus shalt thou say unto the children of Israel, I AM hath sent me unto you.* And God said moreover unto Moses, Thus shalt thou say unto the children of Israel, The LORD God of your fathers, the God of Abraham, the God of Isaac, and the God of Jacob, hath sent me unto you: this is my name for ever, and this is my memorial unto all generations. (Exodus 3:13–15)

    Jesus is God
    Your father Abraham rejoiced to see my day: and he saw it, and was glad. Then said the Jews unto him, Thou art not yet fifty years old, and hast thou seen Abraham? Jesus said unto them, Verily, verily, I say unto you, Before Abraham was, I am. (John 8:56–58)

4. **God is infinite, whereas we are finite:** As finite beings, our perspective is so different from God's. Our knowledge consists only in what we have learned, and factoring in forgetfulness, we don't even know all of that. Our infinite God has complete knowledge

in every sense of the word! In scope, there is not a single piece of information hidden from Him in the entire universe. Regarding time, God is not held in suspense, but knows the end from the beginning. When we pray to God, we are not bringing Him new information, nor are we giving Him a new slant on things. In addition to His perfect knowledge, His presence occupies the entire universe. Nor is there anything that He cannot accomplish. He is totally unlimited, and His thoughts are in a plane that we cannot comprehend.

Infinite in His thoughts and purposes
For my thoughts are not your thoughts, neither are your ways my ways, saith the LORD. For *as* the heavens are higher than the earth, so are my ways higher than your ways, and my thoughts than your thoughts. (Isaiah 55:8–9)

Oh, the depth of the riches and wisdom and knowledge of God! How unsearchable are his judgments and how inscrutable his ways! "For who has known the mind of the Lord, or who has been his counselor?" "Or who has given a gift to him that he might be repaid?" For from him and through him and to him are all things. To him be glory forever. Amen. (Romans 11:33–36)

Within this passage, Paul quotes Isaiah and Job (Isaiah 40:13, Job 35:7; 41:11).

Infinite in His Knowledge (Omniscience)
O LORD, thou hast searched me, and known *me*. Thou knowest my downsitting and mine uprising, thou understandest my thought afar off. Thou compassest my path and my lying down, and art acquainted *with* all my ways. For *there is* not a word in my tongue, *but*, lo, O LORD, thou knowest it altogether. Thou hast beset me behind and before, and laid thine hand upon me. *Such* knowledge *is* too wonderful for me; it is high, I cannot *attain* unto it. (Psalm 139:1–6)

(See also verses 17–18 below)

Infinite in His Presence (Omnipresence)
Whither shall I go from thy spirit? or whither shall I flee from thy presence? If I ascend up into heaven, thou *art* there: if I make my bed in hell, behold, thou *art there. If* I take the wings of the morning, *and* dwell in the uttermost parts of the sea; Even there shall thy hand lead me, and thy right hand shall hold me. If I say, Surely the darkness shall cover me; even the night shall be light about me. Yea, the darkness hideth not from thee; but the night shineth as the day: the darkness and the light *are* both alike *to thee*. (Psalm 139:7–12)

Infinite in His Power (Omnipotence)
For thou hast possessed my reins: thou hast covered me in my mother's womb. I will praise thee; for I am fearfully *and* wonderfully made: marvellous *are* thy works; and *that* my soul knoweth right well. My substance was not hid from

thee, when I was made in secret, *and* curiously wrought in the lowest parts of the earth. Thine eyes did see my substance, yet being unperfect; and in thy book all *my members* were written, *which* in continuance were fashioned, when *as yet there was* none of them. How precious also are thy thoughts unto me, O God! how great is the sum of them! *If* I should count them, they are more in number than the sand: when I awake, I am still with thee. (Psalm 139:13–18)

All Things Possible for God
For with God nothing shall be impossible. (Luke 1:37)

When his disciples heard it, they were exceedingly amazed, saying, Who then can be saved? But Jesus beheld them, and said unto them, With men this is impossible; but with God all things are possible. (Matthew 19:25–26)

5. **God is sovereign, whereas we are subjects:** The Bible is very clear that God is the sovereign over the universe. Through our authority structures on earth, we have learned to be subject to various people in our lives, such as our parents, teachers, employers, military superiors, law enforcement officers, courts, etc. However, there is no hiding from an infinite God, nor is there a higher authority to which we can appeal. During his sufferings, Job longed to present his case before God, but then lamented the futility of that effort.

God's Judgment Cannot Be Appealed
But He is unique and who can turn Him? And what His soul desires, that He does. (Job 23:13 NASB)

Everyone Accountable to God
So then every one of us shall give account of himself to God. (Romans 14:12)

God the Highest Authority
And he hath on his vesture and on his thigh a name written, King of Kings, and Lord of Lords. (Revelation 19:16)

The Sovereign Judge—Great White Throne Judgment
And I saw a great white throne, and him that sat on it, from whose face the earth and the heaven fled away; and there was found no place for them. And I saw the dead, small and great, stand before God; and the books were opened: and another book was opened, which is the book of life: and the dead were judged out of those things which were written in the books, according to their works. And the sea gave up the dead which were in it; and death and hell delivered up the dead which were in them: and they were judged every man according to their works. (Revelation 20:11–13)

6. **God is immutable, whereas we are constantly changing:** We have already discussed God's omniscience, that His knowledge is complete. His perfect knowledge, coupled with His unlimited wisdom and intelligence, makes it inconceivable that He would have a reason to change His mind. He knew the complete outcome of His creation before it ever existed. Aren't we glad that we serve a God who is the same yesterday, today and forever? It is so comforting in this world of change that we live in, that there is *one* constant—God!

God Does Not Change
For I am the LORD, I change not; therefore ye sons of Jacob are not consumed. (Malachi 3:6)

Jesus Does Not Change
Jesus Christ the same yesterday, and today, and forever. (Hebrews 13:8)

No Variance in God
Every good gift and every perfect gift is from above, and cometh down from the Father of lights, with whom is no variableness, neither shadow of turning. (James 1:17)

7. **God is holy, whereas we are sinners:** God's holiness relates to His perfect, righteous character. As we are sinners, this is difficult for us to conceive. We tend to evaluate righteousness in a comparative manner, having never beheld a perfectly righteous man on earth, except for the one revealed in scripture—Jesus Christ, the Son of God. There are numerous references to God's holiness in the scriptures. Note the refrain below from the angel, as he declares the holiness of God as recorded in Isaiah. It is also intriguing that this angel used four of his six wings to cover himself in the presence of a holy God!

Isaiah's Vision of Our Holy God
In the year that king Uzziah died I saw also the Lord sitting upon a throne, high and lifted up, and his train filled the temple. Above it stood the seraphims: each one had six wings; with twain he covered his face, and with twain he covered his feet, and with twain he did fly. And one cried unto another, and said, Holy, holy, holy, *is* the LORD of hosts: the whole earth *is* full of his glory. (Isaiah 6:1–3)

God's Holiness
Sanctify yourselves therefore, and be ye holy: for I am the LORD your God. (Leviticus 20:7)

Sinful Man before a Holy God

If You, LORD, should mark iniquities, O Lord, who could stand? (Psalm 130:3)

God's Righteousness
The LORD is righteous in all his ways, and holy in all his works. (Psalm 145:17)

God's Requirement
Be ye therefore perfect, even as your Father which is in heaven is perfect. (Matthew 5:48)

Our finiteness before an infinite transcendent God causes us innumerable problems. It is very difficult for us to relate to Him on so many levels as we have just noted. It's as if there is a wall of separation between us and Him, needing to be bridged. Our understanding of a transcendent God is not something that can be accomplished in a single session. Perhaps this is why God's Word is a *progressive revelation*. It gives us smaller doses of His infinite nature in earlier chapters of the Bible and then crescendos into fuller revelations in later chapters, particularly in the New Testament. Consider two well-known examples from scripture below, illustrating two extremes of this aspect of the scriptures.

Genesis 18: In the first example, God appears to come on the scene in the form of a man with two other men, who are angels. He talks with Abraham and promises him that he will have a son through Sarah. Then later in the chapter, God, on a more somber note, continues his dialogue with Abraham and says, "Because the cry of Sodom and Gomorrah is great, and because their sin is very grievous; I will go down now, and see whether they have done altogether according to the cry of it, which is come unto me; and if not, I will know" (Genesis 18:20–21). Someone reading this without the complete context of God's total revelation in scripture would have the distinct impression that God is not omniscient, but this would be incorrect. God simply did not choose to reveal this aspect of His nature in this part of His revelation.

Revelation 21: In this second example, Revelation 21 presents a much more glorious view of God. Consider the following descriptors of God in John's description of heaven (the New Jerusalem): "I saw no temple in it, for *the Lord God the Almighty and the Lamb are its temple. And the city has no need of the sun or of the moon to shine on it, for the glory of God has illumined it, and its lamp is the Lamb*" (Revelation 21:22–23). In this passage, we see God being described as the *temple* of the New Jerusalem, the heavenly city, and God's *glory* is all that is needed to light the city, no more need for the sun and moon. Jesus the Lamb of God is the *lamp* of this city. Quite a difference from that Genesis passage, wouldn't you agree?

God's Word can speak to the hearts of spiritually blind and deaf people. Otherwise, it could not speak to us. Jesus, quoting from Isaiah, said, "For the heart of this people has become dull, with their ears they scarcely hear, and they have closed their eyes, otherwise they would see with their eyes, hear with their ears, and understand with their heart and return, and I would heal them" (Matthew 13:14–15, Isaiah 6:9–10). Paul carried it a step further, by telling the Ephesian Christians, "You were dead in your trespasses and sins …" (Ephesians 2:1), which is the reason why Jesus said that we must be born again to see the kingdom of God. We are born into this condition of blindness, deafness and even deadness because of our carnal nature as descendants of Adam the first sinner. Our deadness to the things of God is twofold. First, we do not understand an infinite holy God. This first failure is the reason for the second; we do not understand our own sinfulness. This is the reason people fail to see their need for Christ and His salvation. As we saw in the last chapter, the doctrines of God's holiness and man's sinfulness run parallel through the pages of scripture. So let us transition from the subject of God's transcendence in general to His transcendent character of holiness.

THE CONCEPT OF HOLINESS

Those of us who have grown up in church have heard all our lives that God is holy, but what exactly does this mean? The following is an excerpt from a Bible dictionary under the heading *Holiness, Holy*: "holiness means the pure, loving nature of God, separate from evil, aggressively seeking to universalize itself; that this character inheres in places, times and institutions intimately associated with worship; and that it is to characterize human beings who have entered into personal relations with God …"[2]

What is the significance of God's holiness to us? How does a holy God view sinful man? Perhaps an illustration might help us answer this. Imagine that you are just now seeing a news report of a serial killer suspect being apprehended. He is suspected of killing twenty helpless young women. Although each one begged for mercy during her nightmarish encounter with him, this man brutally abused and murdered every one. After a lengthy trial in which much evidence proving his guilt is presented, you see the latest news report, showing the final verdict being read, "Guilty as charged." What is your reaction to this verdict? Do you pull out your crying towel and begin sobbing uncontrollably for this *poor* man because he will now die by lethal injection? Probably not. Why this lack of compassion on your part? Could it possibly be because you feel that this person actually *deserves* to die? Could it be possible that your horror, shock, and incredulity over the serial killer's crime are based in some measure on a comparison that you have made between the villain and you? Isn't the very thought "How could someone do something like this?" predicated on your inability to conceive of yourself doing it?

The Bible teaches that you and I are both sinners who have rebelled against God. Perhaps one of us is a worse sinner than the other, and the serial killer is a worse sinner than either of us, but this pales in comparison with the fact that we are both sinners compared to a holy God. In fact, this is the very point that Paul made in Romans 3:23, which states, "For all have sinned, and come short of the glory of God." This verse as much as any in scripture points to God's holiness. I wonder if the full meaning of the verse does not elude us as we tend to focus on the problem and consequence of our coming short without realizing the *degree* of our shortcoming. Notice that it does not say, "For all have sinned *greatly* … and come short …" which could imply that God sins only a little; but rather, the point is being made that because we even sin at all, even once (as if that were possible), we come short of His glory. Although people tend to regard their daily actions as being quite reasonable, surely God must view many of them as reprehensible in the same way that we view the most evil among us.

Perhaps you're thinking, "But wait a minute. The serial killer *tortured* and *killed* his victims, whereas we in our worst sins cannot harm an omnipotent God." Oh really? Do you realize the dilemma that our sins placed God in? Because He is holy, God is both just and merciful. He truly *loves* his creation, and His mercy cries out toward us. Consider the pain that God has endured on our behalf. In Genesis 6:6, we read, "The LORD was sorry that He had made man on the earth, and He was grieved in His heart." In Hosea, God laments His dilemma over His people Israel, who had become corrupt and deserved His severest judgment, and bares His heart: "How can I give you up … O Israel? … All My compassions are kindled" (Hosea 11:8). In order for God to reconcile *His mercy,* which compels Him to reach out to sinners in compassion, with *His justice,* which compels Him to administer the justice our sins deserve, our sovereign and holy God had to endure the pain of seeing His very own Son die on a cross in our place! This was the only way that we could be reconciled to Him, and your sins and mine nailed Jesus to that cross, which, incidentally, both *tortured* and *killed* Him! We are told in John 3:16, "For God so loved the world that He gave His only begotten Son that whosoever believeth in Him should not perish but have everlasting life."

One could argue, "Was it not God's choice to save us?" That is a very interesting question, and in one sense, He did make this choice, in fact the Bible teaches that God made this choice before creation itself. Revelation 13:8 refers to "the Lamb slain from the foundation of the world." However, in another sense, the answer may not be as obvious as we might think. While you and I make choices wavering between good and evil, or obedience or disobedience, God in His perfect holiness always chooses good and never evil. Thus, His very nature requires Him to make the *perfect* choice. Thus, if the choice facing God is between doing what is perfect and righteous, although it may be quite painful versus doing what is expedient to avoid the pain, His holy nature compels Him to choose the road of pain over the road of ease. God's holiness is rooted in His absoluteness rather than what is arbitrary. When one considers His transcendence, how could He do otherwise? Indeed, how could a perfect holy being be other than perfect and holy?

One of the chief complaints of unbelievers, particularly agnostics, can be summed up by the question "How could a good God send people to hell?" People who adopt this line of thinking either do not understand or are unwilling to accept the ramifications of a holy God. For those who do not believe in God, the word *good* loses its meaning, as it is reduced to mere relativism. Thus, the only basis for good and evil is the existence of a holy God. Otherwise, who defines what is good or evil? With man, the definition of good and evil varies both geographically and historically. Many things that are today regarded as good, or at least acceptable, were regarded as evil only a few decades earlier. Similarly, there are things regarded as good in this country but regarded as evil elsewhere. The Bible teaches that it is good to love your enemy, whereas the world teaches that it is good to hate him. The natural man makes comparisons between himself and others. He weighs his experience and then processes the information, which leads him to make conclusions about whether a person is good or bad, whether himself or someone else. Given our sinful nature, our evaluations might be akin to a murderer who had killed two people comparing himself to one who had killed ten, and then concluding himself to be good and the other evil. If our standard of righteousness is arbitrary, does it not follow that our conclusions will be faulty? Can right or wrong exist in any meaningful way in the absence of God and an absolute standard of righteousness?

If we who are made in God's image feel anger toward perpetrators of injustice, would it not follow that God must view man's rebellion against His law similar to the way that we view lawbreakers in society? At the heart level, He must also feel incredulous that man, His perfect creation made in His image, could stoop to the wickedness that He sees on earth on a daily basis. Our *natural* actions are the polar opposite of His perfectly righteous heart as the serial killer's actions are so opposite of our view of morality, imperfect as it is. Our elaborate legal system has been set up to punish wrongdoers for the good of society. Note that the Bible teaches that government was established by God.

> Every person is to be in subjection to the governing authorities. For there is no authority except from God, and those which exist are established by God. Therefore whoever resists authority has opposed the ordinance of God; and they who have opposed will receive condemnation upon themselves. (Romans 13:1–2)

Considering the pattern of violence that has existed throughout earth's history, is it even possible that our universe could have survived unless God were the benevolent holy and righteous sovereign that He is? It has been said, "Power corrupts; absolute power corrupts absolutely." What if this saying were true of God? History has repeatedly shown it to be true of man, especially in the last century, with men like Hitler, Mussolini, and Stalin. It has been said that history is His story. The Bible would certainly concur with that statement and indeed is the very basis of it. One need only glance at mankind's history of self-inflicted pain, misery, and destruction to conclude that we would not want to live for eternity in a heaven that resembled that! God has proven throughout His interaction with man that His wisdom transcends ours and He is faithful and just in all His dealings with man. God's very name I Am is a continual reminder to each of us that He is the only self-existent being in the entire universe, and as its Creator, we owe our very existence to Him.

If God is all-powerful and holy as the Bible claims, can He not be trusted to know what is best for His own universe? If His way *is* best, would it not follow that we would all be better off following it? There is a phrase in our holiness definition earlier that is particularly intriguing.

The first half of the definition is here repeated, showing this phrase in italics: "holiness means the pure, loving nature of God, separate from evil, *aggressively seeking to universalize itself ...*[2] Why would God "aggressively seek to universalize His holy nature in the universe?" Although in a very real sense it *is* God's way or the *highway*, He is hardly arbitrary or capricious in His thinking, nor is He selfish. How could the all-powerful God to whom every other being owes his existence be selfish or jealous? Who could compete or contend with Him? Could His insistence on things being His way be based on the simple fact that His way is best for all, for both us and Him? God has been continuously revealing to man His true glory, which has been masked and distorted by Satan throughout history. Consider now the second half of our holiness definition: "that *this character inheres in places, times and institutions intimately associated with worship*; and that *it is to characterize human beings who have entered into personal relations with God ...*"[2] The proper understanding of God's glory will always result in our being drawn to Him and our striving to become more *like* Him. God, whose holiness sets Him apart from man, also desires that His followers be set apart from the world unto Him. Sanctification connotes two ideas: (1) to be set apart and (2) to be made holy. Sanctification is the mode of life for everyone who has come to know Christ. Our responding to Him in faith will ultimately lead to eternal bliss in His presence in the New Jerusalem, which is heaven come down to earth. Additionally, the Christian life is the only way to live life purposefully in the midst of a world system of deceit, which dupes all those who are not led by Christ, Who is the light of the world.

Sanctification is a most difficult and unnatural endeavor. If it were not for the fact that it is a work of God in us, it would be a futile effort. Our abode is in a body that has a carnal nature, which is rebellious against God, surrounded by a people who are also carnal and rebellious against God, with Satan acting as catalyst. In the next chapter, we will see how we got to our current state of fallenness and the ramifications of it.

NOTES (CHAPTER 3)

[1] Stuart Berg Flexner et al., *Oxford American Dictionary, Heald College Edition*, (New York, Avon, 1986), 979

[2] Merrill C. Tenney and J. D. Douglas, *The Zondervan Pictorial Bible Dictionary*, (Grand Rapids: Zondervan, 1999), 357

4

CREATION, SIN, AND THE FALL

IN THE LAST CHAPTER WE LOOKED AT THE HOLINESS OF GOD. ONE MIGHT WELL ASK (indeed, many have), "If God is holy and He created everything, why is our world in such horrible condition, and why is there so much evil in the world?" How did we get to this point? Thankfully, the Bible is not silent on this point. It is very clear from God's Word that we live in a *fallen* world. This means that the world and all its inhabitants have been tainted, corrupted, and perverted from the way that God originally created them. The fall has had dire consequences for both mankind and the universe. The story of Adam and Eve's fall is carefully laid out in the book of Genesis and supplemented by other scriptures in both the Old and New Testament. Let's examine the primary text on this very important Christian doctrine from the early chapters of Genesis, beginning with the creation.

CREATION

In **Genesis 1**, we read about the six days of creation. The first verse begins, "In the beginning God created the heaven and the earth." Below is a short summary of what was created on each of the six days of creation:

Day 1: Creation of the heaven, earth, and light
Day 2: Division of the heaven (atmosphere and outer space) from the global sea
Day 3: Division of the land from the sea, creation of vegetation and its reproduction system
Day 4: Creation of the sun, moon, and stars to divide day from night and to mark seasons
Day 5: Creation of sea life and fowl and their reproduction systems
Day 6: Creation of insects, reptiles, land animals and mankind and their reproduction systems

In the creation account of Genesis 1, the author notes several times that "God saw that it was good," and once at the conclusion of His creation on the end of the sixth day, he notes that "God saw that it was *very* good." At the end of each day's creation is the phrase "the evening and the morning were the *nth* day." Toward the end of the creation account, we see that God made man unique among all His creation. Notice God's special intent for man below in the record of the last day of creation.

> And God said, *Let us make man in our image, after our likeness*: and *let them have dominion over ... all the earth ...* So *God created man in his* own *image, in the image of God created he him; male and female created he them.* And God blessed them, and God said unto them, Be fruitful, and multiply, and *replenish the earth, and subdue it: and have dominion over ... every living thing.* (Genesis 1:26–28)

> And God saw every thing that he had made, and, behold, *it* was very good. (Genesis 1:31)

Being made in the image of God was no small differentiation from the animal kingdom. This means that God created man with a spirit capable of wisdom, reason, reflection, creativity, ingenuity, satisfaction, and capable of deep emotions like love, hate, fear, courage, happiness, joy, sadness, anxiety, anguish, guilt, depression, and a host of other human emotions too numerous to mention. Note that man alone was singled out in Genesis 1:28 to *"replenish the earth, and subdue it: and have dominion over ... every living thing..."* Being God's image bearer came with both privilege and responsibility, as we will see very quickly in Genesis 2.

The creation account continues (Genesis 2:1–3) where, as though a postscript to Genesis 1, we read that God rested on the Sabbath (Genesis 2:2), as a model for us. Afterward in chapter 2, there is a distinct shift in the creation account where the focus turns to man, where we read that God planted a garden in Eden and placed man in the garden, making him the gardener.

> And the Lord God formed man *of* the dust of the ground, and breathed into his nostrils the breath of life; and man became a living soul. And the Lord God planted a garden eastward in Eden; and there he put the man whom he had formed. (Genesis 2:7–8)

What a privilege to be the first man of God's brand-new creation. Adam must have had a field day, no pun intended, exploring the beauty of all the lush vegetation around him and gazing up at the beautiful blue sky and the moon and stars at night. Can you imagine coming to life instantly as an adult with immediate and full cognitive ability? What a glorious surprise to the senses—all these wonderful sights, sounds, fragrances, things to touch, things to taste! With all this, how in the brand-new world could anyone ask for more? Yet there was *one* important thing missing in Adam's life. He was the sole human on this new planet. God, being concerned about the prospect of loneliness, had long ago determined to provide Adam and other living creatures with a helpmate. So God proceeded to parade each of the animals by Adam so that he could name them. However, as Adam was reviewing this seemingly endless parade, he couldn't help feeling that there was just something missing from each one of them. Their outward appearance, their shape, their skin, and hair were so unlike his own. As he petted each one, they all seemed so different from him. As he gazed into each one's eyes and tried earnestly to communicate with them, the only response he could muster was a blank stare, a tilted head, or a grunt, which seemed to say, "No one lives here." As he passed by each successive animal, his hope for true companionship grew more and more dim. There was just no compatibility between him and them, no spirit like his own reflected back to him. It was immediately clear that none of these animals would be suitable for Adam as a friend or confidant.

> And the LORD God said, *It is* not good that the man should be alone; I will make him an help meet for him. And out of the ground the LORD God formed every beast of the field, and every fowl of the air; and brought *them* unto Adam to see what he would call them: and whatsoever Adam called every living creature, that *was* the name thereof. And Adam gave names to all cattle, and to the fowl of the air, and to every beast of the field; but for Adam there was not found an help meet for him. (Genesis 2:18-20)

So God then intervened as Creator turned Great Physician and performed the first surgery in human history, utilizing the first anesthesia and the first sutures. God caused a deep sleep to fall on Adam and took one of his ribs and fashioned Eve. Adam's euphoric reaction to his new helpmate is both predictable and instantaneous: "This is now bone of my bones, flesh of my flesh—she shall be called Woman!" (Genesis 2:23) Thus, theirs was the first marriage in human history, and this glorious union became the pattern for all future marriages.

> Therefore shall a man leave his father and his mother, and shall cleave unto his wife: and they shall be one flesh. And they were both naked, the man and his wife, and were not ashamed. (Genesis 2:24–25)

Life in God's breathtakingly beautiful creation must have been glorious for Adam and Eve. He provided everything the new couple needed for life, liberty, and the pursuit of happiness. The new garden that God had planted was watered by a single river that divided into four rivers. It is noted that this description ties Eden to the area of the earth known as the Fertile Crescent, which is recognized by many historians as the cradle of civilization.

> And out of the ground made the LORD God to grow *every tree that is pleasant to the sight, and good for food; the tree of life* also in the midst of the garden, and *the tree of knowledge of good and evil.* And a river went out of Eden to water the garden; and from thence it was parted, and became into four heads. The name of the first *is* Pison: that *is* it which compasseth the whole land of Havilah, where *there is* gold; And the gold of that land *is* good: there *is* bdellium and the onyx stone. And the name of the second river *is* Gihon: the same *is* it that compasseth the whole land of Ethiopia. And the name of the third river *is* Hiddekel: that *is* it which goeth toward the east of Assyria. And the fourth river

is Euphrates. And the LORD God took the man, and put him into the garden of Eden to dress it and to keep it. And the LORD God commanded the man, saying, Of every tree of the garden thou mayest freely eat: But of *the tree of the knowledge of good and evil, thou shalt not eat of it: for in the day that thou eatest thereof thou shalt surely die.* (Genesis 2:9-17)

Anyone who has ever pondered the creation account has no doubt imagined himself/herself as Adam or Eve in that perfect environment on brand-new planet Earth, with all the beautiful trees, grass, plant life, brilliantly colored flowers, butterflies, birds, incredibly fresh floral scents, friendly nonthreatening animals, no hint of danger, perfect peace and tranquility, and perfect human innocence. Just think—no pollution, no crime, no immorality, no bad news, no sickness or disease, and no death. Mankind never had it so good! Also, note the two very mysterious trees mentioned in the garden, *the tree of life* and *the tree of knowledge of good and evil*. As we will shortly see, one will figure very prominently in the fall of man, and the other will figure very prominently in his redemption.

THE FALL

God's new studies would soon learn the secrets of life, including both the joys and, soon, the pains of human existence. He had conferred upon them the precious privilege of freedom, including the privilege of *free choice*. I'm sure Adam and Eve made many choices during their average day in the garden before the fall—what they would have for breakfast, lunch, and supper; where they would go for their morning and evening walk; what steps they would take in learning their new work of attending to this beautiful garden, and the resulting iterative process of trial and error inherent on every job. In fact, we make the most choices in our lives when we are facing change, as change requires choice. Considering that everything in their life was brand new, their whole life was change—they didn't even have a comfort zone to leave!

God had provided so much for the young couple, and He loved them as any new father would love his children. He wanted to have a meaningful relationship with these precious children of his that bore His resemblance, rather than to just sit idly back in heaven as an unattached observer. As we have all learned, sometimes quite painfully, relationships depend very heavily on trust. Adam and Eve would have to learn how to *trust* God. Could God, the only other friend either of them had besides each other, be trusted? On the other hand, could *they* be trusted? Their fate and the fate of the entire universe hung on the answer to this critically important question. God had certainly given Adam and Eve no reason to doubt Him.

The stage was now set to answer these all-important questions on trust and faithfulness, and the universal implications that would hinge on the answers. An enemy, another one of God's creatures, and a very disenchanted one at that, crept stealthily into the peace and tranquility of Eden. This enemy was about to take Eve and her husband Adam for a ride that they would rather not have gone on. An old adage states that sin always takes us further than we want to go and costs us more than we want to pay and keeps us longer than we want to stay. We are about to witness the first sin in human history. Observe it well and note that the pathology here is the same as for every other sin that has or ever will be committed in human history.

> Now the *serpent was more subtle* than any beast of the field which the LORD God had made. And he said unto the woman, Yea, *hath God said*, Ye shall not eat of every tree of the garden? And the woman said unto the serpent, We may eat of the fruit of the trees of the garden: But of the fruit of the tree which is in the midst of the garden, *God hath said, Ye shall not eat of it*, neither shall ye touch it, lest ye die. And *the serpent said* unto the woman, *Ye shall not surely die:* For God doth know that in the day ye eat thereof, then your eyes shall be opened, and *ye shall be as gods*, knowing good and evil. (Genesis 3:1–5)

Now the couple was faced with a *critical* choice: whether or not to believe the One who had created them and everything around them, the One who had sustained them, the One who had taught them everything they knew and needed to know, *even* which choice to make in this very situation! So now they had a decision to make: "Should we trust God, or should we trust this stranger who says that God cannot be trusted?" You and I might be quick to judge Adam and Eve, but we would do well to consider that they had not been schooled on the subject of lying, as you and I have, both by the hurts we've experienced from the lies of others and the hurts we've experienced from our own lies. How *unfortunate* that their first experience with lying was to be confronted with the greatest lie that has ever been told. How ironic that the only perfectly holy being in the entire universe, the only one who has *never* lied, is now being accused of being the liar. The serpent had baited and set the trap, and the heavenly host must have gasped in utter horror and disbelief as Eve approached the forbidden tree, pondering whether or not to take a bite.

> And when the woman saw that the tree was good for food, and that it was pleasant to the eyes, and a tree to be desired to make one wise, she took of the fruit thereof, and did eat, and gave also unto her husband with her; and he did eat. (Genesis 3:6)

"What will happen now?" must have been Adam and Eve's first question, the moment each of them had eaten the forbidden fruit. They both, no doubt, still felt very alive. As the author of Hebrews notes (Hebrews 11:25), sin certainly brings "pleasures … for a season," and I imagine that the fruit was quite tasty. However, it's the aftermath of sin that kills you. Adam and Eve had failed the *trust* test. They were about to get some quick lessons on death from the One who had done everything divinely possible to satisfy their every need. The first effect of their choice, and the most damning one, was that it had hurt their relationship with God. As we well know, this would be just the first of a host of repercussions from this wrong choice that are still affecting you and me today. Let's observe from scripture how devastating this was to them, and let it be a fresh lesson for us on how devastating sin still is! They got what they wanted, and yet it wasn't. They wanted to know about good and evil, right and wrong, and yet they found this knowledge to be quite scary.

> And *the eyes of them both were opened*, and *they knew that they were naked*; and they sewed fig leaves together, and made themselves aprons. And they heard the voice of the Lord God walking in the garden in the cool of the day: and *Adam and his wife hid themselves from the presence of the Lord God* amongst the trees of the garden. And the Lord God called unto Adam, and said unto him, Where art thou? And he said, *I heard thy voice in the garden, and I was afraid* because I was naked; and I hid myself. And he said, Who told thee that thou wast naked? Hast thou eaten of the tree, whereof I commanded thee that thou shouldest not eat? And *the man said, The woman whom thou gavest to be with me, she gave me* of the tree, and I did eat. And the Lord God said unto the woman, What is this that thou hast done? And *the woman said, The serpent beguiled me,* and I did eat. (Genesis 3:7–13)

We immediately see the effects of their broken relationship with God and the painful consequences of their disobedience. First of all, their *sexuality* had previously been a good and holy thing, but now it had become corrupted, and they were painfully aware of their *nakedness*. Next, we see their feeling of guilt and its corresponding sense of alienation from God. They now felt *dirty* and *unworthy*, and even *afraid* in His presence, something they had never experienced previously, which resulted in their spontaneous and ill-conceived plan to hide from God. Lastly, we see one of the results of their fear of God—dishonesty. When asked *why* they had disobeyed God, we see Eve blaming the serpent. We also see Adam blaming Eve and ultimately even blaming God with his answer, "the woman whom *Thou* gavest … me." The young couple were painfully learning the meaning of God's solemn warning "In the day that thou eatest thereof *thou shalt surely die*" as He pronounced His judgment on them. How this must have blindsided them! This certainly wasn't what they had planned on a short while ago when pondering what seemed like such a reasonable decision.

> And the Lord God said unto the *serpent*, Because thou hast done this, *thou* art *cursed* above all cattle, and above every beast of the field; upon thy belly shalt thou go, and dust shalt thou eat all the days of thy life: And *I will put enmity between thee and the woman, and between thy seed and her seed; it shall bruise thy head, and thou shalt bruise his heel.* Unto the *woman* he said, *I will greatly multiply thy sorrow and thy conception; in sorrow thou shalt bring forth children;* and thy desire shall be to thy husband, and he shall rule over thee. And unto *Adam* he said, Because thou hast hearkened unto the voice of thy wife, and hast eaten of the tree, of which I commanded thee, saying, Thou shalt not eat of it: *cursed* is *the ground* for thy sake; *in sorrow shalt thou eat* of *it* all the days of thy life; *Thorns also and thistles shall it bring forth* to thee; and thou shalt eat

the herb of the field; *In the sweat of thy face shalt thou eat bread, till thou return unto the ground*; for out of it wast thou taken: for dust thou art, and unto dust shalt thou return. (Genesis 3:14–19)

Now, the hammer fell, the verdict was rendered—death and all its accoutrements. God was compelled by His utter hatred of sin and evil to judge Adam, Eve, and the serpent. Note the effects for Eve (discomfort in pregnancy, pain in childbirth) and for Adam, cursed ground—thorns and thistles, to which we could add weeds, briars, beggar lice, cactus, tsunamis, tornadoes, hurricanes, floods, sleet, hail, quicksand, swamps, avalanches, earthquakes, volcanoes, famines, ticks, spiders, scorpions … lions, tigers and bears, oh my, and a host of other curses. The time bomb of *death* had now started ticking, not only for Adam and Eve, but for all of us. Death means so much more than dying at the end of life; it means dying here and now while we live, even under the best of circumstances, and especially under the worst of them, such as war, cancer, injury, poverty, disability, torture, natural disasters, to name a few.

On the other hand, God, not one to be caught off guard, a prerequisite of omniscience, already had a plan. However, the disenfranchised Satan was out of luck since God's plan of redemption was only for *people*. In fact, the plan is revealed in this passage in the middle of God's judgment, of all places! It is, in fact, the first prophecy about Jesus Christ in scripture, as God spoke judgment on the serpent, *"And I will put enmity between thee and the woman, and between thy seed and her seed; it shall bruise thy head, and thou shalt bruise his heel."* (Genesis 3:15). This verse is sometimes referred to as the Protoevangelion, a Latin term that essentially means "first gospel" (*proto* as in prototype, and *evangel* as in evangelism). This verse will be elaborated on later in the book as we delve into the various prophecies and types in the Old Testament.

So now that we have examined the fall of Adam and Eve from scripture, let's briefly discuss some of the ramifications of the fall for people of all ages, as well as the ramifications for our universe: death (physical and spiritual), sickness and disease, a propensity to be at enmity with God and the outworking of that causing enmity in our human relationships, anxiety, fear, anger, violence, greed, dishonesty, striving, arguing, obstinacy, jealousy, bitterness, retribution, vengeance, war, slavery, oppression, and the endless list goes on. This list of *personal woes* also has a *corporate effect*, in that all societies and nations are made up of fallen people. Thus, the destructive tendencies of these people corporately tend toward the destruction of whole communities, nations, and ultimately, even global destruction. That is why nations collapse internally, because of this collective sin effect.

Could this dismal picture of sin, death and destruction possibly be the end of God's wonderful creation? We reflect back on His assessment of each creation day's work, "and God saw that it was *good*," and on the final day, after his work was finished, "and God saw that it was *very good*." Adam and Eve, who had been created in God's image, with His very DNA, have now become his enemies? What a tragic turn of events! How could this true story that had such a wonderful beginning now end so tragically? Could this possibly be the final answer?

What about the mysterious *tree of life* that we read about in **Genesis 2**? Hear the grief in God's voice as He utters His solemn pronouncement at the end of chapter 3.

> And the L{\small ORD} God said, Behold, *the man is become as one of us, to know good and evil:* and now, *lest he put forth his hand, and take also of the tree of life, and eat, and live for ever:* Therefore the L{\small ORD} *God sent him forth from the garden of Eden, to till the ground from whence he was taken.* So he drove out the man; *and he placed at the east of the garden of Eden Cherubims, and a flaming sword which turned every way, to keep the way of the tree of life.* (Genesis 3:22–24)

One of the great ironies of scripture is that a tree was the instrument that brought the fall of man, and a tree was also the instrument that brought about his redemption, and the tree of life will be in the eternal heaven on earth bearing its fruit in every season.

> Christ hath redeemed us from the curse of the law, being made a curse for us: for it is written, Cursed is every one that hangeth on a tree. (Galatians 3:13)

> And he shewed me a pure river of water of life, clear as crystal, proceeding out of the throne of God and of the Lamb. In the midst of the street of it, and *on either side of the river, was there the tree of life, which bare twelve manner of fruits, and yielded her fruit every month: and the leaves of the tree were for the healing of the nations.* (Revelation 22:1–2)

In the next chapter, we will see how God has provided for the redemption of fallen man.

5

JUDGMENT OR REDEMPTION

THE COMING JUDGMENT

IN THE LAST TWO CHAPTERS WE HAVE SEEN THE GREAT GULF BETWEEN GOD'S HOLINESS AND mankind's sinful depravity. At some point in your life, you may have asked yourself how you could possibly bridge this seemingly impossible gulf between you and God, knowing that you are guilty of breaking His perfect law and, therefore, fail to meet His requirement of perfect righteousness. Have you ever dreaded the day that you would stand before your Maker to give an account of your life?

Although there are different views among Bible scholars as to how God's judgment will unfold, there are several Bible passages dealing with this subject. We will look at these scriptures below.

1) **Who Will Judge:** Jesus said that God the Father had appointed Him as mankind's judge, and this was also affirmed by the apostles.

> For *the Father judgeth no man, but hath committed all judgment unto the Son:* That all men should honour the Son, even as they honour the Father. He that honoureth not the Son honoureth not the Father which hath sent him. (John 5:22–23)

> And he commanded us to preach unto the people, and to testify that it is *he which was ordained of God to be the Judge of quick and dead.* (Acts 10:42, see Acts 10:40–43, Peter to Cornelius's household)

> Because *he hath appointed a day,* in which *he will judge the world in righteousness by that man whom he hath ordained;* whereof he hath given assurance unto all men, in that *he hath raised him from the dead.* (Acts 17:31, Paul to the Jews in Athens)

> Let this mind be in you, which was also in Christ Jesus: Who, being in the form of God, thought it not robbery to be equal with God: But made

himself of no reputation, and took upon him the form of a servant, and was made in the likeness of men: And being found in fashion as a man, he humbled himself, and became obedient unto death, even the death of the cross. Wherefore *God also hath highly exalted him, and given him a name which is above every name*: That *at the name of Jesus every knee should bow*, of things in heaven, and things in earth, and things under the earth; And that *every tongue should confess that Jesus Christ is Lord, to the glory of God the Father.* (Philippians 2:5–11, Paul to the Philippians, this passage possibly an early church hymn)

2) **How Many End-Time Judgments:** Generally, those who hold to the premillennial view of the end times believe there will be separate judgments for the lost and for the saved.

And I saw thrones, and they sat upon them, and judgment was given unto them: and I saw the souls of them that were beheaded for the witness of Jesus, and for the word of God, and which had not worshipped the beast, neither his image, neither had received his mark upon their foreheads, or in their hands; and they lived and reigned with Christ a thousand years. But the rest of the dead lived not again until the thousand years were finished. This is the *first resurrection. Blessed and holy is he that hath part in the first resurrection: on such the second death hath no power,* but *they shall be priests of God and of Christ, and shall reign with him a thousand years.* (Revelation 20:4–6)

The above passage speaks of a *first resurrection*, which implies that there is also a *second resurrection* (spoken of in Revelation 20:13). Those resurrected prior to the thousand years are Christians, and those resurrected after the thousand years are the lost who are doomed to hell. Note that those who are part of the first resurrection (1) will reign with Christ for 1,000 years and (2) will not be subject *to the second death.* They will be judged at the Judgment Seat of Christ spoken of below.

So we will see from the following passages how the saved are united with Christ.

AT DEATH WE ARE IMMEDIATELY IN GOD'S PRESENCE

Absent from the body, present with the Lord
Therefore we are always confident, knowing that, whilst we are at home in the body, we are absent from the Lord: (For we walk by faith, not by sight:) We are confident, I say, and willing rather *to be absent from the body, and to be present with the Lord.* (2 Corinthians 5:6–8)

Paul's dilemma

For to me to live is Christ, and to die is gain. But if I live in the flesh, this is the fruit of my labour: yet what I shall choose I wot not. For I am in a strait betwixt two, having a desire to *depart, and to be with Christ*; which is far better: Nevertheless to abide in the flesh is more needful for you. (Philippians 1:21–24)

AT JESUS'S RETURN, WE ARE IMMEDIATELY USHERED INTO HIS PRESENCE

Immediately after the tribulation of those days shall the sun be darkened, and the moon shall not give her light, and the stars shall fall from heaven, and the powers of the heavens shall be shaken: And then shall appear the sign of the Son of man in heaven: and then shall all the tribes of the earth mourn, and they shall see the Son of man coming in the clouds of heaven with power and great glory. And *he shall send his angels with a great sound of a trumpet, and they shall gather together his elect* from the four winds, from one end of heaven to the other. (Matthew 24:29–31)

For this we say unto you by the word of the Lord, that we which are alive and remain unto the coming of the Lord shall not prevent them which are asleep. For the Lord himself shall descend from heaven with a shout, with the voice of the archangel, and with the trump of God: and *the dead in Christ shall rise first*: Then *we which are alive and remain shall be caught up together with them in the clouds*, to meet the Lord in the air: and *so shall we ever be with the Lord*. (1 Thessalonians 4:15–17)

So also is the resurrection of the dead. *It is sown in corruption; it is raised in incorruption*: It is sown in dishonour; it is raised in glory: *it is sown in weakness; it is raised in power*: *It is sown a natural body; it is raised a spiritual body*. There is a natural body, and there is a spiritual body. (1 Corinthians 15:42–44)

Behold, I shew you a mystery; *We shall not all sleep, but we shall all be changed, In a moment, in the twinkling of an eye*, at the last trump: for the trumpet shall sound, and *the dead shall be raised incorruptible*, and *we shall be changed*. For this corruptible must put on incorruption, and *this mortal must put on immortality*. (1 Corinthians 15:51–53)

We see from the above passages from the Olivet Discourse and Paul's first letters to the Corinthians and to the Thessalonians, that when Jesus comes, we will be ushered into His presence. Some see the two passages as representing two comings of Jesus, the latter two referring to the Rapture, and the former as the Second Coming of Christ at the end of the tribulation period. Others see all three passages as referring to the Second Coming. There may be some confusion in the expressions "the dead in Christ shall rise first," and "In a moment, in the twinkling of an eye … we shall be changed" (1 Thessalonians 4:16 and 1 Corinthians 15:52 respectively). How does this reconcile with the foregoing passages in 2 Corinthians 5 and Philippians 1, which indicate that we are immediately ushered into Christ's presence? Many commentators believe that when we die, our spirit will immediately be translated into Christ's presence, and at the Second Coming / Rapture, our spirit will be joined to our immortal body. This is my personal belief.

3) **Judgment of the Saved:** It appears from the foregoing passages that the *saved* will have two advantages over the *lost* on Judgment Day: (1) that they're saved and (2) that they will know ahead of time that they're saved! This is because at death we are immediately ushered into the Lord's presence, and when He returns, those who are alive will immediately be ushered into His presence. This will be our first *meeting* with Him, and judgment will follow that event! Below are passages dealing with Judgment Day for the saved.

The Judgment Seat of Christ

For we must all appear before the judgment seat of Christ; that every one may receive the things done in his body, according to that he hath done, whether it be good or bad. (2 Corinthians 5:10)

The Basis for Believers' Judgment

For other foundation can no man lay than that is laid, which is Jesus Christ. Now if any man build upon this foundation gold, silver, precious stones, wood, hay, stubble; Every man's work shall be made manifest: for the day shall declare it, because it shall be revealed by fire; and the fire shall try every man's work of what sort it is. If any man's work abide which he hath built thereupon, he shall receive a reward. If any man's work shall be burned, he shall suffer loss: but he himself shall be saved; yet so as by fire. (1 Corinthians 3:11–15)

4) **Judgment of the Lost:** On the other hand, the lost will be awakened from their thousand-year-plus slumber of death to appear before the Great White Throne Judgment.

The Great White Throne Judgment

And I saw a great white throne, and him that sat on it, from whose face the earth and the heaven fled away; and there was found no place for them. And I saw the dead, small and great, stand before God; and the books were opened: and another book was opened, which is the book of life: and the dead were judged out of those things which were written in the books, according to their works. And the sea gave up the dead which were in it; and death and hell delivered up the dead which were in them: and they were judged every man according to their works. And death and hell were cast into the lake of fire. This is the second death. And whosoever was not found written in the book of life was cast into the lake of fire. (Revelation 20:11–15)

If you look at this passage by itself, it appears that both the saved and lost are present at this judgment. However, when it is harmonized with Revelation 20:4–6, we see that this judgment involves only the lost. From this passage, we can glean that everyone who ever has or will live on planet earth will be judged by one of two ways—*the books* or *the Book of Life*. Those whose names are written in the Book of Life have previously been judged as righteous by virtue of Christ's imputed righteousness.

Anyone reading this passage should want to know first and foremost, "Is my name written in the Book of Life?" What determines whether our name is recorded in this precious book of God? There is no decision in life that is more critical than our decision concerning our approaching judgment, because it will determine where we will spend eternity.

TWO POSSIBLE ETERNAL DESTINATIONS

The Bible describes two final destinations for every person who has ever lived or will ever live in the future. When each of us departs this life to meet our Maker, His verdict will be final and will determine whether we will be ushered into *heaven* to spend eternity in His presence, or whether we will be sentenced to an eternity in the Lake of Fire, the final *hell*.

HELL

Unless we choose to accept God's provision for our sin, we will be doomed to hell. Since every one of us has sinned against God and broken His holy law, we all *deserve* hell in the same way that those who break the laws of society deserve the punishment that society mandates for the particular crime. God has made it clear in His Word that the final punishment of all the unsaved will be the Lake of Fire. Perhaps you have heard the expression "Ignorance of the law is no excuse." This appears to be God's perspective (Romans 1:18–32, 3:10–19). Although there is scripture that indicates God's punishment may be meted out in degrees relative to what a person should have reasonably known (Luke 12:37–48), I'm not sure how this applies to life in the Lake of Fire. It is difficult for us to imagine the horror of eternal banishment from God's presence and burning in unquenchable fire. Jesus describes hell in the gospels, and the apostle John described it in the book of Revelation. Jesus also notes that hell was prepared for the devil and his angels, which would suggest that it was not God's intended destination for people, though many will end up there.

Hell prepared for the devil and his angels
Depart from me, ye cursed, into *everlasting fire, prepared for the devil and his angels.* (Matthew 25:41)

Urgency of avoiding hell
And if thy right eye offend thee, pluck it out, and cast it from thee: for it is profitable for thee that one of thy members should perish, and not that thy whole body should be cast into hell. And if thy right hand offend thee, cut it off, and cast it from thee: for it is profitable for thee that one of thy members should perish, and not that thy whole body should be cast into hell. (Matthew 5:29–30)

Urgency of Fearing God, Who casts into hell
But I will forewarn you whom ye shall fear: *Fear him, which after he hath killed hath power to cast into hell;* yea, I say unto you, Fear him. (Luke 12:5)

No escape from hell
And in hell he lift up his eyes, being in torments, and seeth Abraham afar off, and Lazarus in his bosom. And he cried and said, Father Abraham, have mercy on me, and send Lazarus, that he may dip the tip of his finger in water, and cool my tongue; for I am tormented in this flame … And beside all this, between us and you *there is a great gulf fixed: so that they which would pass from hence to you cannot; neither can they pass to us, that would come from thence.* (Luke 16:23–24, 16:26)

Hell, a place of eternal torment
If any man worship the beast and his image, and receive his mark in his forehead, or in his hand, The same shall drink of the wine of the wrath of God, which is poured out without mixture into the cup of his indignation; and *he shall be tormented with fire and brimstone* in the presence of the holy angels, and in the presence of the Lamb: And *the smoke of their torment ascendeth up for ever and ever: and they have no rest day nor night,* who worship the beast and his image, and whosoever receiveth the mark of his name. (Revelation 14:9–11)

Life in hell described as death
And death and hell were cast into the lake of fire. This is *the second death.* (Revelation 20:14)

HEAVEN

On the other hand, for those who accept God's program of amnesty for sinners as seen in the passage below, their eternity will be spent in the presence of God in heaven.

> Therefore if any man be in Christ, he is a new creature: old things are passed away; behold, all things are become new. And all things are of God, who hath reconciled us to himself by Jesus Christ, and hath given to us the ministry of reconciliation; To wit, that *God was in Christ, reconciling the world unto himself, not imputing their trespasses unto them*; and hath committed unto us the word of reconciliation. Now then *we are ambassadors for Christ, as though God did beseech you by us: we pray you in Christ's stead, be ye reconciled to God*. For *he hath made him to be sin for us, who knew no sin; that we might be made the righteousness of God in him*. (2 Corinthians 5:17–21)

So, as an ambassador for Christ, may I urge you to receive God's gift of eternal life simply by taking God at His word and, by faith, trusting in Jesus Christ as your Lord and Savior, understanding that His atoning sacrifice fully paid for your sins—past, present and future. Also, as Lord of your life, He promises to give you rest and that His yoke is easy (Matthew 11:29–30), and that He offers life abundantly (John 10:10). After all, who could you trust more than one who has proven His love for you by His sacrificial death on a cross?

Just as the horrors of hell are unimaginable, the beauty of heaven is unimaginable. Although the Bible does not answer every possible question about heaven that we might have, there are passages of scripture that provide significant detail about what heaven will be like. Below are some descriptions of heaven in the New Testament.

Jesus's testimony about heaven:

Heaven is eternal
For God so loved the world, that he gave his only begotten Son, that *whosoever believeth in him should not perish, but have everlasting life*. (John 3:16)

Heaven, a physical place, a social place
Let not your heart be troubled: ye believe in God, believe also in me. *In my Father's house are many mansions*: if it were not so, I would have told you. *I go to prepare a place for you*. And if I go and prepare a place for you, *I will come again, and receive you unto myself; that where I am, there ye may be also*. (John 14:1–3)

Paul's testimony about heaven:

We can't even imagine

But as it is written, *Eye hath not seen, nor ear heard, neither have entered into the heart of man, the things which God hath prepared for them that love him.* (1 Corinthians 2:9)

Paul's visit to heaven

I knew a man in Christ above fourteen years ago, (whether in the body, I cannot tell; or whether out of the body, I cannot tell: God knoweth;) such an one *caught up to the third heaven.* And I knew such a man, (whether in the body, or out of the body, I cannot tell: God knoweth;) How that *he was caught up into paradise, and heard unspeakable words, which it is not lawful for a man to utter.* (2 Corinthians 12:2–4)

Note: first heaven = atmosphere, second heaven = outer space, third heaven = heaven

John's testimony about heaven:

The New Jerusalem, the final heaven

And *I saw a new heaven and a new earth*: for *the first heaven and the first earth were passed away*; and there was no more sea. And *I John saw the holy city, new Jerusalem, coming down from God out of heaven*, prepared as a bride adorned for her husband. And I heard a great voice out of heaven saying, *Behold, the tabernacle of God is with men, and he will dwell with them, and they shall be his people, and God himself shall be with them, and be their God.* And *God shall wipe away all tears* from their eyes; and *there shall be no more death, neither sorrow, nor crying, neither shall there be any more pain*: for the former things are passed away. (Revelation 21:1–4)

And he carried me away in the spirit to a great and high mountain, and shewed me that great city, the holy Jerusalem, descending out of heaven from God, Having the glory of God: and her light was like unto a stone most precious, even like a jasper stone, clear as crystal. (Revelation 21:10–11)

And he that talked with me had a golden reed to measure the city, and the gates thereof, and the wall thereof. And the city lieth foursquare, and the *length is as large as the breadth: and he measured the city with the reed, twelve thousand furlongs. The length and the breadth and the height of it are equal* ... [i.e., the city's length, width, and height are 1,500 miles]. (Revelation 21:15–16 NASB)

And the building of *the wall of it was of jasper*: and *the city was pure gold, like unto clear glass*. And the foundations of the wall of the city were garnished with all manner of precious stones. (Revelation 21:18–19)

And the twelve gates were twelve pearls: every several gate was of one pearl: and *the street of the city was pure gold, as it were transparent glass*. And I saw no temple therein: for the Lord God Almighty and the Lamb are the temple of it. And *the city had no need of the sun, neither of the moon, to shine in it: for the glory of God did lighten it, and the Lamb is the light thereof.* (Revelation 21:21–23)

And he shewed me a pure river of water of life, clear as crystal, proceeding out of the throne of God and of the Lamb. In the midst of the street of it, and on either side of the river, was there the tree of life, which bare twelve manner of fruits, and yielded her fruit every month: and the leaves of the tree were for the healing of the nations. And there shall be no more curse: but *the throne of God and of the Lamb shall be in it*; and *his servants shall serve him*: And *they shall see his face*. (Revelation 22:1–4, italics added)

A CROSSROADS

In our culture, we have all encountered various *ideas* of what heaven and hell would be like, ranging from nonexistent to comical or sarcastic depictions. However, the above comparison is sobering. On that day when we pass from this life to the next, there will be nothing more important than where we will spend eternity! Jesus gave us this solemn warning:

Enter ye in at the strait gate: for *wide is the gate*, and *broad is the way, that leadeth to destruction*, and *many there be which go in thereat*: Because *strait is the gate, and narrow is the way, which leadeth unto life, and few there be that find it.* (Matthew 7:13–14)

Here, Jesus gave us some insight on gaining eternal life. First, we see that only a *few* will be able to enter the gate that leads to eternal life in heaven, whereas the *majority* will enter the gate that ends in destruction and eternal torment in hell. The straight and narrow gate that Jesus referred to is Himself. Today there are many areas of the world where people have never even heard of Jesus Christ. The table below showing 2020 data was obtained from *Religion by Country 2024—World Population Review*.[1]

Below is each religion's estimated population for 2020.

Christianity–2.38 billion
Islam–1.91 billion
Hinduism–1.16 billion
Buddhism–507 million
Folk Religions –430 million
Other Religions–6.1 million
Judaism–14.6 million
Unaffiliated–1.19 billion

Worldwide population–7.60 billion

From this table we can see that only about a third of the world's population *even claims* to be Christian, so nearly 2,000 years after Jesus spoke the words in Matthew 7:13–14, we see the sobering accuracy of His words.

There is probably no other doctrine in the Christian faith that is more offensive to non-Christians than the exclusionary doctrine of salvation by Christ alone, yet to the Christian, this doctrine is axiomatic. When Jesus warned His disciples of His impending death foreordained by God, He told them …

> Jesus saith unto him, I am the way, the truth, and the life: no man cometh unto the Father, but by me. (John 14:6)

Jesus is the *Way*—He is the *means* of pleasing God, and for obtaining heaven.
Jesus is the *Truth*—He is the *embodiment of truth*, the image of the invisible God (Col. 1:15).
Jesus is the *Life*—He is the *life giver*.

In the above verse Jesus referred to Himself as the *Way*, the *Truth*, and the *Life*. In another passage, Jesus referred to Himself as *the door*, and Luke reports in the book of Acts that there is *no other name* whereby we must be saved.

> Then said Jesus unto them again, Verily, verily, I say unto you, *I am the door* of the sheep. All that ever came before me are thieves and robbers: but the sheep did not hear them. *I am the door: by me if any man enter in, he shall be saved,* and shall go in and out, and find pasture. The thief cometh not, but for to steal, and to kill, and to destroy: *I am come that they might have life, and that they might have it more abundantly.* (John 10:7–10)

> Neither is there salvation in any other: for *there is none other name under heaven given among men, whereby we must be saved.* (Acts 4:12)

WAYS THAT PEOPLE RESPOND TO
THE GOSPEL MESSAGE

We saw in chapter 2 that the gospel is the good news that Jesus paid the full penalty for our sins, and that everyone who places his faith in Him receives the gift of eternal life. People respond differently when they hear the gospel message. Jesus told a parable to illustrate this—the Parable of the Sower (Matthew 13:1–9). In this parable, Jesus presents an everyday illustration from life, a sower planting seed. He explains that the seed is God's Word. In this parable, Jesus speaks of the seed falling on four different types of soil. His explanation of the parable is found in Matthew 13:18–23. The following is a summary of the four soils in the parable and the explanation of each:

1. **Wayside Soil**—this soil beside the road is hard and packed from foot traffic, and the birds (representing Satan) eat the seed before it can take root. This represents the distracted hearer—he hears the gospel with his ears, but due to internal or external distractions, he fails to fully comprehend it.

2. **Stony Soil**—this is a thin layer of soil with rock underlying it. Seed falling on this soil takes root; however, with no depth of soil, the only way the plant can grow is up. However, when the sun comes up, there is no adequate root system that can reach groundwater, and the plant quickly burns up and dies. This represents a hearer who joyfully hears the gospel, but when he encounters life's afflictions or persecution for his faith, he becomes disheartened and falls away.

3. **Thorny Soil**—this soil is infested with adverse plants (thorns or weeds that are already established, and they use up the nutrients and moisture from the soil), and the growth above ground blocks out the sun so that this combined effect chokes off growth of the seed. This represents a hearer of the gospel whose ongoing worries or quest for wealth becomes his continual focus, and his original fervor for the gospel becomes merely a peripheral interest in his life.

4. **Good Soil**—this soil is fertile. When the seed hits it, it takes root and produces a crop bearing fruit, and multiplying. This represents a hearer who hears the gospel, understands it, and comprehends that eternal life and subjection to Christ are paramount, and he prioritizes his life accordingly.

OBSTACLES TO SALVATION

There are three obstacles to salvation—the world, the flesh, and the devil. The first of the four soils above involved *the devil* snatching away the gospel message from the distracted hearer. The second soil involves all three of the obstacles—Satan is constantly trying to persecute us from within as we saw him do this to Jesus in the wilderness (Matthew 4), even using God's Word in his attempts. Persecution also comes from other people. Christian persecution is intense in many parts of the world, where being a Christian may even cost you your life. Also, the weakness of our flesh tempts us to give up when persecution arises. I see the third soil type as dealing primarily with the world and the flesh in the distractions of worry and wealth. Finally, in the good soil, we see all these obstacles being overcome.

WAYS PEOPLE RESPOND TO THE GOSPEL

The Way of Unbelief: Since we are all born into sin by virtue of being descendants of Adam the first sinner, every one of us has at one time or other been in this stage of life. In the book of Romans, Paul makes it quite clear mankind does *not* seek God.

> As it is written, There is *none* righteous, no, *not one*: There is *none* that understandeth, there is *none* that seeketh after God. They are *all* gone out of the way, they are together become unprofitable; there is *none* that doeth good, no, *not one*. Their throat is an open sepulchre; with their tongues they have used deceit; the poison of asps is under their lips: Whose mouth is full of cursing and bitterness: Their feet are swift to shed blood: Destruction and misery are in their ways: And the way of peace have they not known: There is no fear of God before their eyes. (Romans 3:10–17)

In this passage, we see the words *none* and *all* used a lot. No one seeks God. All have disregarded God and led immoral lives.

> For I know that in me (that is, in my flesh,) dwelleth no good thing: for to will is present with me; but how to perform that which is good I find not. (Romans 7:18)

> Because the carnal mind is enmity against God: for it is not subject to the law of God, neither indeed can be. So then they that are in the flesh cannot please God. (Romans 8:7–8)

We can see from these passages that man, left to his own devices, is completely unable to seek God. There are some verses in John's gospel where Jesus speaks of this same phenomenon by stating that the Father must intervene in a person's life for him to come to Christ. Jesus's statement to Nicodemus is perhaps the most familiar.

> Jesus answered and said unto him, Verily, verily, I say unto thee, *Except a man be born again, he can not see the kingdom of God.* (John 3:3)

> *All that the Father giveth me shall come to me*; and him that cometh to me I will in no wise cast out ... *No man can come to me, except the Father which hath sent me draw him*: and I will raise him up at the last day. (John 6:37, 6:44)

People who are in a state of unbelief will never seek God. Only God can draw people to Himself, but not everyone to whom He reveals Himself will come to Him. There are obstacles that must be overcome when we are drawn to God and then set out to seek Him.

The Way of Doubt: When people are introduced to God's Word, one very persistent obstacle must be overcome for them to grow in their relationship with God—doubt. This is a critical stage in our spiritual development. Doubt obviously afflicts unbelievers, and it even afflicts believers. After seeing Jesus arrested in the Garden of Gethsemane, Peter was apparently so filled with doubt, or at least confusion, that he denied three times that he even *knew* Jesus. James spoke of the malady of doubt and its paralyzing effects in his epistle.

> If any of you lack wisdom, let him ask of God, that giveth to all men liberally, and upbraideth not; and it shall be given him. But let him ask in faith, nothing wavering. *For he that wavereth is like a wave of the sea driven with the wind and tossed.* For let not that man think that he shall receive any thing of the Lord. *A double minded man is unstable in all his ways.* (James 1:5–8)

Doubt is something that we all struggle with. You may recall the father who came to Jesus on behalf of his demon-possessed son after Jesus's disciples had been unable to cast out the demon. The passage below shows the earnestness of the man in his struggle with doubt.

> but if thou canst do any thing, have compassion on us, and help us. Jesus said unto him, If thou canst believe, all things are possible to him that believeth. And straightway the father of the child cried out, and said with tears, *Lord, I believe; help thou mine unbelief.* (Mark 9:22–24)

Doubt can cause us to waver in our spiritual lives, and it may even paralyze us. Therefore, it is imperative that we move beyond doubt into faith. The Bible teaches us that God's Word is the means for growing our faith.

> So then faith cometh by hearing, and hearing by the word of God. (Romans 10:17)

When our minds fasten onto God's faithfulness instead of depending on our own weak and wayward nature or the unpredictable circumstances of life, we come to realize that our salvation and our life here are fully in His hand. As we read about God and Christ in the scriptures, His Spirit invites our spirit to trust God and walk by faith. As we do this, we begin to see His hand working in our lives, which encourages us toward a cycle of learning about Him and then experientially living in the truth that we've learned by trusting Him to work in our lives.

The Way of Personal Merit: Another obstacle that must be overcome by people who seek a relationship with God is pride. Many people try to seek God by their own merit, which is rooted in pride. They see life as one long ledger with two columns, one that records all their good deeds and the other that records all their bad deeds. In their minds, the secret to having a right relationship with God is simply assuring that the first column is larger than the second. Jesus made clear in his teaching that one of the prerequisites of salvation is a person's realization that it is impossible to obtain insofar as man is concerned.

> Blessed are the poor in spirit: for theirs is the kingdom of heaven. (Matthew 5:3)

> When Jesus heard it, he saith unto them, They that are whole have no need of the physician, but they that are sick: *I came not to call the righteous, but sinners to repentance.* (Mark 2:17)

As we've already seen, Jesus was *not* saying that there are some righteous people who don't need saving, but rather, He was saying that only people who realize their sinful depravity will come to Him for salvation. Other than for physical checkups, do you go to the doctor when you're not sick?

> And he spake this parable unto *certain which trusted in themselves that they were righteous*, and despised others: Two men went up into the temple to pray; the one a Pharisee, and the other a publican. The Pharisee stood and *prayed thus with himself,* God, *I thank thee, that I am not as other men are,* extortioners, unjust, adulterers, or even as this publican. I fast twice in the week, I give tithes of all that I possess. And the publican, standing afar off, would not lift up so much as his eyes unto heaven, but smote upon his breast, saying, God be merciful to me a sinner. I tell you, this man went down to his house justified rather than the other: for every one that exalteth himself shall be abased; and he that humbleth himself shall be exalted. (Luke 18:9–14)

The apostle Paul also related how the obstacle of pride prevented his Jewish kinsmen from receiving Jesus Christ as the promised Messiah, and how this prideful thinking thwarted their efforts to please God.

> But Israel, which followed after the law of righteousness, hath not attained to the law of righteousness. Wherefore? Because they sought it not by faith, but as it were by the works of the law. For they stumbled at that stumblingstone; (Romans 9:31–32)

> Brethren, my heart's desire and prayer to God for Israel is, that they might be saved. For I bear them record that they have a zeal of God, but not according to knowledge. For *they being ignorant of God's righteousness, and going about to establish their own righteousness, have not submitted themselves unto the righteousness of God. For Christ is the end of the law for righteousness to every one that believeth.* (Romans 10:1–4)

The Way of Intellectual Assent: Another obstacle that people must overcome to obtain a faith relationship with God is the trap of depending on *knowledge* for salvation. People who fall into this trap are those who seek to know *about* God without seeking to *know God*. James wrote about this in his epistle.

> But *be ye doers of the word, and not hearers only, deceiving your own selves.* For if any be a hearer of the word, and not a doer, he is like unto a man beholding his natural face in a glass: For he beholdeth himself, and goeth his way, and straightway forgetteth what manner of man he was. But whoso looketh into the perfect law of liberty, and continueth therein, he being not a forgetful hearer, but a doer of the work, this man shall be blessed in his deed. (James 1:22–25)

Here James is saying that a person who *rightly* encounters God's Word will be transformed by it. God's Word will become a part of his thinking, his very life. Paul spoke of two forces in our lives that are in direct opposition—conformation to the world versus transformation by God.

> I beseech you therefore, brethren, by the mercies of God, that ye present your bodies a living sacrifice, holy, acceptable unto God, which is your reasonable service. And be not conformed to this world: but be ye transformed by the renewing of your mind, that ye may prove what is that good, and acceptable, and perfect, will of God. (Romans 12:1–2)

Here Paul is calling us to a life of service to God. The alternative is a passive life that is molded by the worries, pressures, and allurements of life that Jesus alluded to when he explained the thorny ground in Matthew 13.

The Way of Faith: God makes very clear in His Word that the right way to approach Him is by faith. In the chapter on God's holiness, we discussed one aspect of His transcendence being that God is Spirit in lieu of being confined in a body. Thus, there is no other way for us to relate to Him than by faith. We cannot walk up to Him and carry on a conversation like we would with one another. A conversation with God *requires* faith, both in speaking to Him and (even more) in hearing Him. The fact that we cannot see God does not mean that there is no evidence for his existence and that faith is merely a subjective exercise. The Christian faith is built on some very strong evidence such as the Old Testament revelation about Christ, which we will address later, as well as His supernatural presence on earth and His resurrection from the dead, witnessed by over 500 people on one occasion! God's Word has a lot to say about faith.

> But *without faith it is impossible to please him*: for he that cometh to God must believe that he is, and that he is a rewarder of them that diligently seek him. (Hebrews 11:6)

Faith is that fertile soil that Jesus spoke of in the Parable of the Sower, the soil that produces a crop, some a hundredfold, some sixtyfold, and some thirtyfold. Paul said that the seed of the gospel planted in the soil of faith results in salvation (Romans 1:16–17). The way of faith is a relationship with God through His Son Jesus Christ. Jesus spoke of this relationship in John's gospel.

> But he that entereth in by the door is the shepherd of the sheep. To him the porter openeth; and *the sheep hear his voice:* and *he calleth his own sheep by name, and leadeth them out.* And when he putteth forth his own sheep, *he goeth before them, and the sheep follow him: for they know his voice.* (John 10:2–4)

> *I am the door: by me if any man enter in, he shall be saved, and shall go in and out, and find pasture.* The thief cometh not, but for to steal, and to kill, and to destroy: *I am come that they might have life, and that they might have it more abundantly. I am the good shepherd: the good shepherd giveth his life for the sheep … I am the good shepherd, and know my sheep, and am known of mine.* (John 10:9–11, 10:14)

SO WHAT WILL IT BE FOR YOU— JUDGMENT OR REDEMPTION?

The Bible is very clear that those who believe the gospel's message of salvation and receive Jesus Christ as their Savior and Lord will be saved from the coming judgment. On the other hand, those who don't will be judged by their works. The destiny of the former will be eternal life in heaven in the presence of God, but the destiny of the latter will be eternal damnation in the lake of fire away from the presence of God.

NOTES (CHAPTER 5)

[1] *Religion by Country 2024.* World Population Review, https://worldpopulationreview.com/country-rankings/religion-by-country, (accessed 09/13/24)

PART 2
OVERVIEW OF OT MESSIANIC PROPHECY

CHAPTERS

6

NEW TESTAMENT WITNESS TO OT MESSIANIC PROPHECY

THE TIMING OF CHRIST'S COMING

THE BIBLE SAYS THAT IN "THE FULLNESS OF TIME … GOD SENT FORTH HIS SON" (GALATIANS 4:4). So what made the period leading up to Jesus's birth the *fullness of time?* There were characteristics of that period that made it quite suitable for the long-awaited Messiah to come: "This 'time' was when the Roman civilization had brought peace and a road system which facilitated travel; when the Grecian civilization provided a language which was adopted as the *lingua franca* of the empire; when the Jews had proclaimed monotheism and the messianic hope in the synagogues of the Mediterranean world."[1] From our vantage point of looking back at these logistics, it seems quite understandable that this time period was well-suited for God's purpose of sending His Son into the world. However, from the vantage point of the Jews living during that time, the coming of Messiah must have seemed like the farthest thing from a soon-coming event.

In the days leading up to Jesus's birth, the Jews were subject to Roman rule and were no longer the proud nation that had stood from its birth in the exodus from Egypt (1447 BC) through the period of the judges and the kings, which culminated with the Babylonian captivity of the southern kingdom of Judah (586 BC). Babylon fell to the Medo-Persian Empire, which fell to the Grecian Empire, which fell to the Roman Empire. During this period, Rome ruled the day. Divine revelation had ceased for over 400 years, and Israel had ceased to be a sovereign nation for nearly 600 years. God's people were probably tempted to think that He had abandoned them. Their dreams had been shattered. On the other hand, God had clearly promised to send a messiah to the Jews, and the faithful had not given up on that hope.

MESSIANIC EXPECTATION SURROUNDING JESUS'S BIRTH

Particular evidence that the Old Testament portrait of Christ is detailed and accurate is the messianic longing that we see in the gospel accounts. During the troublesome times of first century Judea, the Jews had little to cling to but their proud heritage. They were the sole nation on earth whom God had birthed and called His own people, and their scriptures contained the record of His direct intervention throughout their history. Amid their present darkness and desperation, these captive people still had the promises of God—which were anchored in large part to the arrival of the promised Messiah. He was spoken of throughout their scriptures. No doubt, many of the Jews saw the coming of Messiah as their only hope of deliverance from Roman oppression. The Messiah was prophesied to be a son of David, and God had promised to establish David's throne *forever*. Accordingly, we can readily see how the people living during Jesus's time could be led to expect a political and military messiah. However, Jesus would not fulfill this role until His second coming.

The New Testament record of this messianic longing begins early in the gospel narrative. In the two gospels that relate the story of Jesus's birth, Matthew, and Luke, we are given our first glimpses of this in the accounts surrounding His birth. The accounts of Simeon and Anna in Luke's gospel relate this anticipation in the hearts of God's people. The account of the Magi in Matthew's gospel shows that some knowledge of the Jewish Messiah extended even to the gentile realm over 500 miles away. It has been rightly speculated that this knowledge can be traced back to the prophet Daniel, who had been captured by Nebuchadnezzar in the third year of Jehoiakim's reign (Daniel 1:1) in 606 BC until the first year of Cyrus's reign in Babylon (Daniel 1:21) in 539 BC.[2] We see that Daniel was highly regarded by the rulers he served under. We see reference to this for four of the kings.

1) **Nebuchadnezzar:** After Daniel told Nebuchadnezzar his dream and its interpretation, Nebuchadnezzar "fell on his face and did homage" to Daniel and promoted him "ruler over the whole province" (Daniel 2:46–48). That's hardly a common occurrence, for a king to fall on his face and do homage!

2) **Belshazzar:** The last night of Nebuchadnezzar's grandson Belshazzar's reign, the supernatural hand of God wrote a message on the wall, "Mene', Mene, Tekel, Upharsin," which meant "God has numbered your kingdom, and you have been weighed on the balance and found wanting. Your kingdom has been given to the Medes and the Persians." At this point, Belshazzar appointed Daniel as the third ruler in the kingdom (Daniel 5:24–29).

3) **Darius:** After Belshazzar's death the same night of Daniel's prophecy, Darius the Mede became the king and appointed Daniel as one of three commissioners over 120 satraps.

Daniel began to distinguish himself among the commissioners. The king noticed that Daniel possessed an extraordinary spirit and planned to appoint him over the entire kingdom (Daniel 6:1–3). At this point, the jealousy of Daniel's colleagues was the beginning of the familiar story of Daniel and the lion's den.

4) **Cyrus:** We also see that Daniel enjoyed success in the reign of Cyrus (Daniel 6:28).

Just imagine Daniel's excitement when Cyrus became king. Presumably, Daniel had access to the scroll of Isaiah that contained the following words:

> *Thus saith the* Lord *...* That saith *of Cyrus, He is my shepherd, and shall perform all my pleasure*: even saying to Jerusalem, Thou shalt be built; and to the temple, Thy foundation shall be laid. (Isaiah 44:24, 44:28)

> Thus saith the Lord *to his anointed*, to *Cyrus, whose right hand I have holden, to subdue nations before him*; and I will loose the loins of kings, to open before him the two leaved gates; and the gates shall not be shut; *I will go before thee*, and make the crooked places straight: *I will break in pieces the gates of brass, and cut in sunder the bars of iron*: And *I will give thee the treasures of darkness*, and *hidden riches of secret places, that thou mayest know that I, the Lord, which call thee by thy name, am the God of Israel*. For Jacob my servant's sake, and Israel mine elect, *I have even called thee by thy name: I have surnamed thee, though thou hast not known me*. I am the Lord, and there is none else, there is no God beside me: *I girded thee, though thou hast not known me*. (Isaiah 45:1–5)

Just imagine King Cyrus's excitement when he read those incredible words about himself spoken over 140 years earlier by none other than God!

Immediately after Jesus's birth, Joseph and Mary brought Jesus to the temple for the customary dedication to the Lord of the firstborn male child.

SIMEON

> And when the days of her purification according to the law of Moses were accomplished, they brought him to Jerusalem, to present *him* to the Lord. (Luke 2:22)

> And, behold, there was a man in Jerusalem, whose name *was Simeon*; and the same man *was* just and devout, *waiting for the consolation of Israel*: and the Holy Ghost was upon him. And *it was revealed unto him by the Holy Ghost, that he should not see death, before he had seen the Lord's Christ*. And *he came*

by the Spirit into the temple: and when the parents brought in the child Jesus, to do for him after the custom of the law, Then *took he him up in his arms, and blessed God*, and said, *Lord, now lettest thou thy servant depart in peace, according to thy word: For mine eyes have seen thy salvation, Which thou hast prepared* before the face of all people; A light to lighten the Gentiles, and the glory of thy people Israel. And Joseph and his mother marvelled at those things which were spoken of him. And *Simeon blessed them*, and *said unto Mary* his mother, Behold, *this child is set for the fall and rising again of many in Israel; and for a sign which shall be spoken against; (Yea, a sword shall pierce through thy own soul also,) that the thoughts of many hearts may be revealed.* (Luke 2:25–35, emphasis added)

The following can be gleaned from the wording of this passage: (1) the concept of Messiah (Christ) was familiar to the Jews and, therefore, needed no explanation by Luke, (2) Simeon, no doubt like others of his kinsmen, had a longing for and anticipation of Messiah's coming ("waiting for the consolation of Israel"), and (3) he knew some things about the coming Messiah. We see that the Holy Spirit specifically revealed that Simeon would see the Christ before he died. The account of Anna immediately follows.

ANNA

And there was one *Anna, a prophetess*, the daughter of Phanuel, of the tribe of Aser: she was *of a great age*, and had lived with an husband seven years from her virginity; And *she was a widow of about fourscore and four years*, which *departed not from the temple, but served God with fastings and prayers night and day. And she coming in that instant gave thanks likewise unto the Lord*, and *spake of him [Jesus] to all them that looked for redemption in Jerusalem.* (Luke 2:36–38, emphasis added)

From this passage, we can see that this godly old woman was faithfully serving the Lord in her last days. She is fasting and praying in the temple. Given that she was married seven years and then widowed eighty-four years, she would have been over one hundred years old. Her life is a lesson of faithfulness to each of us. The wording of the passage suggests that she, like Simeon, was anticipating the Messiah's coming and that she was thankful for His arrival and excited to spread the news of Him to all others that shared her longing.

Matthew's gospel records the account of the wise men who traveled from the east to Jerusalem to inquire where to find the Messiah.

WISE MEN

Now when Jesus was born in Bethlehem of Judaea in the days of Herod the king, behold, *there came wise men from the east to Jerusalem, Saying, Where is he that is born King of the Jews? for we have seen his star in the east, and are come to worship him.* When Herod the king had heard *these things*, he was troubled, and all Jerusalem with him. And *when he had gathered all the chief priests and scribes of the people together, he demanded of them where Christ should be born. And they said unto him, In Bethlehem of Judaea: for thus it is written by the prophet, And thou Bethlehem, in the land of Juda, art not the least among the princes of Juda: for out of thee shall come a Governor, that shall rule my people Israel.* Then Herod, when he had privily called the wise men, enquired of them diligently what time the star appeared. And *he sent them to Bethlehem*, and said, Go and search diligently for the young child; and when ye have found *him*, bring me word again, that I may come and worship him also. When they had heard the king, they departed; and, lo, the star, which they saw in the east, went before them, till it came and stood over where the young child was. When they saw the star, they rejoiced with exceeding great joy.

And *when they were come into the house, they saw the young child with Mary his mother, and fell down, and worshipped him:* and *when they had opened their treasures, they presented unto him gifts; gold, and frankincense, and myrrh.* And being warned of God in a dream that they should not return to Herod, they departed into their own country another way. (Matthew 2:1–12, emphasis added)

From this passage we can observe (1) these wise men (magi) are Gentiles, (2) they made inquiry as to the whereabouts of the "King of the Jews," the same title Pilate placed upon Jesus's cross, (3) this title is clearly a messianic reference, (4) the chief priests and scribes (i.e., the scriptural experts) identified Bethlehem as the Messiah's birthplace, (5) upon arrival at the Messiah's house, they worshipped Him and presented Him with lavish gifts.

MESSIANIC EXPECTATION DURING JESUS'S MINISTRY

In addition to these three examples surrounding Jesus's birth, there is a background of messianic expectation that weaves its way through Jesus's ministry. After Jesus grew up and began His ministry, many stories began to circulate about him. The stories were all similar—that He possessed supernatural wisdom, taught with authority, healed people of every conceivable malady, and even raised people from the dead! People began to wonder if these stories could possibly be true. They wondered, "Could this be the One the sacred scriptures have been pointing to all along? Has God finally remembered his people?" Below are examples of this messianic consciousness that we see during Jesus's ministry (note that the term *Christ* below is the Greek form of the Hebrew word *Messiah*):

1. Peter confessed his belief that Jesus was the Christ (Peter's great confession). (Matthew 16:16; Mark 8:29; Luke 9:20)

2. Jesus asked the Pharisees and Sadducees what they gleaned from scripture about the Christ. (Matthew 22:42; Mark 12:35; Luke 20:41)

3. Jesus warned His disciples about false Christs that would appear during the end times. (Matthew 24:5, 24:23–24; Mark 13:6, 13:21–22; Luke 21:8)

4. The Jews at Jesus's trial adjure Him to answer whether He claims to be the Christ. (Matthew 26:63, 26:68; Mark 14:61; Luke 22:67)

5. The chief priests, scribes, crowd, and the two thieves mocked Jesus on the cross as being an impotent Christ. (Mark 15:32; Luke 23:35, 23:39)

6. The people wondered whether John the Baptist was the Christ. (Luke 3:15; John 1:20, 1:25)

7. Jesus led a post-resurrection Bible study about the Christ with two disciples on the Emmaus Road. (Luke 24:26, 24:46)

8. Andrew told Peter that he had found the Christ. (John 1:41)

9. The Samaritan woman wondered whether Jesus was the Christ. (John 4:25, 4:29)

10. The Samaritan townspeople proclaimed that Jesus was the Christ. (John 4:42)

11. Peter still believes that Jesus is the Christ after the crowd deserts Jesus. (John 6:69)

12. The crowd discusses among themselves whether Jesus can be the Christ. (John 7:26–27, 7:31, 7:41–42)

13. The blind man's parents feared to confess Jesus as the Christ because of the Jews. (John 9:22)

14. The Jews in public discourse adjure Jesus to tell whether He is the Christ. (John 10:24)

15. Martha confesses Jesus as the Christ. (John 11:24–27)

16. The crowd discusses characteristics of the Christ from the scriptures. (John 12:34)

Even today, the concept of a Jewish messiah is central to Orthodox Judaism, and they are still awaiting his coming. The point is that Jesus didn't come in a vacuum, but rather, He came to a people who were longing for their Messiah, the One who was repeatedly attested to in the scriptures, the same scriptures that Christians refer to as the Old Testament. Just to be clear, although this messianic expectation existed, many failed to recognize that Jesus was the Messiah when He came, as John shares in His Gospel.

> He was in the world, and the world was made by him, and the world knew him not. He came unto his own, and his own received him not. But as many as received him, to them gave he power to become the sons of God, even to them that believe on his name: (John 1:10–12)

NEW TESTAMENT APPEALS TO THE SCRIPTURES AND PROPHECY

It should be noted here that the word *scripture(s)* in the Bible always refers to the Old Testament. The New Testament, for the most part, was written during the last half of the first century AD, with several of the New Testament books being written within a decade. This period of approximately fifty years is obviously a very compressed time span in comparison to the Old Testament period. By contrast, the Old Testament spanned a period of nearly 4,000 years and its scriptures were written over a 1,000-year period or longer. Given that there were no printing presses at that time, a significant amount of time had to transpire between a book's completion and its adoption into the canon of scripture. This would include time for copying manuscripts and promulgation, time for it to become widely known and accepted as divinely inspired, and time for it to become canonical.

Throughout the New Testament we see specific Old Testament scriptures continually being cited as applying to Jesus. These citations pointed to many specific things about Him—His virgin birth, the location of His birth, His pre-eternal and divine nature, His Sonship with the Father, His ministry, His eternal priesthood, His crucifixion and resurrection, among other things. These OT prophecies were appealed to as validation of His identity as the promised Messiah. To quantify this, a word search was made of the words *scripture(s)* and *prophet(s)* in both their singular and plural forms. In addition, a manual search was made of all the *all-cap* portions of prophetic texts, which is a common feature of modern translations. These three searches were made of the entire New Testament, and the results are shown in table 6.1—Summary of NT References to OT Messianic Prophecies. This table is located at the end of this chapter. From this table we can see a total of 183 times in the New Testament where someone cited an Old Testament passage as pertaining to Jesus. These prophecies pointed either to Christ, the New Covenant in Him, or His Second Coming and final reign on earth. Given that there are 260 chapters in the New Testament, this would correspond to an average citation rate of 183/260 or 70 percent of the chapters in the New Testament. Obviously, since many NT chapters have multiple OT citations, the actual percentage of chapters containing these citations is much lower, but you get the point. From the table, we see that the gospels and Acts alone contain 128 of these references, and the other New Testament books contain the remaining 55 references.

The point is that this was not some peripheral issue with the apostles and New Testament writers, but rather, it was a central part of their message. Virtually everyone in the New Testament who preached or wrote about Jesus cited Old Testament messianic passages as being fulfilled in Him. These references are made by Jesus Himself, John the Baptist, the apostles, and others, with Jesus being the most prolific. The writers of the four gospels and Acts add their own Old Testament references in addition to those of the speakers in their narratives. This is also true of the epistle writers as well, with Paul being the most prolific. Below are a few examples of these references.

Jesus

> Search the scriptures; for in them ye think ye have eternal life: and they are they which testify of me. (John 5:39)

> And beginning at Moses and all the prophets, he expounded unto them in all the scriptures the things concerning himself. (Luke 24:27)

The Gospel Writers

> And with him they crucify two thieves; the one on his right hand, and the other on his left. And the scripture was fulfilled, which saith, And he was numbered with the transgressors. (Mark 15:27–28)

> For these things were done, that the scripture should be fulfilled, A bone of him shall not be broken. And again another scripture saith, They shall look on him whom they pierced. (John 19:36–37)

The Apostles

> Then Peter, filled with the Holy Ghost, said unto them, Ye rulers of the people, and elders of Israel … Be it known unto you all, and to all the people of Israel, that by the name of Jesus Christ of Nazareth, whom ye crucified, whom God raised from the dead, even by him doth this man stand here before you whole. This is the stone which was set at nought of you builders, which is become the head of the corner. Neither is there salvation in any other: for there is none other name under heaven given among men, whereby we must be saved. (Acts 4:8, 10–12, see Psalm 118:22–23)

And Paul, as his manner was, went in unto them, and three sabbath days reasoned with them out of the scriptures, Opening and alleging, that Christ must needs have suffered, and risen again from the dead; and that this Jesus, whom I preach unto you, is Christ. And some of them believed, and consorted with Paul and Silas; and of the devout Greeks a great multitude, and of the chief women not a few. (Acts 17:2–4)

Summary of NT References to OT Messianic Prophecies

Word Search: "Scripture(s)" in the Bible			
No. of References	Total	Messianic	Non-Messianic
Bible	53	43	10
Old Testament	1	0	1
New Testament	52	43	9

Word Search: "Prophet(s)" in the New Testament	
No. of References	157
No. of Messianic References	64
No. of Non-Messianic References	93

Manual Search: "All-Cap" Prophecies in the New Testament	
No. of Messianic References	76

Below is a composite of all messianic references listed from the 3 tables above

(Note: redundancies between the 3 lists were removed)

Combined total of Messianic passages identified by "Scripture(s)" and "Prophet(s)" word search and manual search of All-Caps passages	183

Total appeals to OT messianic prophecies | **183**

Distribution of OT Messianic References in NT	
Gospels	93
Acts	35
Pauline Epistles	30
General Epistles	23
Revelation	2
	183

Distribution of Ref's	
Book	# Ref's
Mat	33
Mar	13
Luk	24
Joh	23
Act	35
Rom	17
1 Cor	2
2 Cor	2
Gal	5
Eph	2
Phil	0
Col	0
1 Ths	0
2 Ths	0
1 Tim	0
2 Tim	2
Tit	0
Phlm	0
Heb	16
Jam	0
1 Pet	3
2 Pet	4
1 Joh	0
2 Joh	0
3 Joh	0
Jude	0
Rev	2
Total	183

Table 6.1 - Summary of NT References to OT Messianic Prophecies

NOTES (CHAPTER 6)

[1] John F. Walvoord and Roy B. Zuck, eds., *The Bible Knowledge Commentary, New Testament* (Colorado Springs: David C Cook, 1983), 601

[2] Daan Nijssen, *Cyrus the Great*, World History Encyclopedia, last modified February 21, 2018, https://www.worldhistory.org/Cyrus_the_Great/ (accessed 09/13/24)

7

THE COVENANTAL ASPECT OF MESSIAH AND HIS LINEAGE

GOD'S PLAN OF SALVATION WAS BEFORE CREATION

IT WAS IN THE HEART OF GOD BEFORE CREATION ITSELF THAT REDEMPTION IN CHRIST WOULD be the means of His salvation for a lost and dying world. There are several scriptures which indicate this. Table 7.1 below is a listing of several scriptures with the italicized portions highlighting the pre-eternal aspect of God's plan.

Table 7.1—God's Foreordained Plan		
Scripture	**Pre-Eternal Proclamation**	**Significance**
Matthew 13:35	That it might be fulfilled which was spoken by the prophet, saying, *I will open my mouth in parables; I will utter things which have been kept secret from the foundation of the world.*	Jesus speaking in parables, planned before creation
Matthew 25:34	Then shall the King say unto them on his right hand, Come, ye blessed of my Father, *inherit the kingdom prepared for you from the foundation of the world.*	Believers saved before creation
John 17:24	Father, I will that they also, whom thou hast given me, be with me where I am; that they may behold my glory, which thou has given me; *for thou lovedst me before the foundation of the world.*	Jesus's high-priestly prayer; He was with God from the beginning
Ephesians 1:4	According as *he hath chosen us in him before the foundation of the world,* that we should be holy and without blame before him in love:	Believers saved before creation

1 Peter 1:20	*Who verily was foreordained before the foundation of the world*, but was manifest in these last times for you …	Jesus's incarnation determined before creation
Revelation 13:8	And all that dwell upon the earth shall worship him *(the beast)*, whose names are not written in the book of life of the *Lamb slain from the foundation of the world.*	Jesus's death foreordained before creation
Revelation 17:8	The beast that thou sawest was, and is not; and shall ascend out of the bottomless pit, and go into perdition; and they that dwell on the earth shall wonder, *whose names were not written in the book of life from the foundation of the world*, when they behold the beast that was, and is not, and yet is.	Believers saved before creation

THE COVENANTS OF GOD

Our God is a covenant God. All relationships involve trust. Since God is a spirit and is therefore invisible (John 4:24), He had to devise a way to communicate with us and to show Himself faithful, so He chose the means of *covenant* to accomplish this. Over the centuries, God has earned the trust of His people through His ongoing covenant relationship with them.

A covenant is simply a binding agreement between two or more parties, wherein each of them agrees to certain stipulations. Because all relationships are based on trust, agreements are part of every relationship. There are different kinds of agreements, formal and informal, verbal and written. Formal agreements are typically reserved for legal matters in our lives such as marriage, major purchases, or wills. However, we use informal agreements daily—these agreements are often verbal, whether in-person, phone/texting, or online. Even for such mundane things as inviting someone to lunch, there is an agreed time that both parties should adhere to. These verbal agreements are a necessary part of life, and we tend to assess people as being trustworthy or unreliable, depending on how they have honored their word to us in the past. The Bible contains the written record of God's covenant relationship with man, and His faithfulness in keeping His Word. In fact, this written record, which spans fifteen or more centuries, written by over forty human authors, is one of the greatest evidences that God is the divine author of the Bible.

There are seven covenants of God recorded in the scriptures. They are outlined in table 7.2, The Covenants of God, at the end of this chapter. We will briefly discuss them below.

The first two covenants were made in the Garden of Eden shortly after creation, approximately 4100 BC.

1. **The Edenic Covenant was made to Adam in the Garden of Eden (Genesis 2:16–17)**

    God told Adam that he may eat of any tree in the Garden of Eden, except the tree that was in the middle of the garden, the Tree of the Knowledge of Good and Evil. God warned Adam that in the day he ate of it, he would surely die. As we are sadly aware, Adam and Eve violated God's covenant with Adam, which ushered in death and a decaying universe.

2. **The Adamic Covenant was made with Adam and Eve after the Fall (Genesis 3:14–19)**

    God relayed to Adam and Eve the consequences of their sin and disobedience. God also cursed the serpent through whom Satan operated. The results of mankind's sin would be pain in childbirth, woman's subordination to her husband, cursed ground—making it difficult to raise vegetation for food, thorns and thistles, and death and burial.

Fast-forward approximately 1,650 years, to around 2459 BC. Mankind has now become utterly corrupt. God relates to Noah His plan to destroy the earth with a global flood, in which He instructs Noah to build an ark for the preservation of his family of eight people.

3. **The Noachian Covenant with Noah (and mankind) after the global flood (Genesis 9:9–17)**

    God promised that He would never again destroy the earth with water. As a sign of His covenant, God would place a rainbow in the clouds after the rain as a reminder to Himself and all mankind of this covenant.

Fast-forward some 467 years to around 1992 BC. Sometime after the seventy-fifth birthday of Abram (Abraham), God calls him out of Ur of the Chaldees to go to a land that He would show him, the land of Canaan. Abraham trusted God and left his homeland and followed God. At this inaugural event in Abraham's life, God commences His multifaceted covenant with Abraham. Thus, the messianic prophetic genealogy jumps from Eve to Abraham.

4. **Abrahamic Covenant with Abraham**

    (Genesis 12:1–7; 13:14–17; 15:1–21; 22:15–18; 26:1–5; 28:10–15)
    God promises to

    *   make Abraham a great nation
    *   make Abraham's name great
    *   make Abraham a blessing
    *   bless those who bless Abraham and curse those who curse him
    *   bless all the families of the earth through Abraham

- give the land of Canaan to Abraham
- multiply Abraham's offspring as stars of heaven and sands of seashore for number
- be a shield for Abraham
- greatly bless him
- cause Abraham's descendants to possess the gates of their enemies
- bless all the nations of the earth by Abraham's descendant

God specifically promised Abraham that this covenant would continue through Isaac and his descendants, and then through Jacob and his descendants. As a seeming footnote of scripture, when Jacob (Israel) blesses his twelve sons just before his death, he comes to Judah (Genesis 49:8–12) and states, "Judah, your brothers shall praise you … Your father's sons shall bow down to you. Judah is a lion's whelp … as a lion, who dares rouse him … the scepter shall not depart from Judah, nor the ruler's staff from between his feet, until Shiloh comes." (Shiloh is believed by many to refer to Messiah.)

Fast-forward some 545 years to around 1447 BC. During their stay of 430 years in Egypt, which included a period of 400 years of enslavement, Israel has now become a nation of 600,000 men, not counting women and children (Genesis 15:13, Exodus 12:37–41). Now we find them making their exodus out of Egypt, led by Moses. Sometime thereafter, at the beginning of their 40 years of wandering in the wilderness, God gives Moses and the Israelite nation the Ten Commandments.

5. Mosaic Covenant with Moses and Israel (Exodus 19:3–6)

God promised Moses and this young nation that if they would obey His voice and keep His covenant, then they would be His own possession among all the peoples and they would be a kingdom of priests and a holy nation.

Fast-forward some 396 years later to around 1051 BC, when David became king of Israel. Then, some 7 1/2 years into his reign, around 1044 BC, he captures the city which became Israel's capital, Jerusalem (2 Samuel 5:5). After successfully relocating the Ark of the Covenant to Jerusalem, he proposes his plan to Nathan the prophet to build a permanent temple to house the Ark of the Covenant. It is at that time that God tells him, due to the bloodshed of David's many wars, that He would use David's son after him, a man of peace, to build the temple. We know that this prophecy was fulfilled through Solomon. During God's announcement to David through Nathan, He makes a covenant with David.

6. Davidic Covenant with David and Israel (2 Samuel 7:8–16)

God promised David that

- He would appoint a place for His people Israel and plant them
- He would give David rest from all his enemies
- He would make a house for David

- He would raise up David's son after him
- He would establish his son's kingdom
- David's son would build a house (temple) for God's name
- God will establish the throne of his (son's) kingdom forever
- God will be a father to him (David's son), and he will be a son to Him
- God will correct David's son with the strokes of men
- God's lovingkindness will not depart from David's son
- David's house and kingdom will endure before God forever
- David's throne will be established forever

If we review these Old Testament covenants, we can see how they each point in some way to Jesus Christ. The Edenic covenant was made with Adam while he was in paradise before there was a need for a savior. The Mosaic covenant, from which we get the term Old Testament, was a problematic covenant due to the sinfulness of man. Let's quickly review.

Number	Covenant	Messianic Significance
1	Edenic	The Fall and need for Messiah was hinted at by the Tree of Knowledge.
2	Adamic	Conflict between the seed of the woman and serpent points to Christ.
3	Noachian	The ark is a picture of redemption in Christ.
4	Abrahamic	Abraham's "sacrifice" of Isaac is a picture God's sacrifice of Jesus.
5	Mosaic	Only Christ perfectly fulfilled the Law.
6	Davidic	David's life is a type (picture) of Christ. Christ a descendant of David.

Through this covenantal process, God established in history His plan of redemption that He had determined before time began, and He established some credentials that the promised Messiah would have to meet. These are all fulfilled in Jesus Christ. Also, for anyone seeking the truth today, fulfilled prophecy is one of the greatest evidences of God's inspiration of the Bible.

Fast-forward approximately 1,073 years to around AD 30, where we join a group of men reclining in an upper room around a table. The men are Jesus and His disciples. As the men are gathered around the table, they are in the process of observing the Passover meal. Jesus had been explaining to them that He would be killed by evil men and that the time was fast approaching, and that this would be His last Passover meal with them. However, as He was breaking the unleavened bread to pass it around, I'm sure their jaws must have dropped at His next statement. He says to them, "Take, eat; this is My body which is given for you." Again, when He passes the cup, He says, "Drink from it, all of you; for this is My blood of the *(new)* covenant, which is poured out for many for forgiveness of sins" (Matthew 26:26–28).

In the gospels, there are numerous references of Jesus telling His disciples that He would die at the hands of evil men. However, I have not found many references *before* the Last Supper where

He explained to His disciples *why* He would die. One example is when Jesus told the disciples that He would *give His life as* a *ransom* for many (Matthew 20:28, Mark 10:45). Another is in His shepherd discourse, where He says, "I am the good shepherd; the good shepherd lays down His life for the sheep" (John 10:11). However, they could easily have taken that to mean His dying to protect them from some physical harm rather than as an atoning sacrifice. There is also the reference where Jesus says, "Greater love has no one than this, that one lay down his life for his friends" (John 15:13)—we obviously know that He was talking about His sacrificial death, but did they know that? There may be others that I am not aware of. Here, Jesus is revealing to His disciples through the living drama of Passover that His impending death is necessary for their sins to be forgiven! Can you imagine the moment? This is, in fact, the seventh and final covenant of God with man.

7. **New Covenant (Matthew 26:26–30, Luke 22:14–23, Mark 14:22–26)**

Take, eat; this is My body which is given for you.

Drink from it, all of you; for this is My blood of the (new) covenant, which is poured out for many for forgiveness of sins.

We see that the Old Testament era was one of works, beginning from the Fall and continuing throughout the Old Testament period. This is epitomized by the Mosaic Law, which was alluded to in the Mosaic covenant, which came just prior to God giving Moses and Israel the Ten Commandments and the various other laws. Throughout the Old Testament, however, we see this thread of hope is also woven through it—one day, the Messiah would come. I believe few in Israel understood what that meant, as many were looking for a conquering king. However, because of the New Testament record, there is no confusion to those who have placed their faith in this glorious Messiah. table 7.3, Covenants Timeline, located at the end of this chapter, shows the timeline of these seven covenants.

JESUS'S LINEAGE

Along highways, transportation officials often place signs of upcoming features, whether intersecting roadways, curves, or travel-related businesses at interstate exits. Additionally, there are various billboards placed by private interests, which also serve to alert drivers to various things. These billboards are larger than life and are designed to get people's attention. God placed many messianic *billboards* along the *highway* of the Old Testament. These billboards reveal Messiah's lineage and portray various characteristics of Him, God's plan of redemption, and the new covenant. In the next chapter, we will look at the various *types* of these billboards. God placed an incredible number of these *signs* throughout the Old Testament. These signs helped the people to look forward to the Messiah and prepared them to recognize Him when He came.

As we can see in the Abrahamic and Davidic covenants, they allude to this coming Messiah, whom we now know as Jesus, being a descendant of both Abraham and David. At this point, let's look at some bullets from these two covenants that point to the coming Messiah.

Abrahamic Covenant

- God promised to bless all the families of the earth through Abraham.
- God promised to bless all the nations of the earth by Abraham's descendant.

Davidic Covenant

- God would make a house for David.
- God would establish his son's kingdom.
- God will establish the throne of his (son's) kingdom forever.
- David's house and kingdom will endure before God forever.
- David's throne will be established forever.

PROPHETIC GENEALOGY AND GENEALOGIES IN THE GOSPEL RECORD

Two of the gospels, Matthew and Luke, contain genealogies of Jesus. The importance of these genealogies would have been significant for the early church. Obviously, part of the Messiah's credentials would be his descent from the Davidic line. It is the opinion of many that Matthew's gospel gives the royal lineage of Jesus through His stepfather Joseph and that Luke's gospel gives his human lineage through His virgin mother Mary. This would signify that Jesus is qualified both legally and biologically to be Israel's long-awaited Messiah. Since God promised David that He would establish his throne forever, the Messiah would have to be a physical descendant of David, and Jesus was often addressed as Son of David during his earthly ministry.

Matthew's genealogy runs forward from Abraham to Jesus, while Luke's genealogy runs backward from Jesus to Adam (and even to God)! Both genealogies can be seen in table 7.4, *The Genealogies of Jesus Christ*, located at the end of this chapter. This table also includes the prophetic genealogy of Messiah from the Old Testament—that Messiah will be a descendant of Eve, Abraham, Isaac, Jacob (Israel), Judah, Jesse, and David. Below is a diagram of the prophetic genealogy of Jesus, showing the scriptures supporting each person listed. Although the messianic line runs from Adam through Seth all the way to Jesus, by prophetic genealogy of Jesus, I am referring to those people specifically designated in scripture by God that Jesus would be a descendant of.

Person	Scripture
Eve ↓	the seed of the woman (Gen. 3:15)
Abraham ↓	In your seed, all the nations … shall be blessed (Gen. 22:18, Gal. 3:16)
Isaac ↓	In your seed, all the nations … shall be blessed (Gen. 26:4)
Jacob (Israel) ↓	In your seed, all the nations … shall be blessed (Gen. 28:14)
Judah ↓	The scepter shall not depart from Judah, nor the ruler's staff (Gen. 49:10)
Jesse ↓	a shoot will spring from … Jesse … a branch from his roots (Isa. 11:1)
David ↓	your house … kingdom shall endure … forever (2 Sam. 7:16)
Jesus	and the Word was made flesh and dwelt among us (John 1:14)

Additionally, table 7.5, *Comparison of Biblical Genealogies of Judah's Line,* located at the end of this chapter, compares the genealogies in Matthew and Luke with those in Genesis, 1 and 2 Kings, and 1 Chronicles.

There are some confusing points in these genealogies, which are summarized below:

1. Both Matthew's and Luke's genealogy appear to run through Joseph (see table 7.4)

2. Both genealogies list Shealtiel and Zerubbabel (see table 7.4)

3. Matthew's genealogy indicates that there are three groups of fourteen generations listed; however, there are only forty-one names instead of forty-two (see table 7.4)

4. Matthew's genealogy is much shorter than Luke's, indicating possible gaps (see table 7.4)

5. Matthew's genealogy has gaps when compared to the kings' genealogies in 2 Kings and 1 Chronicles (see table 7.5)

6. Matthew's genealogy lists Jeconiah, but Jeconiah is cursed (see tables 7.4 and 7.5)

7. Cainan in Luke's genealogy is missing from the Genesis genealogy (see table 7.5)

8. In the NASB and at least one other translation, Admin is in Luke's genealogy but missing from the Genesis genealogy (see table 7.5). However, in the KJV and several other translations, Admin is *not* listed in Luke's genealogy.

Each of these points is discussed below, giving explanations for these apparent disparities.

1. **Both Matthew's and Luke's genealogy appear to run through Joseph** (see table 7.4)

This has no doubt confused a multitude of Bible students. I know that the first time I discovered this, I had heard previously that one of the genealogies was Jesus's genealogy through Joseph and the other one was through Mary. Although it does appear that both run through Joseph, it is the opinion of many that Luke's genealogy is through Mary's lineage. Note that Luke went to great detail to explain that Jesus's birth was through the Virgin Mary prior to her sexual union with Joseph. Given the Bible's general pattern of listing the fathers in genealogies, this is the probable explanation for the form of Luke's genealogy. It should be noted from the Bible's own footnotes that the phrase "son of" literally means "of."[1] Thus, Luke's genealogy would read, "Joseph of Heli, of Matthat, of Levi …," etc. Accordingly, two explanations follow:

a) Luke's intent may have been to list Joseph as the son-in-law of Heli, rather than as his son, with it being understood that Mary was Heli's daughter and Jesus's mother, since Luke had already explained Jesus's virgin conception by Mary.

b) Joseph's mention in the genealogy appears to be merely a parenthetical insertion. Accordingly, the phrase "being *as was supposed*, the son of Joseph" is just an aside. Thus, without the parenthetical expression, you would have "Jesus … of Heli, of Matthat, of Levi …," etc. In this case, Jesus would be descended from Mary's father Heli (the last male), with Mary simply being skipped in the genealogy since she was a woman and since Luke's account had already made it clear that Mary was Jesus's virgin mother.

2. **Both genealogies list Shealtiel and Zerubbabel** (see tables 7.4 and 7.5)

Do both genealogies converge at these two men and diverge afterward, or are the Shealtiel and Zerubbabel in Luke different people than those in Matthew? If they are different, this eliminates the problem. What if they are the same two men?

How is this possible that Matthew lists Shealtiel's father as Jeconiah, while Luke lists his father as Neri? It is possible that Shealtiel was the literal son of one and the adopted son of the other: "That Zerubbabel was called both the son of Shealtiel and the son of Shealtiel's brother Pedaiah (1 Chronicles 3:17–19) is probably due to a levirate marriage

(Deuteronomy 25:5–10). After Pedaiah died, his brother Shealtiel may have taken Pedaiah's widow to be his wife and to them was born Zerubbabel."[2] It is possible that something similar may explain the convergence of both genealogies at Shealtiel, with Neri being the biological father of Shealtiel while Jeconiah was his adoptive father. This would make sense in light of the curse on Jeconiah and his descendants outlined under point no. 6 below. The divergence after Zerubbabel can be explained by Zerubbabel having multiple sons, with one being in Matthew's genealogy and the other being in Luke's.

3. **Matthew's genealogy indicates that there are three groups of fourteen generations listed; however, there are only forty-one names instead of forty-two** (see table 7.4)

The three groupings are Abraham to David, David to Deportation, Deportation to Christ. One possibility is that the three groupings of fourteen was simply a memory aid, with it being understood that David or Jeconiah was being counted twice to make it work.

4. **Matthew's genealogy is much shorter than Luke's, indicating possible additional gaps** (see table 7.4)

From table 7.4, there are twenty-seven names listed in Matthew's genealogy after David, while there are forty-two names listed in Luke's. Given that David's reign was from 1011 to 971 BC (table 1.4, The Kings of Israel and Judah), this would yield approximately 1,000 years from the time of David to Jesus's birth. This would yield an average age of twenty-four for each father at the time his son is born (Luke's genealogy). By contrast, the average age of each father in Matthew's shorter genealogy would be thirty-seven. Also, it can be seen (point no. 5 below) that there are clearly gaps in Matthew's genealogy when compared to the Old Testament genealogies. Accordingly, it is not difficult to believe that there could be additional gaps, which is inconsequential since Matthew is simply trying to tie Jesus to David's line through his stepfather Joseph.

5. **Matthew's genealogy has gaps when compared to the kings' genealogies in 2 Kings and 1 Chronicles** (see table 7.5)

Since Matthew's genealogy gives the royal lineage of Jesus, all it need do is tie to the genealogy of Judah's kings. Since it makes this tie, the genealogical record of the kings is available to fill in those gaps. This would establish Jesus's right to the throne of David as a legal descendant of David, thus establishing that aspect of His messianic credentials.

6. **Matthew's genealogy lists Jeconiah, but Jeconiah is cursed** (see table 7.5)

Jeremiah (Jeremiah 22:24–30) prophesied that Jeconiah (King Jehoiachin) was cursed and forsaken of God.

Thus says the LORD, "Write this man down childless, A man who will not prosper in his days; for no man of his descendants will prosper sitting on the throne of David or ruling again in Judah." (Jeremiah 22:30)

According to Jeremiah 22:28 and 1 Chronicles 3:17–18, Jeconiah did have children:

Though Jeconiah's sons never occupied the throne, the line of rulership did pass through them. If Jesus had been a physical descendant of Jeconiah, He would not have been able to occupy David's throne. Luke's genealogy made it clear that Jesus was a physical descendent of David through another son named Nathan.[3]

7. **Cainan in Luke's genealogy is missing from the Genesis genealogy** (see table 7.5)

The explanation for this is found in Matthew Henry's Commentary in which he states, "It is sufficient to say that the seventy interpreters, who, before our Saviour's time, translated the Old Testament into Greek, for reasons best known to themselves inserted that Cainan; and St. Luke, writing among the Hellenistic Jews, was obligated to make use of that translate, and therefore to take it as he found it."[4] Accordingly, it appears that the name Cainan was inserted in the Genesis genealogy in the Septuagint, and Luke included it in his genealogy.

8. **Admin in Luke's genealogy is missing from the Genesis genealogy** (see table 7.5)

Tables 7.4 and 7.5 were developed using the NASB '95 translation, the one I personally use, which includes the name Admin in Luke's genealogy, but not in the overlapping Genesis genealogy. I found this name in one other translation of the Bible. However, in the KJV and several modern translations including the NIV, the name Admin was not present. So this disparity is explained by different manuscript groupings utilized by the various Bible translations and is not present in the majority of translations that I checked.

Hopefully, this clarifies some of the mystery of these genealogies. In closing, Jesus Christ was the covenant-promised Messiah, who existed with God before creation but was willing to die on a cross for the sins of the world, according to the foreordained plan of God.

As noted earlier, our God is a God of covenants. The Bible is made up of two testaments or *covenants*, the Old Testament and the New Testament. Perhaps one of greatest visual illustrations of the importance of God's covenants is found within the confines of the wilderness tabernacle which we will explore in the chapter on Exodus. Within the tabernacle enclosure, the most sacred ground is found within the Holy of Holies. Within this very room dwelt the presence of God manifested in the pillar of cloud by day and the pillar of fire by night. So where was the point where this pillar touched down? Above the *Mercy Seat*, which was the lid of the gold-plated wooden box, which was called the Ark of the *Covenant*. Is this not fascinating that the *Mercy Seat* which so vividly points to Christ was sandwiched between the presence of God and the Ark of the *Covenant*?

The Covenants of God

Covenant	Scripture	Covenant Promise	Messianic Significance
Edenic	Gen 2:16-17	You may eat of every tree...but from the tree that is in the middle of the garden you shall not eat...(or)...you shall surely die	The Fall triggered God's fore-ordained plan of redemption in Christ
Adamic	Gen 3:14-19 (15)	And I shall put enmity between you and the woman, and between your seed and her seed; He shall bruise you on the head, and you shall bruise Him on the heel	Proto Evangelion - first gospel (first messianic prophecy in scripture)
Noahic	Gen 8:22	While the earth remains, seedtime and harvest...shall not cease	The redemption of Noah's family from the flood foreshadows its ultimate redemption and restoration through Christ. The ark is a picture of redemption.
	Gen 9:9-17	...I...establish My covenant with you and...your descendants...and...every living creature...All flesh shall never again be cut off by...water of the flood, neither shall...a flood...destroy the earth...I set My bow in the cloud	
Abrahamic	Gen 12:1-7	Go forth from your country...relatives...father's house to the land I will show you. And I will make you a great nation...bless you...make your name great...you shall be a blessing...I will bless those who bless you...curse those who curse you...in you all the families of the earth will be blessed...to your descendants I will give this land	Abraham's faith foreshadows all who will have faith in Christ (see Rom 4:9-25)
	Gen 13:14-17	...all the land which you see, I will give it to you and to your descendants forever. I will make your descendants as the dust of the earth...	This promised land will one day be an eternal kingdom
	Gen 15:1-21	...Do not fear, I am a shield to you. Your reward will be very great...Know for certain that your descendants will be strangers in a land that is not theirs, where they will be enslaved and oppressed four hundred years. But I will judge the nation whom they will serve, and afterward they will come out with many possessions...Then in the fourth generation they will return here...to your descendants I have given this land, from the river of Egypt as far s the great river...Euphrates	God prophesies the Israelite enslavement from which God births the nation of Israel
	Gen 22:15-18	...I will greatly bless you...and...multiply your seed...in your seed all the nations of the earth shall be blessed because you have obeyed My voice	in your seed shall all the nations of the earth be blessed - has its fulfillment in Christ of Abraham's lineage. Abraham, by his willingness to offer his son to God, is a breathtaking type of God the Father who offered His Son Jesus on a Cross for our sins (Gal 3:16, Rev 5:9-10)
	Gen 26:1-5	**To Isaac:** ...I will be with you and bless you, for to you and to your descendants I will give all these lands, and I will establish the oath...I swore to your father Abraham...I will multiply your descendants as the stars from of heaven...by your descendants shall all the nations of the earth be blessed	
	Gen 28:10-15	**To Jacob:** ...I am the Lord...of your father Abraham...of Isaac; the land on which you lie, I will give it to you and to your descendants...Your descendants will...be like the dust...in you and...your descendants shall all the families of the earth be blessed	

Table 7.2 - The Covenants of God

The Covenants of God.xlsx

The Covenants of God

Covenant	Scripture		Covenant Promise	Messianic Significance
Abrahamic	Gen	49:8-12	**To Judah:** Judah...thy brethren shall praise...thy father's children shall bow down before thee...Judah is a lion's whelp...he couched as a lion...the scepter shall not depart from Judah...until Shiloh come... (Abraham's blessing of his children before his death)	Judah is the son of Jacob (Israel) that Messiah will be descended from
Mosaic	Ex	19:3-6	...If you...obey My voice and keep My covenant, then you shall be My own possession among all the peoples...and you shall be to Me a kingdom of priests and a holy nation....	The Law - its requirements fulfilled by the New Covenant in Christ
Davidic	2 Sam 7:8-16 1 Chr 17:3-14		I will raise up your descendant after you...and I will establish the throne of his kingdom forever...Your house and your kingdom shall endure before Me forever; your throne shall be established forever	David's throne established forever
	Isa	1:24-28	...Zion will be redeemed with justice...	The New Jerusalem
	Psa	89	...I have made a covenant with My chosen; I have sworn to David My servant, I will establish your seed forever and build up your throne to all generations...My faithfulness and My lovingkindness will be with him, and in My name his horn will be exalted...He will cry to Me "You are my Father, My God, and the rock of My salvation....	David's seed shall indeed be established forever in Jesus the final and eternal king of David's line
The New Covenant in Jesus Christ	Jer	31:31-34	...I will make a new covenant with the house of Israel...Judah...I will put My law within them and on their heart I will write it; and I will be their God and they shall be My people. They will not teach again..."know the Lord", for they will all know Me, from the least...to the greatest of them, for I will forgive their iniquity, and their sin I will remember no more.	What was prophesied by Jeremiah the Prophet, was later fulfilled by Christ on the cross, and introduced by Him in The Last Supper. The Lord's Supper beautifully reminds us of this New Covenant (New Testament) we have through the shed blood of Christ
	Mat	26:26-28	...Jesus took some bread...and after a blessing, He broke it and gave it to the disciples, and said, "This is My body", and when He had taken a cup and given thanks, He gave it to them, saying, "Drink from it all of you; for this is My blood of the covenant, which is poured out for many for forgiveness of sins..."	

Table 7.2 - The Covenants of God

The Covenants of God.xlsx

Timeline of God's Covenants in the Bible

Time	Period	God's Covenants			Result / Significance	Messianic Signifiance
		Name	With	Promise(s)		
BC 4100	After Creation prior to Sin and the Fall	1 Edenic	Adam	Warning not to eat of Tree of Knowledge of Good & Evil, or Death	Adam & Eve's disobedience	disobedience brings need **Eve**
4000 3900		2 Adamic	Adam & Eve	The Curse, banishment from Garden, 1st Messianic Promise	The Curse, banishment from Garden, 1st Messianic Promise	(the Mother of all living)
3800 3700 3600 **3500** 3400 3300 3200 3100 **3000** 2900 2800 2700 2600 **2500**	Pre-Flood	3 Noahic	Noah	God promises flood to destroy earth, commands Noah to build an ark to save him and his family		The fallen race of Adam promised a Savior / The ark is a picture of redempton in Christ
2400 2300 2200 2100	Post-Flood				The global flood destroys all life outside the ark (only 8 people, animals on ark & sea life remain), Mankind preserved thru Noah's family	
2000 1900 1800 1700 1600 **1500**	Patriarchal Period	4 Abrahamic	Abraham Isaac Jacob Judah (revealed in Jacob's blessing of Judah)	I will establish My covenant with you and your descendants. I will make you a great nation. I will bless you and make your name great. I will bless those who bless you and curse those who curse you. In you all the families of the earth will be blessed. I will give this land to your descendants. In your seed shall all the nations of the earth be blessed.	Messiah will be of Abraham's line / Messiah will be of Isaac's line / Messiah an Israelite of Jacob's line / Messiah a Jew of Judah's line	**Abraham** **Isaac** **Jacob** **Judah**
1400 1300 1200 1100	Enslavement / Moses / Judges	5 Mosaic	Moses & Israel	If you obey My voice and keep My covenant, then you shall be My own possession among all the nations…and you shall be to Me a kingdom of priests and a holy nation.	Moses, of the family of Levi, was not in Jesus' lineage of Judah's line. Although no one has been able to keep the Law of Moses, Jesus Christ fulfilled it perfectly.	
1000 900 800 700 600 **500** 400	Period of the Kings / Captivity / Restoration	6 Davidic	David	I will raise up your descendant after you…and I will establish the throne of his kingdom forever. Your house and your kingdom shall endure before Me forever; your throne shall be established forever.	The Messiah Will be a king of David's line	**David**
300 200 100 **0** ~ 30 AD	Inter-Testamental Period	7 New Covenant	Jesus Christ *	Jesus took some bread…and after a blessing, He broke it and gave it to the disciples, and said, "This is My body", and when He had taken a cup and given thanks, He gave it to them, saying, "Drink from it all of you; for this is My blood of the covenant, which is poured out for many for forgiveness of sins."	All who place their trust in Jesus Christ will be saved for all eternity	**Jesus Christ**

↓ **Begin New Testamemt Period**   * Covenant made by Jesus with Believers

Table 7.3 - Covenants Timeline

Jesus' Genealogies in Matthew & Luke (compared with Genesis Genealogy)

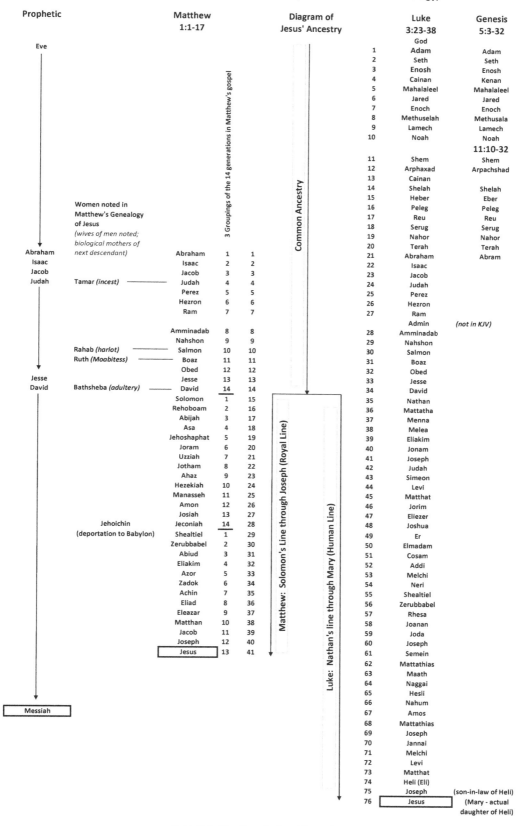

Prophetic		Matthew 1:1-17			Diagram of Jesus' Ancestry		Luke 3:23-38	Genesis 5:3-32
Eve							God	
						1	Adam	Adam
						2	Seth	Seth
						3	Enosh	Enosh
						4	Cainan	Kenan
						5	Mahalaleel	Mahalaleel
						6	Jared	Jared
						7	Enoch	Enoch
						8	Methuselah	Methusala
						9	Lamech	Lamech
						10	Noah	Noah
								11:10-32
						11	Shem	Shem
						12	Arphaxad	Arpachshad
						13	Cainan	
						14	Shelah	Shelah
		Women noted in				15	Heber	Eber
		Matthew's Genealogy				16	Peleg	Peleg
		of Jesus				17	Reu	Reu
		(wives of men noted;				18	Serug	Serug
		biological mothers of				19	Nahor	Nahor
Abraham		*next descendant)*				20	Terah	Terah
Isaac			Abraham	1	1	21	Abraham	Abram
Jacob			Isaac	2	2	22	Isaac	
Judah			Jacob	3	3	23	Jacob	
	Tamar *(incest)*		Judah	4	4	24	Judah	
			Perez	5	5	25	Perez	
			Hezron	6	6	26	Hezron	
			Ram	7	7	27	Ram	
							Admin	*(not in KJV)*
			Amminadab	8	8	28	Amminadab	
			Nahshon	9	9	29	Nahshon	
	Rahab *(harlot)*		Salmon	10	10	30	Salmon	
	Ruth *(Moabitess)*		Boaz	11	11	31	Boaz	
			Obed	12	12	32	Obed	
Jesse			Jesse	13	13	33	Jesse	
David	Bathsheba *(adultery)*		David	14	14	34	David	
			Solomon	1	15	35	Nathan	
			Rehoboam	2	16	36	Mattatha	
			Abijah	3	17	37	Menna	
			Asa	4	18	38	Melea	
			Jehoshaphat	5	19	39	Eliakim	
			Joram	6	20	40	Jonam	
			Uzziah	7	21	41	Joseph	
			Jotham	8	22	42	Judah	
			Ahaz	9	23	43	Simeon	
			Hezekiah	10	24	44	Levi	
			Manasseh	11	25	45	Matthat	
			Amon	12	26	46	Jorim	
			Josiah	13	27	47	Eliezer	
	Jehoichin		Jeconiah	14	28	48	Joshua	
	(deportation to Babylon)		Shealtiel	1	29	49	Er	
			Zerubbabel	2	30	50	Elmadam	
			Abiud	3	31	51	Cosam	
			Eliakim	4	32	52	Addi	
			Azor	5	33	53	Melchi	
			Zadok	6	34	54	Neri	
			Achin	7	35	55	Shealtiel	
			Eliad	8	36	56	Zerubbabel	
			Eleazar	9	37	57	Rhesa	
			Matthan	10	38	58	Joanan	
			Jacob	11	39	59	Joda	
			Joseph	12	40	60	Joseph	
			Jesus	13	41	61	Semein	
						62	Mattathias	
						63	Maath	
						64	Naggai	
						65	Hesli	
						66	Nahum	
						67	Amos	
						68	Mattathias	
						69	Joseph	
						70	Jannai	
						71	Melchi	
						72	Levi	
						73	Matthat	
						74	Heli (Eli)	
Messiah						75	Joseph	(son-in-law of Heli)
						76	Jesus	(Mary - actual daughter of Heli)

Vertical labels within diagram: "3 Groupings of the 14 generations in Matthew's gospel"; "Common Ancestry"; "Matthew: Solomon's Line through Joseph (Royal Line)"; "Luke: Nathan's line through Mary (Human Line)"

Table 7.4 - The Genealogies of Jesus Christ

Comparison of Biblical Genealogies of Judah's Line

Time BC	Period	Genesis	1 & 2 Kings (taken from Kings Table)	1 Chronicles 2:3-15 & 3:1-24	Matthew 1:1-17		Luke 3:23-38	
		5:3-32						God
~ 4100		Adam					1	Adam
		Seth					2	Seth
		Enosh					3	Enosh
		Kenan	Matthew Henry, p 618 - "…it is sufficient to				4	Kenan
		Mahalaleel	say that the seventy interpreters, who, before				5	Mahalaleel
		Jared	the Saviour's time, translated the Old				6	Jared
		Enoch	Testament into Greek, for reasons best				7	Enoch
		Methuselah	known to themselves inserted that Cainan, St.				8	Methuselah
		Lamech	Luke, writing among the Hellenistic Jews,				9	Lamech
2500	Flood	Noah	was obligated to make use of that				10	Noah
		11:10-32	translation…to take it as he found it"					
		Shem					11	Shem
		Arpachshad					12	Arphazad
			Cainan not in Genesis genealogy ←				13	Cainan
		Shelah	(see explanation above)				14	Shelah
		Eber					15	Heber
		Peleg					16	Peleg
		Reu					17	Reu
		Serug					18	Serug
		Nahor					19	Nahor
		Terah					20	Terah
2100	Patriarchal Perid	Abram			Abraham	1	21	Abraham
		Isaac			Isaac	2	22	Isaac
		Jacob			Jacob	3	23	Jacob
		Judah		Judah	Judah	4	24	Judah
		Perez		Perez	Perez	5	25	Perez
				Hezron	Hezron	6	26	Hezron
				Ram	Ram	7	27	Ram
			(Note: Admin not in KJV listing in Luke) ←					Admin
				Amminadab	Amminadab	8	28	Amminadab
				Nahshon	Nahshon	9	29	Nahshon
				Salma	Salmon	10	30	Salmon
				Boaz	Boaz	11	31	Boaz
				Obed	Obed	12	32	Obed
				Jesse	Jesse	13	33	Jesse
	Saul		David	David	David	14	34	David
			Solomon	Solomon	Solomon	1	35	Nathan
			Rhehoboam	Rhehoboam	Rehoboam	2	36	Mattatha
			Abijah	Abijah	Abijah	3	37	Menna
			Asa	Asa	Asa	4	38	Melea
			Jehoshaphat	Jehoshaphat	Jehoshaphat	5	39	Eliakim
			Jehoram	Joram	Joram	6	40	Jonam
			Ahaziah	Ahaziah	**Gap**		41	Joseph
			Jehoash (Joash)	Joash			42	Judah
			Amaziah	Amaziah			43	Simeon
			Azariah (Uzziah)	Azariah	Uzziah	7	44	Levi
			Jotham	Jotham	Jotham	8	45	Matthat
			Ahaz	Ahaz	Ahaz	9	46	Jorim
			Hezekiah	Hezekiah	Hezekiah	10	47	Eliezer
			Manasseh	Manasseh	Manasseh	11	48	Joshua
			Amon	Amon	Amon	12	49	Er
			Josiah	Josiah	Josiah	13	50	Elmadam
			Jehoahaz, Jehoikim, Mattaniah (Zedekiah)	Johanon, Jehoikim, Zedekiah	**Gap**		51	Cosam
			Jehoichin (Jeconiah)		Jeconiah	14	52	Addi
586	Babylonian Captivity						53	Melchi
							54	Neri
			* Haggai 1:1 mentions Zerubbabel,	Shealtiel ** Pedaiah	Shealtiel	1	55	Shealtiel
			governor or Judah (and son of Shealtiel).					
			Haggai's message was addressed to him	* Zerubbabel	Zerubbabel	2	56	Zerubbabel
			and other leaders of Judah. These were	Hananiah			57	Rhesa
			apparently the same Shealtiel and	?			58	Joanan
			Zerubbabel in the 1 Chronicles,	Shemaiah			59	Joda
			Matthew's genealogies. Whether these	Neariah			60	Josech
			same names in Luke's genealogy refer to	Elioenai			61	Semein
			the same two people or different people				62	Mattathias
			of the same name is uncertain.				63	Maath
							64	Maggai
							65	Hesli
			** That Zerubbabel was called both the				66	Nahum
			son of Shealtiel and the son of Shealtiel's		Abiud	3	67	Amos
			brother Pedaiah (1 Chro 3:17-19) is		Eliakim	4	68	Mattathias
			probably due to a levirate marriage		Azor	5	69	Joseph
			(Deut 25:5-10). After Pedaiah died his		Zadok	6	70	Jannai
			brother Shealtiel may have taken		Achim	7	71	Melchi
			Pedaiah's widow to be his wife and to		Eliud	8	72	Levi
			them was born Zerubbabel. The Bible		Eleazar	9	73	Matthat
			Knowledge Commentary, by Walvoord &		Matthan	10	74	Eli (Heli)
	Birth of		Zuck, p 1539		Jacob	11	75	Joseph (Mary)
~ 4 BC	Jesus				Joseph	12		
					Jesus	13	76	Jesus

Note (in left boxed column): Jehoahaz (Johanon), Jehoikim and Mattaniah (Zedekiah) were Josiah's sons, while Jehoichin (Jeconiah) was his grandson (Jehoikim's son).

Period of the Kings

Table 7.5 - Comparison of Biblical Genealogies of Judah's Line

NOTES (CHAPTER 7)

[1]   *NASB Side-Column Reference Edition*, (Anaheim, The Lockman Foundation, 1996), footnote for Luke 3:23, 94

[2]   John F. Walvoord and Roy B. Zuck, eds., *The Bible Knowledge Commentary, Old Testament*, (Colorado Springs: David C Cook, 1985), 1539

[3]   John F. Walvoord and Roy B. Zuck, eds., *The Bible Knowledge Commentary, New Testament* (Colorado Springs: David C Cook, 1983), 18

[4]   Matthew Henry, *Matthew Henry's Commentary on the Whole Bible, Volume V – Matthew to John* (New Jersey: Fleming H. Revell Company, 1975), 618

8

MECHANICS OF OT MESSIANIC PROPHECY

IN OUR OVERVIEW OF OLD TESTAMENT MESSIANIC PROPHECY THUS FAR, WE'VE COVERED THE New Testament's witness to it in chapter 6 and the covenantal aspect of it in chapter 7. In this concluding chapter of our overview, we will look at the various *prophetic devices* used to convey information about Messiah in the Old Testament. Below is a listing of these devices and an explanation of each.

TYPES OF PROPHETIC DEVICES

1. **Prophecy**—predictive statements about Messiah or related to Him.

2. **Types and Shadows**—pictures embedded in the Old Testament narrative that point to the Messiah.

3. **Dreams and Visions**—prophetic information pointing to the Messiah revealed in dreams or visions.

4. **Theophany**—God appearing in a physical form.

5. **Christophany**—Christophanies are theophanies that are Christ specific. They are actual appearances of the pre-incarnate Christ in a physical form.

6. **Messianic Prophetic Genealogy**—consists of the names within the messianic line that are prophetically designated as persons whom Christ would be descended from, as we saw in the last chapter.

7. **Old Testament Language and Culture**—the very language and culture of the Old Testament points to a messianic fulfillment and served to prepare God's people for the Messiah's coming. This language and culture is embedded in the Old Testament law as noted by the author of Hebrews.

As a student of the Bible, I have long been amazed by the evidence of God's divine inspiration of the scriptures. His hand can readily be seen through the intricate details recorded by the various human authors who penned the scriptures. The messianic prophetic tapestry that is interwoven throughout the Old Testament is both extensive and varied. I believe that every one of the thirty-nine books of the Old Testament has some messianic connection. We will see that starting in the next chapter on Genesis, as we begin our march through the Pentateuch, examining each prophetic element one at a time as we encounter it.

These prophetic puzzle pieces vary in scope and size from as little as one verse to whole chapters. They may be concise and powerful like Micah 5:2, which testifies of Jesus's birthplace, His future rule over Israel, and His pre-eternality. On the other hand, they may be broad and detailed. I remember being blown away when I was first told that there are entire chapters in the Old Testament that are about Jesus. Perhaps the most familiar of these are Psalm 2 (about the Son of God) and Psalm 22 (about Jesus's crucifixion), and Isaiah 53 (about Jesus the suffering servant). Also, the prophetic elements vary in clarity. Some are more cryptic in nature, such as the *protoevangelium* in Genesis 3:15, while others are quite clear and detailed, as in the case of the whole-chapter prophecies mentioned above.

Some prophecies deal directly with the Messiah Himself, while others deal with matters related to the Messiah's coming, such as salvation, the outpouring of the Holy Spirit, the New Covenant, the inclusion of the Gentiles, His millennial and eternal reign, as examples. One interesting aspect of prophecy is that it is often written in past tense, as though the prophet is describing something that he has seen, even though he is speaking of a future event. Below is a discussion of each prophetic device, giving examples of each.

DISCUSSION AND EXAMPLES OF EACH PROPHETIC DEVICE

1. **Prophecy:** Prophecy is simply a promise expressed in textual form. The New Testament is simply the record of the establishment of the New Covenant in Christ that was foretold throughout the Old Testament. Of all the prophetic elements, prophecy is the most obvious, the most easily understood, and the most voluminous. The largest part of messianic prophetic information comes in the form of prophecy. Examples are shown below:

   Genesis 3:15—the protoevangelium foretells the seed of the woman versus the seed of Satan, and the woman's seed's ultimate victory over Satan.

   Genesis 22:18—foretells that Abraham's offspring will bless all the nations of earth. In Galatians 3:8, 16, Paul makes it clear that this refers to Christ.

Psalm 2—the entire chapter is about Christ, who is alternately referred to as God's anointed, God's king, and God's Son.

Isaiah 7:14—prophesies Christ's virgin birth

Micah 5:2—foretells Messiah's birthplace, His future rule of Israel, and His pre-eternality.

2. **Types and Shadows:** This prophetic element involves pictures of Christ that are interwoven through the Old Testament narrative. Some of these pictures are subtle and may present themselves as small details of a larger story. Others are more dramatic such as Passover, the Day of Atonement, and the story of Ruth. Some are less obvious, while others are quite obvious. Types and shadows come in various forms—person types, event types, Mosaic Law types, and others that we will explore as we go.

Some of these types and shadows are commented on in the New Testament. Also, their existence in general is spoken of by the author of Hebrews. Note in the examples below from the book of Hebrews the words *copy*, *shadow*, and *type*. Each of these passages is referring to prophetic types in the Old Testament that are *pictures* of the New Covenant in Christ. The author of Hebrews is laying out the argument that the new covenant in Christ is far superior to the old covenant made at Sinai.

> Now if He were on earth, He would not be a priest at all, since there are those who offer the gifts according to the Law; who serve a *copy* and *shadow* of the heavenly things, just as Moses was warned *by God* when he was about to erect the tabernacle; for, "SEE," He says, "THAT YOU MAKE all things ACCORDING TO THE PATTERN WHICH WAS SHOWN YOU ON THE MOUNTAIN." (Hebrews 8:4–5)

> The Holy Spirit is signifying this, that the way into the holy place has not yet been disclosed while the outer tabernacle is still standing … Therefore it was necessary for the *copies* of the things in the heavens to be cleansed with these, but the heavenly things themselves with better sacrifices than these. For Christ did not enter a holy place made with hands, *a mere copy* of the true one, but into heaven itself, now to appear in the presence of God for us. (Hebrews 9:8, 9:23–24)

> For the Law, since it has only *a shadow* of the good things to come and not the very form of things, can never, by the same sacrifices which they offer continually year by year, make perfect those who draw near. (Hebrews 10:1)

> By faith Abraham, when he was tested, offered up Isaac, and he who had received the promises was offering up his only begotten *son; it was he* to

whom it was said, "IN ISAAC YOUR DESCENDANTS SHALL BE CALLED." He considered that God is able to raise *people* even from the dead, from which he also received him back *as a type*. (Hebrews 11:17–19)

Perhaps, when you were smaller, you may have picked up a *Highlights* magazine, possibly in a doctor's office waiting room (especially if you're older). A regular feature of this magazine, which I loved, was the hidden-picture puzzle. There would be a full-page picture, and within this large picture there were several smaller hidden pictures of various objects embedded in the large picture. In much the same way, when we read the Old Testament, these messianic types and shadows begin to appear to us in stunning clarity. The amazing thing is that when you would first look at the large *Highlights* picture, you may not see any of the smaller object pictures, but as you would study it carefully, you could begin to pick them out one at a time. Similarly, a casual reading of the Old Testament may miss many or even all the prophetic types and shadows found within its pages. However, careful subsequent readings will increasingly reveal them. I believe the Holy Spirit calls our attention to them as we read. For me personally, the discovery of these prophetic types and shadows in the Old Testament has been one of my most joyful experiences in reading through the Bible. I seriously doubt that anyone has ever plumbed all the depths of this intricate subject. Below are examples.

Manna (Exodus 16:31)—Manna was sent by God to sustain the Israelites in the wilderness and is a picture of Christ, who said, "I am the Bread of Life," after feeding the 5,000 (John 6:48).

Abraham's Commanded Sacrifice of His Son (Genesis 22)—Abraham was willing to follow God's command to sacrifice his son until God stopped him. Abraham is a picture of God the Father and Isaac is initially a picture of Christ, until the ram caught in the thicket becomes the replacement sacrifice and thus becomes the picture of Christ.

Passover (Exodus 12)—God commanded Moses to have the people slay a lamb and paint its blood on the doorposts and lintel of their house so that when God came to slay the firstborn males in the Egyptian homes, He would see the blood on the Israelite homes and pass over them. Similarly, by our trust in Him, Jesus's shed blood is applied to our heart. Then instead of being objects of God's wrath, we become His children (John 1:12).

Day of Atonement (Leviticus 16)—This annual offering could only be offered by the High Priest and would cleanse the people of all their sins from the past year. This is a rich picture of what Christ does for us, as we will see when we go through Leviticus.

3. **Dreams and Visions:** Dreams and visions are scattered through the Old Testament and really need no explanation. However, many of them contain prophetic elements, and some point specifically to Messiah. Examples are below.

Jacob's Ladder—Jacob, after running away from his angry brother Esau, had a dream of angels ascending and descending on a ladder that reached from earth to heaven, with God standing above the ladder, telling Jacob that He is the God of Abraham and Isaac (Genesis 28:12–15). Nearly 2,000 years later, Jesus calls Nathaniel as a disciple and tells him that he will see the heavens opened and angels ascending and descending upon the Son of Man (John 1:51), and we see angels ministering to Jesus after His temptation in the wilderness (Matthew 4:11). So they are ascending and descending from heaven on Jesus and on His human progenitor Jacob in a dream nearly 2,000 years prior.

Nebuchadnezzar's Dream—The king dreamed of a giant statue with a head of gold, breast and arms of silver, belly and thighs of bronze, legs of iron, and feet of iron and clay. The statue was decimated by a stone made without hands. Daniel told the king both his dream and its interpretation, explaining that Nebuchadnezzar's kingdom was represented by the gold head. The stone destroying the statue represents God's final ushering in of His eternal kingdom, which is Christ's Second Coming to end man's kingdoms and set up His own eternal one.

Daniel's Vision—Daniel saw a vision of One like a Son of Man coming up to the Ancient of Days, who gave him glory, a kingdom, and an everlasting dominion. This clearly pictures God the Son coming before God the Father to receive His eternal kingdom! (Compare Daniel 7:13–14 to Revelation 5.)

4. **Theophanies:** Theophanies are actual physical appearances of God to people. There are various types of theophanies—God appeared in human form, angelic form, and other forms. This is a special category of types that foreshadow Immanuel, whose name means "God with us." Some theophanies are more dramatic, such as the burning bush or the pillar of cloud or fire, while some are more natural like God's visit to Abraham, where He appears in the form of a man accompanied by two angels who also appear in the form of men. Examples below.

a)	God's appearance to Abraham as a man	Genesis 18
b)	Jacob wrestles with a supernatural man	Genesis 32:24–32
c)	Pillar of cloud and fire	Exodus 13:21
d)	Balaam and his donkey visited by the angel of the Lord	Numbers 22:21–35
e)	Gideon visited by the angel of the Lord	Judges 6:11–24
f)	Manoah and his wife visited by the angel of the Lord	Judges 13:3–23

It should be noted that the phrase "the angel of the Lord" is a manifestation of God Himself, because the angel of the Lord always speaks in first person for God as though it is God Himself speaking.

5. **Christophanies:** As stated earlier, Christophanies are theophanies that are Christ specific.

Below are examples.

Captain of the Lord's Hosts: This supernatural man appears to Joshua just after the manna had ceased in Canaan. Joshua was by Jericho when the man appears with his sword drawn. Joshua asks him, "Are you for us or for our adversaries?" He replies, "No; rather I indeed come now as captain of the host of the Lord" (Joshua 5:13–15).

Fiery Furnace Appearance: When Nebuchadnezzar had Shadrach, Meshach, and Abednego bound and thrown into the fiery furnace, he saw them walking unharmed in the midst of the furnace, accompanied by a mysterious fourth man. He answered and said, Lo, I see four men loose, walking in the midst of the fire, and they have no hurt; and the form of the fourth is like the Son of God (Daniel 3:25).

6. **Messianic Prophetic Genealogy:** The Old Testament specifically named certain people whom the Messiah would be descended from. This was covered in the last chapter. We see this prophetic genealogy extends from Eve to David and ultimately ends with Jesus. The prophecy below in 2 Samuel 7 is about Solomon and ultimately Jesus, who would become the final eternal king.

And thine house and thy kingdom shall be established for ever before thee: thy throne shall be established for ever. (2 Samuel 7:16)

The Messianic prophetic genealogy is repeated below from the last chapter:

Eve > Abraham > Isaac > Jacob > Judah > Jesse > David > Jesus

7. **Old Testament Language and Culture:** In my personal study of Old Testament messianic prophecy, a very fascinating discovery was revealed to me—that our Christian terminology, which we may take for granted, is firmly rooted in Old Testament concepts. This can be seen in table 8.1, New Testament Words of the Old Testament, shown at the end of this chapter. The point is that the everyday language of the Old Testament in many ways pointed to the coming Messiah. Similarly, the various offices of prophet, priest, king, kinsman redeemer, etc., have their ultimate fulfillment in Jesus Christ. The daily language, culture, and terminology of the Old Testament, which was ordained by God, comprise a special category of prophetic type. The Old Testament language and culture is laced with messianic symbology and terminology.

The table referenced above lists several words in alphabetical order. Below the root words are shown in logical order with similar words grouped together. Each word or grouping will be shown to point to Jesus Christ in some way. This special language and culture prepared the Jews to recognize their Messiah when He came.

a) **Anoint**—this word refers to the ritual of anointing someone to set them apart for God's service, such as kings and priests, which typically involved pouring oil upon the person's head. It also refers to a person who is set apart by God for a special purpose and/or to be endued with divine power. If we take Saul, for example, Samuel, at God's instruction, anointed Saul as the first king of Israel (1 Samuel 9:27, 10:1). On the other hand, even though Saul later attempted to murder David out of jealous paranoia, David refused to "stretch his hand against the Lord's anointed," though he had two opportunities to kill his would-be murderer (1 Samuel 24:3–6, 26:3–13). So we see in these passages both senses of the word *anoint*. Psalm 2:1–2 speaks of the rulers of this world taking counsel against God and His anointed. This is clearly speaking of Christ, who is also referred to as God's king and as God's Son in the same psalm.

b) **Messiah**—appears to be the primary word used to refer to God's special anointed One who would one day arise on earth on behalf of his people. Although this word is only found twice in the Old Testament, both instances in Daniel 9:25–26, which speaks of the end time, the word *Christ* is used repeatedly throughout the New Testament to refer to Jesus, perhaps most notably in Peter's great confession. Jesus asked the disciples, "Who do you say that I am?" Peter responds, "You are the Christ, the Son of the Living God." (Matthew 16:16). "Christ" is English for the Greek *Christos*, "anointed one." [1] Christ is the English word for the Hebrew word *messiah*. The word *Christ* is used over 500 times in the New Testament!

c) **Atone, Offer, Ransom, Sacrifice**—these words are all associated with the payment of a price to make sinners acceptable to a holy God.

1) **Atone**—means to make amends or reparation for a past wrong. This was the purpose of every sacrifice offered to God in the Old Covenant. The Day of Atonement was the one day of the year when the high priest would make the necessary offerings such that all the Israelites' sins would be removed and everyone would start with a clean slate.

2) **Offer**—sacrifices are voluntary and therefore are offered by the one making them. Similarly, Christ offered Himself as a once-for-all sacrifice for sins.

3) **Ransom**—a ransom is a price paid for the life of another.

4) **Sacrifice**—the Old Covenant involved multiple sacrifices that would cleanse the sinner of a particular sin, or in the case of the Day of Atonement, the worshippers would be cleansed from every sin committed in the past year.

The point being made here is that when Christ came to offer Himself as the once-for-all sacrifice for all sins, the idea of sacrifice, ransom, and atonement for sins was not a new concept. In fact, it was so familiar that two of the problems in the early church were (1) the Judaizers trying to infuse elements of the law into Christianity, and (2) that some of the Christians were enticed to abandon their faith and return to the Mosaic system that they grew up with. This problem was addressed by Paul in his letter to the Galatians (see chapter 3) and by the writer of Hebrews, who showed the superiority of the New Covenant in Christ over the old Mosaic Covenant.

d) **Clean, Justify, Sanctify**—these words speak of the cleansing that is required for worshippers of God. God is holy, and those who worship Him are commanded to be holy.

   1) **Clean**—the sacrifices brought under the Mosaic system cleansed the worshippers of sins committed. There were specific offerings for specific sins, and the Day of Atonement cleansed from all sins previously committed.
   2) **Justify**—man's greatest need in the Old Testament and now in the church age is to be justified before God.
   3) **Sanctify**—sanctification in the Old Testament involved both people and objects. The priests had to observe a rite of sanctification, and the objects of the tabernacle also required a rite of sanctification. Sanctification connotes two ideas: (1) being set apart, and (2) being made holy.

Christians today are cleansed in two ways. First, by the once-for-all imputed righteousness of Christ through His shed blood, we are *justified* before God. Second, by the indwelling presence of the Holy Spirit, we are *being sanctified*, which is an ongoing process of being *conformed* to the image of Christ by God.

e) **Deliver, Redeem, Save**—in the Old Testament, all these words involve people being rescued from something.

   1) **Deliver**—this word speaks of people being delivered from something bad, whether death, sickness, or some catastrophic threat.
   2) **Redeem**—this word means to buy back. A redemption price could be paid to buy a slave's freedom in scripture. It also connotes the idea of restoring value. For example, we can redeem points to purchase items (the points are worthless until redeemed). Years ago, people could earn stamps from purchases, then they could take the stamps to a redemption center to get cash or make a purchase. The redeemed person is redeemed *from* something. As Christians, we are redeemed from sin and death.

3) **Save**—just like in the two preceding words, when a person is saved, he is saved from something—an unfruitful, wasted life and the penalty of eternal damnation. On the day of Pentecost, 3,000 souls were *saved* after Peter's sermon.

f) **Covenant**—as was discussed in the previous chapter, God relates to us on the basis of *covenant*. Our Bible is composed of two testaments, the Old and the New, which refer to the old Mosaic Covenant, which was based on works, versus the New Covenant in Christ, which is based on salvation by grace through faith in Him (Ephesians 2:8–9).

The point being made by these Old Testament words that have their fullest meaning in the New Testament is that this language and culture is one more thing in the Old Testament that pointed to Christ. The idea of appeasing a holy God who is offended by sin and the means of appeasement being sacrificial offerings were all rooted in Old Testament concepts. Another point is that the law contained a provision for a kinsman redeemer. This role was beautifully portrayed in the book of Ruth, where Boaz, Naomi's near kinsman, married Ruth the Moabitess, performing the role of kinsman redeemer and buying back Elimelech's land. This is a beautiful *type* of Christ our Redeemer who purchased our ransom by His own blood.

We are now finished with our overview of Old Testament Messianic Prophecy, so we are now ready to begin our journey through the Pentateuch and mine the treasures of messianic prophecies and types.

Words Related to New Testament Theology Found in the Old Testament

Root Word	Additonal Word Variations of Root Word								Total
anoint 30	anointed 86	anointedst 1	anointest 1	anointing 25					143
atone 0	atonement 80	atonements 1							81
clean 114	cleaness 5	cleanse 27	cleansed 30	cleanseth 2	cleansing 8	unclean 162	uncleaness 29	uncleanesses 1	378
covenant 272	covenanted 2	covenants 0							274
deliver 267	deliverance 14	deliverances 1	delivered 218	deliveredst 1	deliverer 8	deliverest 2	delivereth 13	delivering 0	524
justify 7	justification 0	justified 12	justifier 0	justifieth 2	justifying 2				23
messiah 2									2
offer 219	offered 115	offereth 15	offering 713	offerings 265					1327
ransom 10	ransomed 3								13
redeem 49	redeemed 55	redeemedst 1	redeemer 18	redeemeth 2	redeeming 1	redemption 9			135
sacrifice 194	sacrificed 30	sacrificedst 1	sacrifices 65	sacrificeth 6	sacrificing 2				298
sanctify 64	sanctification 0	sanctified 46	sanctifieth 0						110
save 170	saved 47	savest 3	saveth 7	saving 7	saviour 13	salvation 119			366

Table 8.1 - New Testament Words in the Old Testament

NOTES (CHAPTER 8)

[1] Chad Brand et al., eds., *Holman Illustrated Bible Dictionary* (Nashville: Holman Bible Publishers, 2003), 284

PART 3
EXPLORING THE OT MESSIANIC PROPHECIES

CHAPTERS

9

JESUS IN GENESIS

Now we have completed our overview of the Bible and our overview of OT messianic prophecy. So let's begin our journey through the Old Testament's prophetic portrayal of the Messiah. As we look at the various pieces of this prophetic tapestry, the prophetic *device(s)* of each entry will be identified in parentheses (prophecy, type/shadow, dreams/ visions, theophanies/Christophanies, Messianic prophetic genealogy, or OT language/culture). We will begin our journey at the most logical place—in Genesis, the book of beginnings.

1. **The Holy Trinity** (OT Language and Culture)

> In the beginning God created the heavens and the earth. (Genesis 1:1)

> And God said, Let *us* make man in *our* image, after *our* likeness: and let them have dominion over the fish of the sea, and over the fowl of the air, and over the cattle, and over all the earth, and over every creeping thing that creepeth upon the earth. So God created man in his own image, in the image of God created he him; male and female created he them. (Genesis 1:26–27)

> And the LORD God said, Behold, the man is become *as one of us*, to know good and evil: and now, lest he put forth his hand, and take also of the tree of life, and eat, and live for ever. (Genesis 3:22)

> And the LORD came down to see the city and the tower, which the children of men builded. And the LORD said, Behold, the people is one, and they have all one language; and this they begin to do: and now nothing will be restrained from them, which they have imagined to do. Go to, *let us go down*, and there confound their language, that they may not understand one another's speech. So the LORD scattered them abroad from thence upon the face of all the earth: and they left off to build the city. Therefore is the name of it called Babel; because the LORD did there confound the language of all the earth: and from thence did the LORD scatter them abroad upon the face of all the earth. (Genesis 11:5–9)

It should be noted that none of these texts is a prophetic promise about the Messiah, nor is it a type or shadow (i.e., a picture) of Him. For this reason, I am classifying it under the language and culture category. All four of these texts illustrate the plurality of God, although the first one is not at all obvious. So let us examine them one at a time. The very language of these passages suggests the plural aspect of the godhead—that there is *one* God; however, He exists in *multiple* (three) persons. Since one of those persons is Christ, it is messianic in that sense. Although the word *trinity* is not in the Bible, the doctrine of the Trinity is, and its first hint in scripture is in these passages.

Genesis 1:1: The word *God* translates the Hebrew name Elohim, which is listed as being a plural form of "god" in Strong's Hebrew dictionary.[1] How is that for being early in the biblical narrative as a hint concerning Messiah—the very first verse of the Bible! We don't have to go far in Genesis to see this aspect of the godhead being developed in clear English.

Genesis 1:26–27: In these verses, we see God being alternately described in the singular and the plural, with the latter first. "Let *Us* make man in *Our* image …" is followed by "So God created man in *His* own image … in the image of God created *He* him; male and female created *He* them." I know for me personally, I had previously envisioned God as talking to the angels in Genesis 1:26 when I read this passage. However, the plain language of "Let us make" suggests a team effort, and Genesis 1:1 does not read, "In the beginning God and the angels created the heavens and the earth," but that God alone did.

Genesis 3:22: We continue just prior to Adam and Eve's banishment from the Garden, with God's internal discussion, "the LORD God said, Behold, the man is become as *one of us*, to know good and evil." Here, God again speaks of Himself in the plural, "*One of Us …*"

Genesis 11:5–9: In this passage concerning the Tower of Babel, where man attempted to construct a tower reaching from earth to heaven, we find the words "*let Us go down*, and there confound their language." Once again, God is having this internal conversation within Himself as multiple persons within the godhead.

In addition to the above examples, we see an additional passage in Isaiah in the year of King Uzziah's death when God commissioned Isaiah as a prophet.

> Also *I heard the voice of the Lord, saying*, Whom shall I send, and *who will go for us*? Then said I, Here am I; send me. (Isaiah 6:8)

Once again, we see God speaking of Himself in the plural.

Accordingly, even though the Protoevangelium below is credited with being the *first evangel* or *gospel*, these passages of God speaking of Himself in the plural are the first hints of Christ— Whom we know as the second person of the Trinity. The Protoevangelium, which we will look at next, *is* the first messianic *prophecy*.

2. **The Protoevangelium** (Prophecy)

> And I will put enmity between thee and the woman, and between thy seed and her seed; it shall bruise thy head, and thou shalt bruise his heel. (Genesis 3:15)

What is the Protoevangelium? First we have *proto* as in prototype (first of its kind), joined by *evangelium*, from the root word *evangel*, or gospel. Thus, the Protoevangelium is the first prophecy of the gospel in scripture. It has been said that there is a scarlet thread of redemption that runs throughout the Bible. The Protoevangelium is simply the beginning of that thread.

Before we look at this prophecy in detail, let's first backpedal one chapter in scripture, when God forbade Adam to eat of the Tree of the Knowledge of Good and Evil (Genesis 2:16–17), adding that in the day that he would eat thereof he would surely die. After this very sin in the opening of chapter 3, Adam and Eve suddenly realized for the first time their physical nakedness and suddenly felt estranged from God as He called for them, which appears to have been His customary practice. At this point, there is dialogue back and forth between God, Adam, and Eve, which involved finger-pointing by the latter two, in a futile attempt to shift the blame. At this point, God begins to foretell the curse that will result from the disobedience of the couple. Now, let's examine the following points concerning the curse, which contains this prophecy:

a) **First Addressed:** The Lord first addresses the serpent (Satan). Note, He begins by saying, "Because you have done this, cursed are you more than all ..." Only after beginning with Satan does God proceed next to Eve and afterward to Adam.

b) **Timing:** Note God's timing in placing the first glimmer of the gospel—immediately after the fall of man! Yes, Adam and Eve, you really messed up royally, but God has provided a plan of redemption.

c) **Enmity:** "I will put enmity between you and the woman, and between your seed and her seed." Thus, the continuing conflicts between God and Satan and God and man have been ongoing from that moment until now. Peter speaks of this struggle in his first epistle, "Be sober, be vigilant; because your adversary the devil, as a roaring lion, walketh about, seeking whom he may devour:" (1 Peter 5:8). This verse speaks of the battle between Satan and the woman, and between Satan and her descendants. So, what about the battle between "your seed and her seed"? Let's first address "your seed" (Satan's seed). Jesus identifies Satan's seed in John's gospel. He is addressing the Pharisee's claim that they are children of Abraham (John 8:33–44). He concludes by telling them, "*Ye are of your father the devil*, and the lusts of your father ye will do. He was a murderer from the beginning, and abode not in the truth, because there is no truth in him. When he speaketh a lie, he speaketh of his own: for he is a liar, and the father of it." Accordingly, Satan's seed are people who follow him, rather than physical offspring.

d) **Her seed:** It is interesting, this phrase "her seed." Throughout the Bible, the practice concerning genealogies is that they are given through men, not women. It is notable that even in Matthew's genealogy of Jesus, where four women are mentioned, the genealogy still passes through the men. Note from the excerpt below:

Judah was the father of Perez and Zerah *by Tamar* … Salmon was the father of Boaz *by Rahab*, Boaz was the father of Obed *by Ruth* … David was the father of Solomon *by Bathsheba*. (Matthew 1:3, 1:5–6)

So what did God mean by *her seed?* Many expositors believe this is nothing less than a reference to the *virgin birth* of Jesus! In this powerful prophecy we see the Old Testament summed up by the compressed genealogy: Eve's seed, Mary's seed—Jesus. As noted earlier, I should point out that many expositors believe that Matthew's genealogy, which is the royal line through David's son Solomon, passes through Joseph, while Luke's genealogy, through David's son Nathan, is believed to be Jesus's biological line through Mary. Accordingly, the compressed genealogy above would apply to Luke's genealogy, which begins with Jesus and concludes with Adam: "Seth, the son of Adam, the son of God" (Luke 3:38). Therefore, Jesus's humanity begins with Eve, the mother of all living (Genesis 3:20) (and Adam) and concludes with the Virgin Mary.

e) **Bruised head / heel:** This speaks of the continuing conflict between Satan and mankind. Now the passage turns to the battle between Satan and God, and, more specifically, between Satan and Christ, and Christ's ultimate victory. Note "between thy seed and her seed; it shall bruise thy head, and thou shalt bruise his heel." Here we see that Satan's *seed* refers to the agency of man, as noted above, and Eve's *seed* refers to Christ.

So what does this mean: "*it* [Christ] shall bruise thy head [fatal blow], and *thou* [Satan] shalt bruise his [Christ's] heel [not *fatal*—although Jesus died from His passion/ crucifixion, He rose from the dead]. We see that this speaks of the final and ultimate victory of God and Christ over Satan and his followers, which is summed up in the last book of the Bible, Revelation.

3. **Garments of Skin** (Type/Shadow)

Unto Adam also and to his wife did the Lord God make coats of skins, and clothed them. (Genesis 3:21)

Here God is *covering* Adam's and Eve's *physical nakedness* after their sin, which is a *picture* of their *spiritual nakedness* before Him (they *knew* that they were naked). Note what Paul says in 2 Corinthians 5:4, "For indeed *while we are in this tent*, we *groan*, being *burdened*, because *we do not want to be unclothed but to be clothed*, so that what is mortal will be swallowed up by life." Paul is saying this even as a believer in this life! Back to the story—it is conceded that our omnipotent God could create animal skins without slaying an animal. However, the plain language of the text would tend to suggest that the *coats of skins* did involve an animal killing—a blood sacrifice. This is the first recorded blood sacrifice in the Bible, and look who made it—God! Also, note what this blood sacrifice replaced—the fig-leaf clothing made by Adam and Eve (Genesis 3:7), which is a *picture* of works—accordingly, this fits the picture of salvation by *grace*, and not by works. So we see that God is using a blood sacrifice to provide a physical covering for Adam and Eve, born out of their first-time discomfort with their nakedness as a result of their sin. This *picture* of our sins being covered by the blood of Jesus is brought out in Jesus's Parable of the Marriage Feast, Matthew 22:1–14, which climaxes with an unsuspecting guest who had failed to wear the *appropriate* wedding garment supplied by the king being thrown out of the banquet hall.

4. Cain's and Abel's Offering (Type/Shadow)

> And in process of time it came to pass, that Cain brought of the fruit of the ground an offering unto the LORD. And Abel, he also brought of the firstlings of his flock and of the fat thereof. And the LORD had respect unto Abel and to his offering: But unto Cain and to his offering he had not respect. And Cain was very wroth, and his countenance fell. (Genesis 4:4–5)

Cain, the firstborn, and Abel, the second-born son of Adam and Eve both brought their offerings to God. Cain's grain offering was not acceptable. Abel's lamb offering was. Why? Was it Abel's offering or his attitude that was superior? These questions are not directly addressed in the text, and there is no recorded prior instruction from God regarding the type or even the necessity of offerings. After all, this is over 2,500 years prior to the Mosaic Law! A quick review of the early chapters in Leviticus, table 11.1 in chapter 11, reveals five general offering types: (1) burnt offering (animal), (2) grain offering (vegetative), (3) peace offering (animal), (4) sin offering (animal), and (5) guilt offering (animal). See the summary below:

Animal sacrifice	– Offering types 1, 3, 4, 5
Vegetative sacrifice	– Offering type 2
Involved sin or guilt	– Offering types 1, 4, 5
Expressed thanksgiving or devotion to the Lord	– Offering types 2, 3

So we see from this that four of the five offering types involved animal sacrifice, and provision for sin was only accomplished by animal sacrifice. So God's acceptance of the blood offering over the grain offering is another *type* that points to Jesus the perfect sacrifice.

5. Genealogies (Covenantal Genealogy)

Any new student of scripture who has ever read through the genealogies in the Bible has no doubt found it to be somewhat of a boring exercise. The question could be raised, "Why are the genealogies in the Bible?" Credible answers to this question would include the following:

1) The short answer is that God wanted them there.

2) Adam and Eve would have wanted to explain mankind's origin, their expulsion from the Garden of Eden, and their changed relationship with God afterward.

3) The first people on earth would logically want to preserve history.

4) They would want to explain Cain's expulsion and preserve the covenant lineage.

5) They would later want to preserve the narrower messianic lineage to record the fulfillment of the prophecy about the seed of the woman in Genesis 3:15.

So God's inspiration was working in concert with human logic in recording the genealogies.

Figure 9.1 on the adjacent page shows diagrammatically that the gospel was in the mind of God before creation. This diagram ties to table 7.1 – God's Foreordained Plan at the beginning of chapter 7. The prophetic genealogy connects the dots of the various named individuals in the messianic line that Jesus would be descended from, beginning with Eve in the protoevangelium in Genesis 3:15. After Eve we skip to Abraham, followed by his descendants, Isaac, Jacob and Judah. Then we encounter Jesse and David, and then Mary the mother of Jesus (as we saw in Luke's genealogy in figure 7.4 and the notes explaining it at the end of chapter 7), and finally we end with Jesus.

The Gospel In the Mind of God

Jesus slain *(in the mind of God)* before creation
John 17:5, Acts 2:22-24, Romans 16:20, Ephesians 1:4-5, 2 Timothy 1:9, 1 Peter 1:18-20

The Proto Evangelium
(first gospel, first messianic prophecy)
Genesis 3:15
"And I will put enmity between you and the woman,
and between your seed and <u>her seed</u>.
He shall bruise you on the head,
And you shall bruise Him on the heel."

(connect with Isa 7:14 below)
(Eve's Seed - Christ)

*(Note the timing of this - God speaking to
the serpent in the presence of Adam & Eve,
immediately after their fall)*

(Serpent's Seed - those who reject
Christ & follow Satan, especially
those involved w/ crucifixion)
(see John 8:44)

Jesus' Prophetic Genealogy

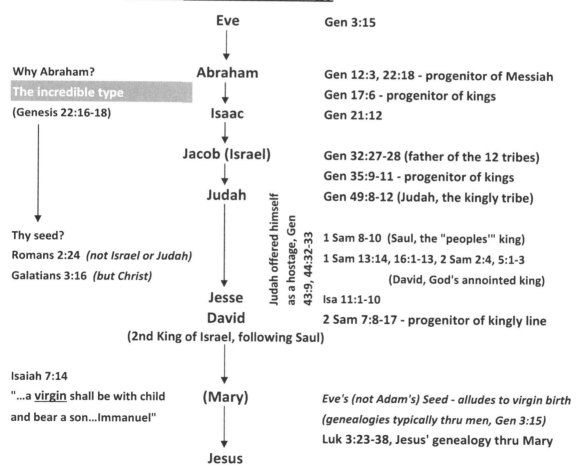

Eve — Gen 3:15

Why Abraham?
The incredible type
(Genesis 22:16-18)

Abraham — Gen 12:3, 22:18 - progenitor of Messiah
Gen 17:6 - progenitor of kings

Isaac — Gen 21:12

Jacob (Israel) — Gen 32:27-28 (father of the 12 tribes)
Gen 35:9-11 - progenitor of kings

Judah — Gen 49:8-12 (Judah, the kingly tribe)

Judah offered himself as a hostage, Gen 43:9, 44:32-33

Thy seed?
Romans 2:24 *(not Israel or Judah)*
Galatians 3:16 *(but Christ)*

1 Sam 8-10 (Saul, the "peoples'" king)
1 Sam 13:14, 16:1-13, 2 Sam 2:4, 5:1-3
(David, God's annointed king)
Isa 11:1-10

Jesse
David — 2 Sam 7:8-17 - progenitor of kingly line
(2nd King of Israel, following Saul)

Isaiah 7:14
"...a <u>virgin</u> shall be with child
and bear a son...Immanuel"

(Mary) — *Eve's (not Adam's) Seed - alludes to virgin birth*
(genealogies typically thru men, Gen 3:15)
Luk 3:23-38, Jesus' genealogy thru Mary

Jesus

Figure 9.1

6. Enoch's Rapture (Type/Shadow)

> Enoch lived sixty-five years, and became the father of Methuselah. Then *Enoch walked with God* three hundred years after he became the father of Methuselah, and he had *other* sons and daughters. So all the days of Enoch were three hundred and sixty-five years. *Enoch walked with God; and he was not, for God took him.* (Genesis 5:21–24)

It is a common euphemism to speak of a person's passing by stating that God *took* the person. However, in Hebrews 11, which lists many of the Old Testament heroes of the faith, the author makes it very clear that Enoch was raptured (did not see death).

> By faith Enoch was *taken up so that he would not see death;* AND HE WAS NOT FOUND BECAUSE GOD TOOK HIM UP; for he obtained the witness that before his being taken up he was pleasing to God. (Hebrews 11:5)

Enoch is one of two men in the Bible who did not taste death—the other being Elijah. This amazing gem is hidden within the *cemetery* of Genesis 5, which contains the genealogy that extends from Adam to Noah. It is a *picture* of both the *resurrection* and the *rapture* of the New Testament, and is messianic in that sense—since Jesus is the means for both.

7. Noah's Ark (Type/Shadow)

The account of Noah's Ark (Genesis 5:32–9:17) is a beautiful picture of salvation. God gives Noah the ominous prophecy of the earth's and mankind's destruction 120 years in the future, with Noah and his family being the only survivors.

> Then the LORD said, "My Spirit shall not strive with man forever, because he also is flesh; nevertheless *his days shall be one hundred and twenty years.*" The Nephilim were on the earth in those days, and also afterward, when the sons of God came in to the daughters of men, and they bore *children* to them. Those were the mighty men who *were* of old, men of renown. Then the LORD saw that the wickedness of man was great on the earth, and that every intent of the thoughts of his heart was only evil continually. The LORD was sorry that He had made man on the earth, and He was grieved in His heart. The LORD said, "*I will blot out man whom I have created from the face of the land, from man to animals to creeping things and to birds of the sky; for I am sorry that I have made them.*" (Genesis 6:3–7)

However, aren't we thankful for the next verse (Genesis 6:8) – But Noah found favor in the eyes of the Lord!

God then instructs Noah to build an ark (Genesis 6:14–16). To paraphrase, God instructs Noah to build the ark out of gopher wood, with rooms; coat it inside and out with pitch; make it 300 cu × 50 cu × 30 cu (or 450' × 75' × 45') (see figure 9.2 next page); make a window 1 cubit (1.5') from the top; place the door in the side of the ark; and make it with three decks. As a retired civil engineer, I truly marvel at Noah's accomplishment of this task and am inclined to think that the construction of the ark and its successful voyage were both miracles! After all, the voyage lasted a year and seventeen days. Assuming a lunar year of 360 days (used elsewhere in scripture), would yield 377 days. This was no three-day cruise!

This story is a beautiful *picture* of salvation—note the following similarities:

Noah's Ark	**Salvation**
God's warning (Noah and ark's construction*)	God's warning—the law, prophets, Jesus
God's pending judgment (worldwide flood)	God's pending judgment (hell and lake of fire)
God's plan (the ark)	God's plan (Christ's atoning crucifixion)
One way (only one door in the ark)	One way (faith in Christ) (John 14:6)
God *closed* the ark's door (Genesis 7:13–16)	God *sent* His Son Jesus (the Door) (John 10:9)

*120-year long warning

Let me add a personal note of interest. One day I was teaching a series of lessons in a Bible study class, about the very subject of this chapter—Old Testament prophecies and pictures of Christ in the Pentateuch. As we were discussing the story of Noah's ark being a *type*, a class member, Wayne Deer, who had been to seminary, asked me, "Have you ever looked up the word *pitch* in the Hebrew dictionary of a Strong's Concordance?" I told him that I had not.

> Make thee an ark of gopher wood; rooms shalt thou make in the ark, and shalt *pitch it* within and without with *pitch*. (Genesis 6:14 KJV)

Note that the word *pitch* is used in both the verb and noun form—see Strong's listings below:

> "*Pitch* it" (verb) *3722—kaphar* (kaw-far'); a primary root; to cover (specially with bitumen); fig. to *expiate* or condone, to *placate* or cancel; - *appease*, make (an) *atonement*, cleanse, disannul, *forgive*, be merciful, *pacify*, *pardon*, *purge* (away), put off, (make) *reconcile* (-iation).[2]

> "With *pitch*" (noun) *3724—kopher* (ko' fer); from 3722; prop. A cover, i.e. (lit.) a village (as covered in); (spec.) bitumen (as used for coating), and the henna plant (as used for dyeing); fig. a *redemption price*; – bribe, camphire, pitch, *ransom*, satisfaction, sum of money, village.[3]

Notice the word meanings in both the verb and noun forms of pitch in Hebrew (italics mine) – expiate, placate, appease, atonement, forgive, pacify, pardon, purge, reconcile/reconciliation, redemption price, ransom. To be somewhat concise from this word listing, we have the astonishing fact that

The ark was coated inside and out with *atonement* and *redemption*! What a beautiful picture of the Lord Jesus Christ—our Eternal Savior and high priest!

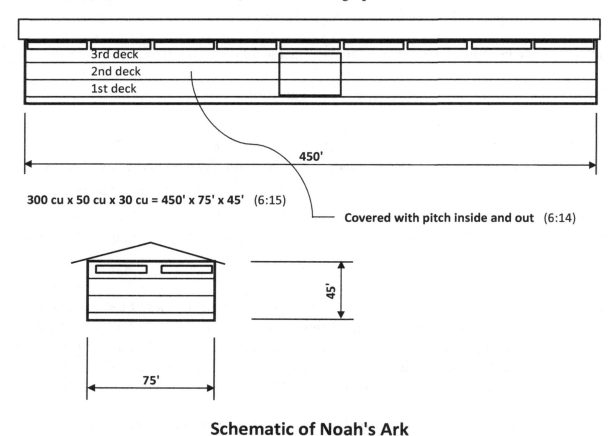

Schematic of Noah's Ark

Figure 9.2

8. **Abraham** (Prophecy, Prophetic Genealogy)

> Now the LORD had said unto Abram, Get thee out of thy country, and from thy kindred, and from thy father's house, unto a land that I will shew thee:
> And I will make of thee a great nation, and I will bless thee, and make thy name great; and thou shalt be a blessing:
> And I will bless them that bless thee, and curse him that curseth thee: and *in thee shall all families of the earth be blessed.* (Genesis 12:1–3)

In this prophecy, God commands Abram to leave his home country and journey to a land that God would show him. God promises seven things to Abraham: (1) to make of him a great nation, (2) to bless him, (3) to make his name great, (4) to make him a blessing, (5) to bless those that bless him, (6) to curse those who curse him, and (7) to bless all the families of the earth through him. Promises 1–6 relate to Abraham and the Jewish nation. However, promise 7 is messianic and relates specifically to Jesus Christ, speaking of the blessing of salvation that would one day be available to all nations through His atoning work on the cross and His eternal priesthood.

When we get to Genesis 22, we will see an incredible prophetic *picture* of God's plan (John 3:16), played out in a mini drama in the life of Abraham and Isaac. We shall also see how this *picture* connects in a remarkable way to Jesus's prophetic genealogy. Abraham is the second person in Jesus's prophetic genealogy.

Eve

Abraham

9. **Melchizedek** (Type/Shadow or Christophany?)

> Then after his return from the defeat of Chedorlaomer and the kings who were with him, the king of Sodom went out to meet him at the valley of Shaveh (that is, the King's Valley). And *Melchizedek king of Salem* brought out *bread and wine*; now he was a *priest of God Most High*. He *blessed him* and said,
> "*Blessed be Abram of God Most High*,
> Possessor of heaven and earth;
> And blessed be God Most High,
> Who has delivered your enemies into your hand."
> He gave him a tenth of all. (Genesis 14:17–20)

After Abraham rescued his nephew Lot in a great military victory, he met Bera, the king of Sodom, and Melchizedek, the king of Salem. Melchizedek is a fascinating figure who seems to spring out of nowhere. Note the following concerning Melchizedek:

He was the *king* of *Salem* (former name of Jerusalem (see below); Salem means Shalom or peace)
He was a *priest* of God Most High
He brought out *bread* and *wine* (Last Supper, Bread of Life, True Vine (John 6:30–58; 15:1)
He *blessed Abram* of God Most High, possessor of heaven and earth
He *blessed God Most High*
Abram *gave him a tenth* of all (the first tithe recorded in scripture, > 600 years before the law)

Note what the author of Hebrews says about Melchizedek in Hebrews 7:1–3:

> For this Melchizedek, king of Salem, priest of the Most High God, who met Abraham as he was returning from the slaughter of the kings and blessed

him, to whom also Abraham apportioned a tenth part of all *the spoils, was first of all, by the translation of his name, king of righteousness*, and then also *king of Salem*, which is *king of peace. Without father, without mother, without genealogy, having neither beginning of days nor end of life, but made like the Son of God, he remains a priest perpetually.*

Could it be that this mysterious figure Melchizedek is none other than the preincarnate Christ? Salem appears to be the same geographic area as Jerusalem (see Psalm 76:1–2). Who is without genealogy and has neither beginning of days nor end of life other than God? Also, note that the author of Hebrews states that his name means "king of righteousness." Who else could be deserving of a title like that?

Note also Psalm 110:1–4 (NASB), authored by David:

> The Lord says to my Lord:
> "Sit at My right hand
> Until I make Your enemies a footstool for Your feet."
> The Lord will stretch forth Your strong scepter from Zion, *saying*,
> "Rule in the midst of Your enemies."
> Your people will volunteer freely in the day of Your power;
> In holy array, from the womb of the dawn,
> Your youth are to You *as* the dew.
> The Lord has sworn and will not change His mind,
> *"You are a priest forever*
> According to the order of Melchizedek."

David is saying in verse 1, *"The Lord says to my Lord* [the Messiah], Sit at My right hand until I make Your enemies a footstool for Your feet." Note that the pronoun *Your* is capitalized, signifying deity. In verse 4, David is saying that God has sworn that this Messiah "is *a priest forever* according to the order of Melchizedek."

Jesus, conversing with the Pharisees, asks them a couple of questions, "What do you think about the Christ, whose son is He?" They answered, "The son of David." Jesus responds, "Then how does David call Him 'Lord'?" Here, Jesus is referring to Psalm 110:1, revealing the truth that the Messiah is both human and divine.

For many years, I was convinced that Melchizedek was none other than the preincarnate Christ (*a Christophany*), because this event happened over 600 years prior to the Levitical priesthood. Jesus holds the titles prophet, priest, and king, so Melchizedek is an amazing *picture* of Christ as priest and king in the early pages of the Old Testament. However, it appears that the consensus among Bible scholars is that Melchizedek was merely a man. This view holds that the Hebrews 7 statement that Melchizedek was "without father, without mother, without genealogy, having neither beginning of days nor end of life" is simply making the point that Melchizedek is a *type* of Christ. According to this view, these details were merely omitted from the Genesis account of him, as he appears to just pop out of nowhere, rather than being true in a literal sense.

10. Visitation of Abraham by God (Theophany)

> And *the* LORD *appeared unto him* in the plains of Mamre: and he sat in the tent door in the heat of the day; And *he lift up his eyes and looked, and, lo, three men stood by him:* and when he saw them, he ran to meet them from the tent door, and bowed himself toward the ground, And said, *My* LORD, if now I have found favour in thy sight, pass not away, I pray thee, from thy servant: Let a little water, I pray you, be fetched, and wash your feet, and rest yourselves under the tree: And I will fetch a morsel of bread, and comfort ye your hearts; after that ye shall pass on: for therefore are ye come to your servant. And they said, So do, as thou hast said. (Genesis 18:1–5)

It is clear from this passage and the remaining text that the three *men* visitors are the Lord and two angels. So the three men show up at Abraham's residence, and he entreats them to stay and eat a meal with him and hastily has Sarah prepare it. During the meal, God promised that barren Sarah would have a son. After the meal, the three men (the Lord and two angels) begin walking toward Sodom, where the Lord reveals to Abraham that He is going to investigate Sodom regarding the evil report about them. Abraham, who is quite concerned about his nephew Lot who is living in Sodom, has a remarkable conversation in which he progressively petitions the Lord not to destroy Sodom if there are at least ten righteous people living there. We know from chapter 19 that unfortunately, there were less than ten righteous people living there. However, the two angels rescued Lot and his two daughters. Lot's wife, who was initially part of the rescue party, was unfortunately turned into a pillar of salt for later disobeying the angels' clear instructions (Genesis 19:26).

The Bible teaches us that God is omniscient, omnipresent, and omnipotent—all-knowing, everywhere-present, and all-powerful, respectively. Perhaps the most notable passage on these characteristics of God is Psalm 139. Also, you may recall that in Jesus's conversation with the Samaritan woman at the well (John 4:7–28), He told her, "*God is Spirit*, and those who worship Him must worship Him in spirit and truth" (John 4:24). Further, the apostle Paul tells us in his letter to the Colossians (1:15), that Jesus is the *image of the invisible God*. Accordingly, the only way that we can *see* the invisible *Spirit* God is for Him to *manifest* Himself to us in some way.

In Isaiah 7:14, Isaiah prophesies the virgin birth that we will look at later in detail: "A virgin will be with child and bear a son, and she will call His name *Immanuel.*" Looking this up in Strong's Hebrew Dictionary and in Matthew's gospel, where he cites this prophecy (1:23), we see that the name Immanuel means "God with us." Accordingly, Jesus, when he walked this earth was quite literally God with us. When He returns at the second coming, He will reign with us as king for a thousand years, at the end of which He will reign eternally on the New Earth as God with us! Accordingly, the physical manifestation of God to man in this story is what theologians refer to as a *theophany.* Theophanies are like prophetic snapshots of Christ. So once again in Genesis, we see through this theophany a prophetic foretelling of Jesus as the God-man, God's holy Son!

11a. Birth of Isaac (Prophetic Genealogy, Type/Shadow)

Genesis 21: Isaac is the third person in Jesus's prophetic genealogy as noted below. Isaac's birth was miraculous. He was born to a ninety-year-old barren woman, fathered by a one-hundred-year-old man (Genesis 17:16, 21:5)! However, the story of how Isaac came to be born is a circuitous maze of human failure. Paul even uses a portion of this story as a picture contrasting false salvation with true salvation.

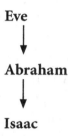

11b. Hagar / Sarah Allegory (Prophetic Allegory of Mt. Sinai vs. Jerusalem)

We saw in item 8 above that God promised to make of Abram (later Abraham) a great nation. However, there was one huge obstacle that stood in the way of that promise being fulfilled—Sarah was barren. So as we are sometimes inclined to do, Abraham doubted God and took it upon himself to *help* God fulfill His promise. Abraham's first attempt at helping was a plea to God to let Abraham's servant Eliezer be his heir. However, God refused (Genesis 15:2–4), telling Abraham that "one who will come forth from your own body, he shall be your heir." Next, Sarai (later Sarah), thought of a way to *help* God. In God's aforementioned conversation with Abraham, God said nothing about one coming forth from *Sarah's* body, so she hatched a *brilliant* scheme (Genesis 16:1–4), suggesting that Abraham lay with her maid Hagar to have a child, which Sarah would claim as her own, and so, Ishmael was born—thus beginning the fulfillment of God's prophecy to make of Abraham a great nation (or so they thought).

A tremendous price is still being paid until this day for their tragic and misguided decision—the centuries-old ongoing conflict between the Jews and the Arabs, and the false religion of Islam, which was birthed in Arabia. In fact, there is an amazing prophecy in Genesis 16:11–12, in which God spoke to a downcast Hagar, fearful for her life and the life of her son, after being sent away by a jealous Sarah. God comforted Hagar by telling her that Ishmael would "be a wild donkey of a man. His hand will be against everyone, and everyone's hand will be against him; and he will live to the east of all his brothers." Today, we are seeing Islamic terrorist groups literally fulfilling this prophecy today on a scale that previously would've been unimaginable. The most notable was al-Qaeda's 9/11/01 attack on the World Trade Center and the Pentagon building, with the fourth intended attack being a target in Washington, DC, possibly the US Capitol. However, it was foiled by some courageous men on that plane who gave their lives, resulting in the plane crashing in rural Pennsylvania. This attack was responsible for 2,977 fatalities.[4] In addition, there were thousands of injuries, and substantial long-term health consequences.

Centuries later, Paul wrote a letter to the Galatians, who had fallen away from simply trusting Christ for their salvation and sanctification but had fallen back into the futility of works of the Law to *earn* their salvation. Paul, in his letter, contrasted true salvation by faith with false salvation by works of the law. He wrote the following, citing the above Old Testament story of Sarah and Hagar as a *type* of true salvation by faith (Galatians 4:22–31):

> For it is written, that *Abraham had two sons*, the *one by a bondmaid, the other by a freewoman*. But he who was of the bondwoman was born after the flesh; but he of the freewoman was by promise. *Which things are an allegory*: for *these are the two covenants; the one from the mount Sinai*, which gendereth to bondage, which is Agar. For this Agar is mount Sinai in Arabia, and answereth to Jerusalem which now is, and is in bondage with her children. *But Jerusalem which is above is free*, which is the mother of us all. For it is written, Rejoice, thou barren that bearest not; break forth and cry, thou that travailest not: for the desolate hath many more children than she which hath an husband. Now we, brethren, as Isaac was, are the children of promise. But as then he that was born after the flesh persecuted him that was born after the Spirit, even so it is now. Nevertheless what saith the scripture? Cast out the bondwoman and her son: for the son of the bondwoman shall not be heir with the son of the freewoman. *So then, brethren, we are not children of the bondwoman, but of the free.*

Note that Agar above is the KJV New Testament spelling of Hagar, and Paul was making the point that just as Ishmael persecuted Isaac, the Judaizers were persecuting the church in attempt to infuse works into the gospel.

Meanwhile, back to the story of Isaac's birth: Abraham was seventy-five years old when God called him to leave Ur of the Chaldees and journey to "the land which I will show you" (Genesis 12:1–4), and promised to make of him a great nation. He was at least eighty-five years old when Ishmael was born (Genesis 16:3). After this, when Abraham is ninety-nine and Sarah eighty-nine years old, God promised Abraham that within a year, Sarah would conceive and give birth to a son (Genesis 17:1–22). During this conversation, again God tells Abraham that he will be father of a multitude of nations and that he would be the father of kings. God establishes His covenant with Abraham, instructing him that every male among them be circumcised—not only his relatives, but even his servants. Finally, twenty-five years after God called Abraham, promising to make of him a great nation, Sarah gives birth to Isaac. So imagine being a mom and dad at the age of ninety and one hundred, respectively! Interestingly, in Genesis 22, which we will look at next, God refers to Isaac as Abraham's "only son," even though Isaac was born approximately fifteen years after Ishmael. One chapter earlier, God had told Abraham, "In Isaac shall thy seed be called" (Genesis 21:12), because through Isaac's lineage both the Jewish nation and the Messiah would be born.

In the caption for this entry, it was noted that Isaac is a type/shadow of Christ. However, this will be explored in the next entry.

12. Abraham and Isaac, Human Sacrifice (Type/Shadow, Prophetic Genealogy)

This is one of the most astounding stories in the Bible. We read earlier about the twenty-five-year journey of Abraham and Sarah, which culminated with the long-awaited and miraculous birth of Isaac. Also, we saw how their faith was tested and how it waxed and waned along the way. With that backdrop, imagine the horror and confusion in Abraham's heart and mind when God said to him, "Take now thy son, thine only son Isaac, whom thou lovest, and get thee into the land of Moriah; and offer him there for a burnt offering upon one of the mountains which I will tell thee of" (Genesis 22:2). Can you imagine being given that mandate from God? There is no indication in the account that Sarah knew anything about this. So early the next morning, dutiful Abraham arose and began preparations—saddling his donkey, instructing two of his servants, splitting the wood for the sacrifice, taking Isaac, and setting off for the most horrific journey of his entire life.

Abraham, Isaac, two servants, and a donkey begin their three-day trip to Mount Moriah. Nothing is said about the journey itself. But can you imagine what that must've been like for Abraham? Imagine the difficulty of Abraham holding his emotions in check, so as not to alert Isaac. If he starts sobbing, this will no doubt arouse Isaac's curiosity: "Why are you crying, Daddy?" On the other hand, how do you conduct a three-day journey with the son that you are intending to slay, the one you love so dearly, the future of your patriarchy, and pretend that nothing is wrong? Perhaps there were occasions where Abraham broke down, and when questioned by Isaac, he just lied about the reason. Perhaps, to distract himself from his overwhelming grief, he attempted pleasant conversation with Isaac. "Isaac, do you remember the time …?" whereupon he would launch into various anecdotes about times he and Isaac had together. Perhaps Abraham was even able to feign laughter in telling some of those stories. After all, these were Isaac's last moments on earth, and Abraham wanted them to be happy ones for both Isaac and him! This was no doubt the longest three days of Abraham's life.

Finally, the dreaded day and moment arrived, when they reached the foot of the mountain. Abraham then instructs his servants to wait there with the donkey, while he and Isaac ascend the mountain to offer the sacrifice. So one journey ends, and another even more difficult one begins. Abraham places the firewood on Isaac, presumably on his back, and Abraham carries the fire and the knife. As they ascend the mountain, Isaac asks a very reasonable question, which must've been the most painful conversation thus far insofar as Abraham was concerned. "Daddy, you have the fire and the knife, and I have the wood, but where is the lamb for the burnt offering?" If you're Abraham, how in the world do you answer that? He thinks for a moment and responds, "God will provide for Himself the lamb for the burnt offering, son."

As they are nearing the summit, one can only imagine the inner conflict that is churning inside of Abraham. He is no doubt plotting what is going to happen when Isaac realizes his *true* intent, the moment of truth! Will Isaac start screaming and flailing wildly in an attempt to escape his now-apparent nightmarish fate? It is difficult enough to apprehend and restrain an innocent lamb before plunging the knife into his chest, but how can he bring himself to stab his own son? The Bible doesn't give us any of these details. However, there is no indication that Isaac resisted his father! So now the moment has arrived. It can be postponed no longer. Abraham places his hand on Isaac or ties him down, and raises the knife!

Suddenly, a voice calls to him from heaven. "Abraham, Abraham!" He responds, "Here I am." The voice continues, "Do not stretch out your hand against the lad, and do nothing to him, for now I know that you fear God, since you have not withheld your son, *your only son*, from Me." In the next instant, Abraham looks over and sees a ram caught in the thicket by his horns. Abraham quickly releases Isaac, captures and slays the ram, and offers him as a burnt offering in place of his son. The now-jubilant Abraham euphorically names this holy place Jehovah Jireh, which means "The Lord will provide, just as He did today! In the mount of the Lord, it will be provided!"

There is far more going on here than might appear to the casual reader. Why would God command Abraham to commit such a seemingly abominable act? Can anyone read this story in scripture and *not* ask that question? Over the years, I have heard various attempts to answer this question. Did God doubt Abraham's sincerity? Was He testing Abraham for His own sake? Was He testing Abraham for Abraham's sake? Not only is this story one of the greatest *types* of Christ within the pages of the Old Testament, as we will see shortly, but when you combine this with the fact of who Abraham is in the Messianic genealogy, this is quite astounding! You see, Abraham is listed second in the prophetic genealogy of the Messiah. Do you remember who is first? Eve, the mother of all living (Genesis 3:20), the one whose descendant would be aligned against Satan and his followers, as we see in that powerful first messianic prophesy of Genesis 3:15. So for Christ to be born as a babe in a manger, He would, of necessity, be descended from Eve. But what about the next person whom God says Christ will descend from? That person is Abraham. Earlier in Genesis, God said to Abraham, "In you all the families of the earth will be blessed." Wouldn't you say that is a pretty incredible statement? However, as we continue this story, we're going to see a critical detail of *how* all the families of the earth will be blessed in Abraham.

And the angel of the LORD called unto Abraham out of heaven the second time, And said, *By myself have I sworn,* saith the LORD, for *because thou hast done this thing, and hast not withheld thy son, thine only son*: That in blessing I will bless thee, and in multiplying I will multiply thy seed as the stars of the heaven, and as the sand which is upon the sea shore; and thy seed shall possess the gate of his enemies; And *in thy seed shall all the nations of the earth be blessed; because thou hast obeyed my voice.* So Abraham returned unto his young men, and they rose up and went together to Beersheba; and Abraham dwelt at Beersheba. (Genesis 22:15–19)

Centuries later, the apostle Paul adds some insight to this.

And the scripture, foreseeing that God would justify the heathen through faith, *preached before the gospel unto Abraham,* saying, *In thee shall all nations be blessed.*

Now *to Abraham and his seed were the promises made.* He saith not, *And to seeds, as of many; but as of one,* And to *thy seed, which is Christ.* (Galatians 3:8, 3:16)

In John's gospel, Jesus made a remarkable statement about Abraham just before revealing His true identity—that He is God. In John 8:56–59, we read:

Your father Abraham rejoiced to see my day: and he saw it, and was glad. Then said the Jews unto him, Thou art not yet fifty years old, and hast thou seen Abraham? Jesus said unto them, Verily, verily, I say unto you, *Before Abraham was, I am.* Then took they up stones to cast at him: but Jesus hid himself, and went out of the temple, going through the midst of them, and so passed by.

So we see that this bizarre story in scripture was an incredible *type* of the gospel story! Who would God's second selection on the Messianic prophetic genealogy be? Well, He selected the only man recorded in human history who was willing to do for God what God would turn around and do for all mankind—sacrifice *his only son*! In this story, we see the following incredible *types* of the gospel!

1) **Sacrifice of Son**: Abraham's willful offering of Isaac is a picture of God's willful offering of Jesus for the sins of the world.

2) **Miraculous Birth**: Isaac had a miraculous birth—he was born of a ninety-year-old barren woman. Jesus had a miraculous birth—He was born of a virgin.

3) **Son of Promise**: Isaac was a son of promise (God's twenty-five-year promise to Abraham and Sarah. Jesus was the Promised Son of God (see Psalm 2).

4) **Only Son**: Both were *only* sons—Isaac was the only son God recognized to continue the Jewish and Messianic lineage. Jesus was God's only begotten Son.

5) **Place of Sacrifice**: Isaac was sacrificed on Mount Moriah. Golgotha, the place where Jesus was sacrificed is also on Mount Moriah near the Jerusalem temple (2 Chronicles 3:1).

6) **Wood of Sacrifice**: Isaac carried the wood for his sacrifice up Mount Moriah. Jesus carried the wooden cross for His sacrifice up the Via Doloroso.

7) **Obedient**: Isaac was obedient to his father to the point of death. Jesus was obedient to His Father to the point of death.

8) **Both were raised by God**: Isaac was *symbolically* raised from death in that God restrained Abraham (Hebrews 11:17–19). Jesus was literally raised from the dead.

13. Jacob, Israel—Father of the Jewish Nation (Prophetic Genealogy)

Jacob is the fourth person in Jesus's prophetic genealogy as noted below. Jacob, Abraham's grandson and Isaac's son, will become the father of twelve sons, whose descendants will become the twelve tribes of Israel.

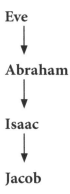

Eve

Abraham

Isaac

Jacob

The story of Jacob begins before his birth in Genesis 25, when because of the twins struggling in Rebekah's womb, she inquired of the Lord why this was so. God answered that two nations were in her womb and that the older would serve the younger. So the day came for Rebekah to give birth, and the first child, a redhead, pops out, followed by his younger brother, who pops out holding on to his brother's heel. Jacob, whose name means "supplanter," begins to live up to his name as a young adult. When Esau came home famished after a hunting trip, Jacob talks his older-by-seconds brother into selling his birthright to Jacob in exchange for some stew. The Bible's epitaph on Esau's foolish act is "Thus, Esau despised his birthright" (Genesis 25:34). The birthright, given to the oldest son, was important during the patriarchal period—it came with both privilege and responsibility. The privilege was that the brother with the birthright received a double portion of the inheritance. The responsibility was that this person would become the next family leader after his father's death. Later, as the time is nearing for Jacob to pass on, he instructs his eldest son Esau to go hunting and return to cook Jacob a delicious meal so that Jacob, in return, will bless Esau before his death. So to seal the deal of earlier securing Esau's birthright, Jacob, at Rebekah's prompting after she overheard Isaac's conversation with Esau, disguises himself as Esau. He then presents Rebekah's prepared meal from the livestock to his visually impaired father, who unwittingly pronounces Esau's blessing on Jacob (Genesis 27:1–29).

Afterward, Jacob is warned by Rebekah that Esau is enraged at him, and she sends him back to her homeland. On the way, Jacob has a dream about a ladder reaching from earth to heaven, with the Lord standing above it, and the angels ascending and descending on it. In the dream, God promises him Canaan and the extension of the Abrahamic Covenant. Jacob awakes and names the place Bethel, the House of God, and promises to give God a tenth of his possessions if God keeps His promise to bless and protect him (Genesis 28:11–19).

While in his homeland, he is quickly enrolled in God's course Deception 101, aka "whatsoever a man soweth, that shall he also reap." Jacob experiences, at the hands of his future father-in-law Laban, a deception comparable to that which he pulled on Esau and Isaac. Jacob, who was smitten by Laban's daughter Rachael, agrees to work seven years for him as the price for Rachael's hand in marriage. So on the wedding night, Jacob is deceived into marrying Rachael's more homely-looking sister Leah, who was slipped into the honeymoon tent by Laban. So Jacob, who is still in love with Rachael, then agrees to serve Laban for an additional seven years (Genesis 29:1–28). Between Jacob's two wives and their maids, who became his concubines, Jacob had twelve sons and a daughter named Dinah. Meanwhile, Jacob has become quite prosperous working for Laban and decides to return to his homeland, where he hopes to be reconciled with Esau.

On the way there, Jacob concocts a scheme to appease Esau and hopefully protect his wives and children. The night before the reunion, a man wrestles with Jacob all night. The angelic being touched the socket of Jacob's thigh just before daybreak and dislocated it. When the angel commands Jacob to let him go, Jacob says, in effect, "Not unless you bless me." The angel says, "Henceforth, your name will be called Israel for you have striven with God and man and prevailed" (Genesis 32:24–32).

Some years later, Jacob is enrolled in God's second course, Deception 102, when eleven of his sons sell his favorite son Joseph as a slave to some Midianite traders on their way to Egypt. Then they dipped Joseph's beautiful coat of many colors in animal's blood and brought it to Jacob to deceive him into thinking that Joseph had been killed by a wild animal.

In this bad news about Joseph, God is actually preparing a way for Israel to survive a coming famine. We see this played out in Genesis 39–47 and culminating in his glorious reunion with his beloved son Joseph, who within the space of thirteen years (Genesis 37:2, 41:46), went from being a slave, to a prisoner, to second-in-command to Pharaoh!

14. Joseph (Type/Shadow)

We are introduced to Joseph in Genesis 37. Joseph is not included in the prophetic genealogy of Christ, nor the larger messianic lineage. We will see in the next entry that of Jacob's twelve sons, Judah is the one from whom Jesus Christ will be a descendant. However, if we could pretend to go back in time (not knowing the end of the story) and we were asked the question "Which one of Jacob's twelve sons would *you* vote for that Christ would be a descendant of?" we would likely have voted for Joseph. He is an example of a personal *type* of Christ. Earlier, we saw how Isaac, who is included in the prophetic messianic genealogy, was a *type* of Christ. Some of the ways he *typified* Christ were played out in the real-life drama of him being a human sacrifice, though saved at the last moment.

We are introduced to Joseph in Genesis 37 and 39–50. We meet Joseph as a seventeen-year-old teenager. As the firstborn son of Jacob's beloved wife Rachel, Joseph was loved by his father, who made him a coat of many colors. Joseph was a bit of a tattletale, and his brothers hated him. He had two dreams, which he shared with his brothers, sharing the second dream with his father, who rebuked him. So when Joseph was sent on an errand by Jacob to check on his brothers, they conspired against him and threw him into a pit, initially planning to kill him. However, as a Midianite caravan happened to pass by, his brothers decided to sell him to them and deceived Jacob into believing Joseph had been killed by a wild animal.

Joseph's ensuing thirteen years are spent first as a slave to Potiphar, an Egyptian officer in Pharaoh's army. Later, he is sent to a dungeon, because of Potiphar's lying wife who claimed that Joseph attempted to rape her. At the end of his thirteen-year imprisonment, Joseph, by the clear hand of God, is exalted to a high position by Pharaoh. This was because Joseph interpreted Pharaoh's dream, which predicted seven years of plenty followed by seven years of famine, and gave him an action plan. So Pharaoh appointed thirty-year-old Joseph as his second in command to carry out that plan. Later, his brothers came and bowed down to Joseph, fulfilling his dream of thirteen years earlier. So Jacob and his clan of seventy move to Egypt, thus surviving the famine. Below is the synopsis of Joseph's life and how it parallels Jesus's life

Joseph	Jesus	
Beloved of his father, Gen. 37:3	Beloved of His Father	John 5:20
Betrayed by his brothers, Gen. 37:18–28	Betrayed by His brothers	John 1:10–11
Wrongly imprisoned, Gen. 40:14–15	Wrongly imprisoned	Acts 2:22-23
Did not yield to temptation, Gen. 39:6–20	Jesus never yielded to temptation	Heb. 4:15

Second to Pharaoh, Gen. 45:8	At the right hand of God	Heb. 10:11–14
Authority of Pharaoh, Gen. 41:40–44; 45:9	Authority of His Father	Matt. 28:18
Loved his brothers who betrayed him, 50:21	Loved those who crucified Him	Luke 23:24
Forgave his betraying brothers, Gen. 45:5	Forgave those who crucified Him	Luke 23:24
Saved his people from famine, Gen. 50:20	Saves from spiritual death	John 3:16
Joseph's splendor in Egypt, Gen. 45:13	Jesus's glory in heaven	John 17:24

15. Judah (Prophetic Genealogy, Type/Shadow)

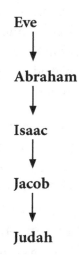

Eve

Abraham

Isaac

Jacob

Judah

Just before Jacob died, he gathered all his sons around his bed and prophesied over each of them. Jacob's prophecy over Judah shows God's choice of him as the lineage from which the kings will be born, and ultimately, the Last King, the Eternal King, the King of kings—Jesus Christ. Jacob's prophecy over Judah is shown below:

> Judah, thou art he whom thy brethren shall praise: thy hand shall be in the neck of thine enemies; *thy father's children shall bow down before thee. Judah is a lion's whelp*: from the prey, my son, thou art gone up: he stooped down, *he couched as a lion*, and *as an old lion*; who shall rouse him up? *The sceptre shall not depart from Judah, nor a lawgiver from between his feet, until Shiloh come; and unto him shall the gathering of the people be. Binding his foal unto the vine*, and *his ass's colt* unto the choice vine; *he washed his garments in wine, and his clothes in the blood of grapes*: His eyes shall be red with wine, and his teeth white with milk. (Genesis 49:8–12)

Isn't it interesting that Joseph's brothers and his father Jacob all bowed down to him during his life, yet God chose Judah as the royal line? If we were to choose the son of Jacob to whom Jesus would be descended from, would we not have all chosen Joseph? Yet God, in His omniscience, chose Judah for His sovereign purpose. It is interesting to note that Judah is the one of Joseph's brothers who offered himself as a hostage for the sake of his brother

Benjamin. This makes him an interesting *mini-type* of Christ, who gave His life as a ransom for many (Matthew 20:28).

Notice the phrases in the prophecy (in italics), expounded on below, that point to Judah's line as being the kingly line and how they relate to the Lord Jesus Christ:

1) Thy father's children shall bow down before thee (*before the kings and the King of kings*).

2) Judah is a lion's whelp (cub); he couched as a lion; as an old lion (*Jesus, the Lion of Judah*).

3) The scepter shall not depart from Judah, nor the ruler's staff (NASB) from between his feet. (*After the people, guided by God, chose Saul from the tribe of Benjamin (based on outward appearance—he was the tallest of the tribe of Benjamin) as their first king; God rejected Saul and anointed David from the tribe of Judah, a man after His own heart, as the next king, and promised him that one of his descendants would become the Eternal King* (2 Samuel 7:12, 16).

4) Until Shiloh comes. (*Many attribute the name Shiloh as a reference to the Messiah; other translations of the word are "peace and rest" or "peace-giver." Certainly, the millennial and eternal reign of Christ will be a time of perpetual peace*).

5) Unto him shall the gathering of the people be (*before kings and before the King of kings*)

   Wherefore God also hath highly exalted him, and given him a name which is above every name: That at the name of Jesus *every knee should bow*, of things in heaven, and things in earth, and things under the earth; And that *every tongue should confess* that Jesus Christ is Lord, to the glory of God the Father. (Philippians 2:9–11)

   That will be quite a gathering!

6) Binding his foal … his ass's colt unto the vine. (*Jesus rode into Jerusalem on the foal of a donkey to present Himself as Messiah*, Zechariah 9:9, John 12:14).

7) He washed his garments in wine … in the blood of grapes. (*In the Last Supper, Jesus shared the broken bread and the wine with His disciples, symbols of His crucified body and blood, respectively.* Also, in Revelation 19:11–16, Jesus returns on a white horse and his vesture (or robe) is "dipped in blood." Many think this blood represents the blood of His enemies; however, one source gives an alternate interpretation that it may represent His own blood shed for our atonement.)

In Genesis 17:6 and 35:11, and again in Deuteronomy 17:14–20 and 28:36, we see God's plan for the kings of Israel and Judah. Centuries before, the men of Shechem prematurely ask for a king in Judges 9:6, and Israel later asks Samuel for a king in 1 Samuel 8. Those verses, except for the better-known text in the 1 Samuel passage are shown below:

> And I will make thee exceeding fruitful, and I will make nations of thee, and kings shall come out of thee. (Genesis 17:6)

> And God said unto him, I am God Almighty: be fruitful and multiply; a nation and a company of nations shall be of thee, and kings shall come out of thy loins. (Genesis 35:11)

> When thou art come unto the land which the LORD thy God giveth thee, and shalt possess it, and shalt dwell therein, and shalt say, I will set a king over me, like as all the nations that are about me; Thou shalt in any wise set him king over thee, whom the LORD thy God shall choose: one from among thy brethren shalt thou set king over thee: thou mayest not set a stranger over thee, which is not thy brother. But he shall not multiply horses to himself, nor cause the people to return to Egypt, to the end that he should multiply horses: forasmuch as the LORD hath said unto you, Ye shall henceforth return no more that way. Neither shall he multiply wives to himself, that his heart turn not away: neither shall he greatly multiply to himself silver and gold. And it shall be, when he sitteth upon the throne of his kingdom, that he shall write him a copy of this law in a book out of that which is before the priests the Levites: And it shall be with him, and he shall read therein all the days of his life: that he may learn to fear the LORD his God, to keep all the words of this law and these statutes, to do them: That his heart be not lifted up above his brethren, and that he turn not aside from the commandment, to the right hand, or to the left: to the end that he may prolong his days in his kingdom, he, and his children, in the midst of Israel. (Deuteronomy 17:14–20)

> The LORD shall bring thee, and thy king which thou shalt set over thee, unto a nation which neither thou nor thy fathers have known; and there shalt thou serve other gods, wood and stone. (Deuteronomy 28:36)

> And all the men of Shechem gathered together, and all the house of Millo, and went, and made Abimelech king, by the plain of the pillar that was in Shechem. In this passage, the wicked men of Shechem asked for a wicked king to rule over them, who slew his 70 brothers after all the military victories that Gideon his father had won for the people of Shechem, but God quickly destroyed him and the people of Shechem. (Judges 9:6)

No claim is being made that we have identified all the messianic prophetic elements herein, but below is a list of the items covered:

Summary of Messianic Prophetic Elements in Genesis

1.	The Holy Trinity	(OT Language and Culture)
2.	Protoevangelium, *Eve*	(Prophecy, Messianic Prophetic Genealogy)
3.	Garments of Skin	(Type/Shadow)
4.	Cain and Abel's Offering	(Type/Shadow)
5.	Messianic Genealogy	(Messianic Prophetic Genealogy)
6.	Enoch's Rapture	(Type/Shadow)
7.	Noah's Ark	(Type/Shadow)
8.	*Abraham*	(Prophecy, Messianic Prophetic Genealogy)
9.	Melchizedek	(Type/Shadow)
10.	Visitation by God	(Theophany)
11a.	*Isaac*	(Prophecy, Messianic Prophetic Genealogy)
11b.	Hagar/Sarah Allegory	(Prophetic Allegory of Mt Sinai vs. Jerusalem)
12.	Abraham's Sacrifice of Isaac	(Type/Shadow, Messianic Prophetic Genealogy)
13.	*Jacob;* Israel—Father of Jewish Nation	(Messianic Prophetic Genealogy)
14.	Joseph	(Type/Shadow)
15.	*Judah*	*(Messianic Prophetic Genealogy)*

NOTES (CHAPTER 9)

[1] James Strong, *The New Strong's Expanded Exhaustive Concordance of the Bible, Red Letter Edition* (Nashville: Thomas Nelson, 2010), Entry #430 of Hebrew Dictionary, 17

[2] Ibid., Entry #3722 of the Hebrew Dictionary, 135

[3] Ibid, Entry # 3724 of the Hebrew Dictionary, 135

[4] Clare Mulroy, "How Many Died in 9/11? A Look at the Tragic Attack 23 Years Ago," *USA Today*, September 11, 2024, http:// www.usatoday.com/story/news/2024/09/10/how-many-people-died-in-911/75150354007/ (accessed 09/20/24)

10

JESUS IN EXODUS

In this chapter, we will turn our attention to the book of Exodus. This book records Israel's birth as a nation in Egypt and its exodus from there. You recall that we left Genesis at the point where Joseph had become second in command to Pharaoh. Jacob's family moved to Egypt and reunited with him, during the famine. Jacob's family (he and his descendants) were seventy in number (Genesis 46:26–27, Exodus 1:5), including Joseph and his two sons. In this book, God calls Moses and Aaron to deliver Israel out of Egypt, leads them through the wilderness to Sinai, gives them the Ten Commandments and various other laws, instructs them on building the tabernacle, and concludes with its erection and God's abiding presence thereon.

1. Moses as a Type (Type/Shadow)

Moses wrote the first five books of the Bible, Genesis through Deuteronomy, known as the Pentateuch. It should be noted here that Moses is not in Jesus's genealogy, being born of the tribe of Levi, the priestly tribe, rather than Judah, the royal tribe, from which Christ is descended. We are introduced to Moses in Exodus 2. Moses's mother, adoring her beautiful son, when she could hide him no longer as a three-month-old baby, placed him in a wicker basket covered with pitch and placed it among the reeds near the bank of the Nile River (Exodus 2:2–3). Moses's sister stood at a distance to determine what would happen to her baby brother. By the grace of God, Pharaoh's daughter, coming to bathe in the Nile, saw the basket among the reeds and felt compassion for the baby. As she retrieved him from the river, Moses's sister walked up, offering to call a nurse from the Hebrew women. Thus, Moses's mother was able to nurse her own son and receive wages for the privilege.

This began the first of three forty-year periods of Moses's life, in which he grew up in Pharaoh's palace, with all the royal perks, including a great education. This first period ended when he attempted to break up a fight between two of his Hebrew kinsmen, when the offender asked, "Are you intending to kill me as you killed the Egyptian?" whom Moses had killed a day earlier for brutalizing a Hebrew slave. Moses, being made aware that his deed had become known, fled from Pharaoh to the land of Midian.

At this point, Moses met the seven daughters of the priest of Midian at a well. He was invited to live with Reuel aka Jethro (Exodus 2:15–18, 3:1) the priest, who gave Moses his daughter Zipporah to marry. This began the second forty-year period of Moses's life. One day while pasturing the flock, Moses sees an incredible sight—a bush is on fire, but it is not being consumed! So he walks over to examine it, at which point God begins a conversation with him—calling Moses to return to Egypt and lead the Israelites out of Egyptian bondage. God gives the reluctant Moses his older brother Aaron (Exodus 7:7) to be his spokesman when he will confront Pharaoh.

Moses is joined by Aaron en route to Egypt. Their arrival in Egypt began the third and final forty-year period of Moses's life, as leader of the Israelite people. The transition period between Midian and the forty-year desert wandering involved Moses's confrontation of Pharaoh and God's miraculous plagues that He inflicted on the Egyptians to bend Pharaoh's stubborn will. The last plague is the death of the firstborn male, at which Pharaoh finally relents, leading to the exodus and forty-year wilderness wandering. Below are the aspects of Moses's life that make him a *person-type* of Christ. Within this broader story of Moses, there are individual prophetic elements of Christ in each of the three forty-year periods of Moses's life. We will look at these as we journey through Exodus and the remainder of the Pentateuch.

Type	Moses	Christ
Miraculous deliverance from a monarch as a child	Exod. 2:2–10	Matt. 2:14–15
The Burning Bush (I Am)	Exod. 3:13–15	John 8:56–59
Moses celebrated Passover; Christ became our Passover	Exod. 12:3–32	Luke 22:14–23
Both had direct access to God	Num. 12:6–8	John 5:20, 17:5, 10, 21
Both established memorials	Exod. 12:14	Luke 22:19
Both were mediators of a covenant	Deut. 5:1–5	John 1:17, Luke 22:19
Both worked miraculous signs	Deut. 34:10–12	Mark 1:21–34
Both exercised supernatural power over the sea	Exod. 14:1–31	Matt. 8:23–27; 14:22–23
Both fed a multitude	Exod. 16:1–15	Matt. 14:13–21
Both fasted forty days	Exod. 34:28	Matt. 4:1–11
Both glowed supernaturally	Exod. 34:29–35	Matt. 17:1–9
Both were discredited at home	Num. 12:1–2	Mar 6:1–6
Both endured murmurings	Exod. 15:22–24	Matt. 9:32–34
Both had seventy helpers	Num. 11:16–17	Luke 10:1–20
Both were intercessors to their own peril	Exod. 32:30–33	John 17
Both were prophets	Deut. 18:15–19	Mark 6:4
Both of their lives were taken by God	Deut. 34:1–7	John 3:16
Both reappeared after death	Matt. 17:1–3	Acts 1:3

2. Moses's Deliverance from Death as a Baby (Type/Shadow)

Exodus 1:8, 15–22; 2:1–9: Moses was persecuted by the King of Egypt as a baby, just as Jesus was persecuted by King Herod as a toddler (Matthew 2:16, 2:1–23). Both were miraculously delivered—Moses by a wise mother's desperate plan and a compassionate daughter of Pharaoh, and Jesus by angelic counsel to Joseph (Matthew 2:13). Both escaped a slaughter of male children by the evil monarch who intended to kill them. So Moses's narrow escape from the king of Egypt's command to slaughter all the Hebrew male babies prefigures Jesus's escape from King Herod's command to slaughter all the male children two years old and under. Both Moses and Jesus were God's spokesmen—Moses, an anointed vessel of God, and Jesus, God's Holy Son.

3. The Burning Bush (Theophany, Prophecy)

Exodus 3:1–4:17

> Now Moses kept the flock of Jethro his father-in-law, the priest of Midian: and he led the flock to the backside of the desert, and came to the mountain of God, even to Horeb. And *the angel of the LORD appeared unto him in a flame of fire out of the midst of a bush: and he looked, and, behold, the bush burned with fire, and the bush was not consumed.* And Moses said, I will now turn aside, and see this great sight, why the bush is not burnt. And when the LORD saw that he turned aside to see, *God called unto him out of the midst of the bush, and said, Moses, Moses. And he said, Here am I.* (Exodus 3:1–4)

Theophany: The burning bush was a physical manifestation of God's presence to Moses. We see this from the language in the verses—"the Lord appeared unto him in a flame of fire out of the midst of a bush" and "God called unto him out of the midst of the bush." Theophanies are all types of Christ in the sense that He is Immanuel—God with us (Matthew 1:23). On this subject of theophanies, it would be good to pause and consider a couple of scripture passages—namely, John 4 and Psalm 139. The former records Jesus's conversation with a Samaritan woman at the well, and the latter describes attributes of the eternal God, most notably, His omnipresence.

> The woman saith unto him, Sir, I perceive that thou art a prophet. Our fathers worshipped in this mountain; and ye say, that in Jerusalem is the place where men ought to worship. Jesus saith unto her, Woman, believe me, the hour cometh, when ye shall neither in this mountain, nor yet at Jerusalem, worship the Father. Ye worship ye know not what: we know what we worship: for salvation is of the Jews. *But the hour cometh, and now is, when the true worshippers shall worship the Father in spirit and in truth: for the Father seeketh*

such to worship him. God is a Spirit: and they that worship him must worship him in spirit and in truth. (John 4:19–24)

We see from Jesus's conversation with this woman that God exists as a *Spirit*. Therefore, when we see God revealed in any physical manifestation, it is only by His direct revelation to us. The climactic revelation of God in physical form is Jesus Christ! John so wonderfully reveals this in his gospel—in his opening chapter (1:1, 14), Jesus's seven "I Am" statements, plus an eighth "I Am" statement we will examine in connection with the Burning Bush passage above, plus His response to Phillip (14:7–9) in His farewell discourse.

O Lord, thou hast *searched* me, and *known* me. Thou *knowest* my downsitting and mine uprising, thou *understandest* my thought afar off. Thou *compassest* my path and my lying down, and art *acquainted* with all my ways. For there is not a word in my tongue, but, lo, O Lord, *thou knowest it altogether*. Thou hast beset me behind and before, and laid thine hand upon me. *Such knowledge* is *too wonderful for me*; it is high, I cannot attain unto it.

Whither shall I go from thy spirit? or whither shall I flee from thy presence? If I ascend up into *heaven, thou art there*: if I make my bed in *hell*, behold, *thou art there*. If I take the wings of the morning, and dwell in the *uttermost parts of the sea; Even there shall thy hand lead me*, and thy right hand shall hold me. If I say, Surely the darkness shall cover me; even the night shall be light about me. Yea, *the darkness hideth not from thee*; but the night shineth as the day: the *darkness and the light are both alike to thee.*

For *thou hast possessed my reins*: thou hast covered me in my mother's womb. I will praise thee; for *I am fearfully and wonderfully made: marvellous are thy works*; and that my soul knoweth right well. *My substance was not hid from thee*, when I was *made in secret*, and curiously wrought in the lowest parts of the earth. Thine eyes did see my substance yet being unperfect; and *in thy book all my members were written*, which *in continuance were fashioned, when as yet there was none of them. How precious also are thy thoughts* unto me, O God! how great is the sum of them! If I should count them, they are more in number than the sand: when I awake, I am still with thee. (Psalm 139:1–18)

A simple outline of this passage is that verses 1–6 speak of God's *knowledge*, verses 7–12 speak of God's *presence*, verses 13–18 speak of God's *power*, and verses 19–24 (not shown) speak of our response to God. Theologians have a word for each of these qualities of God—namely, they refer to God's *omniscience*, His *omnipresence*, and His *omnipotence*—that is, God is all-knowing, everywhere-present, and all-powerful. This was discussed in the previous chapter on God's holiness.

Prophecy:

The Exodus passage mentioned above (3:1–4:17) records God's conversation with Moses from the burning bush, wherein God is instructing Moses to lead His people out of Egypt: After God revealed to Moses His particular assignment for him, Moses asks God a very pertinent question.

> Come now therefore, and I will send thee unto Pharaoh, that thou mayest bring forth my people the children of Israel out of Egypt. And Moses said unto God, Who am I, that I should go unto Pharaoh, and that I should bring forth the children of Israel out of Egypt? And he said, Certainly I will be with thee; and this shall be a token unto thee, that I have sent thee: When thou hast brought forth the people out of Egypt, ye shall serve God upon this mountain. And *Moses said unto God, Behold, when I come unto the children of Israel, and shall say unto them, The God of your fathers hath sent me unto you; and they shall say to me, What is his name? what shall I say unto them?* And God said unto Moses, I AM THAT I AM: and he said, Thus shalt thou say unto the children of Israel, I AM hath sent me unto you. And God said moreover unto Moses, Thus shalt thou say unto the children of Israel, the LORD God of your fathers, the God of Abraham, the God of Isaac, and the God of Jacob, hath sent me unto you: *this is my name for ever, and this is my memorial unto all generations.* (Exodus 3:10–15)

The above passage is prophetic. You see, Jesus clearly claimed this name, God's name, God's memorial name to all generations, for Himself! In the seven I Am statements of Jesus referenced below, each of them has an object. In each one, Jesus is claiming to be God, and the object is revealing a particular aspect of His deity. They are listed below:

I Am the Bread of Life	John 6:35, 48
I Am the Light of the World	John 8:12, 9:5
I Am the Door	John 10:9
I Am the Good Shepherd	John 10:11
I Am the Resurrection and the Life	John 11:25
I Am the Way, the Truth, and the Life	John 14:6
I Am the True Vine	John 15:1

However, in John 8, Jesus makes an astounding claim about His identity in an eighth I Am statement. The conversation is shown below:

> Your father Abraham rejoiced to see my day: and he saw it, and was glad. Then said the Jews unto him, Thou art not yet fifty years old, and hast thou seen Abraham? Jesus said unto them, Verily, verily, I say unto you, Before Abraham

was, I am. Then took they up stones to cast at him: but Jesus hid himself, and went out of the temple, going through the midst of them, and so passed by. (John 8:56–59)

Notice when Jesus made the assertion about Abraham, who lived over 2,000 years earlier, *rejoicing to see His day*, and that *he saw it and was glad*," that the Jews seem to be mocking Him. However, when Jesus says, *"Before Abraham was, I Am,"* the tone quickly changes—they took up stones to cast at Him. They regarded Jesus's latter statement as blasphemy, because they failed to see that Jesus *is* God.

Accordingly, this passage is prophetic in that sense—that it looks forward to, sets the stage, if you will, for Jesus's claim to be God.

4. The Passover (Type/Shadow)

God's plan to lead His people out of Egypt by the hand of Moses, as He said in the Burning Bush conversation, has now reached its zenith. Moses, with the help of his brother Aaron, is about to confront Pharaoh for the last time prior to the exodus march. The tenth and final plague will be the death of all firstborn males in Egypt, including men, boys, slaves, free, and even firstborn male animals! However, at the same time this chaos and grief is going on in Egypt, the Israelites will be spared—because they obeyed God's command through Moses.

> And the LORD spake unto Moses and Aaron in the land of Egypt saying, This month shall be unto you the beginning of months: it shall be the first month of the year to you. Speak ye unto all the congregation of Israel, saying, In the tenth day of this month they shall *take to them every man a lamb*, according to the house of their fathers, *a lamb for an house*: And if the household be too little for the lamb, let him and his neighbour next unto his house take it according to the number of the souls; every man according to his eating shall make your count for the lamb. *Your lamb shall be without blemish, a male of the first year*: ye shall take it out from the sheep, or from the goats: And ye shall keep it up until the fourteenth day of the same month: and *the whole assembly of the congregation of Israel shall kill it in the evening*. And *they shall take of the blood, and strike it on the two side posts and on the upper door post of the houses, wherein they shall eat it*. And *they shall eat the flesh* in that night, roast with fire, *and unleavened bread*; and *with bitter herbs* they shall eat it. Eat not of it raw, nor sodden at all with water, but roast with fire; his head with his legs, and with the purtenance thereof. And ye shall *let nothing of it remain until the morning*; and that which remaineth of it until the morning ye shall burn with fire. And thus shall ye eat it; with your loins girded, your shoes on your feet, and your staff in your hand; and ye shall eat it in haste: it is the LORD's passover. *For I will pass through the land of Egypt this night, and will smite all*

147

the firstborn in the land of Egypt, both man and beast; and against all the gods of Egypt I will execute judgment: I am the LORD. And *the blood shall be to you for a token* upon the houses where ye are: and *when I see the blood, I will pass over you*, and *the plague shall not be upon you to destroy you*, when I smite the land of Egypt. And *this day shall be unto you for a memorial*; and ye shall keep it a feast to the LORD throughout your generations; ye shall keep it a feast by an ordinance for ever. (Exodus 12:1–14)

The apostle Paul, in his rebuke of the Corinthian church for its failure to confront an incestuous man, testified that the Passover is a *type* of Christ in 1 Corinthians 5:6–8:

Your glorying is not good. Know ye not that a little leaven leaveneth the whole lump? Purge out therefore the old leaven, that ye may be a new lump, as ye are unleavened. For even *Christ our passover* is sacrificed for us: Therefore let us keep the feast, not with old leaven, neither with the leaven of malice and wickedness; but with the unleavened bread of sincerity and truth.

Here, Paul is intimating the truth that in the same way the Passover lamb's blood kept the death angel from afflicting the Israelites, Christ's blood on the cross saves us from eternal death and separation from God. Also, one of the names of Jesus is the *Lamb of God*—we see this in Isaiah's messianic prophecy of the suffering servant (Isaiah 53:4–7). The apostle John in his gospel speaks of "the Lamb of God" (John 1:29, 36), and in Revelation, John speaks of the Lamb as referring to Christ numerous times—Revelation 5:6, 6:9, 7:17, 14:10, 15:3, 19:9, 21:23, 22:1, 22:3.

So let's examine *how* the Passover is a type of Christ.

- An *unblemished* male lamb *one year* old—this points to Christ's *sinlessness* and His crucifixion *in the prime of His life*.
- Blood on *wooden* or stone *doorpost and lintel* (KJV "upper door post")—Jesus's blood on the *vertical* and *horizontal* members of a wooden cross (wood doorpost suggested by Exodus 21:5–6)
- Death angel *prevented* from harming household *with the blood*—those who trust in the *atoning blood* of Christ are *protected* from eternal death
- Passover lamb eaten with *unleavened* bread—leaven in the Bible represents *sin*; this also points to the *sinlessness* of Christ
- Passover lamb eaten with *bitter* herbs—a picture of the *bitter agony* of Jesus's passion
- Jesus gives new meaning to the Passover at the Last Supper—as noted below

Note that when Jesus gave his disciples instructions to prepare for their last supper, He told them to prepare for the Passover—Matthew 26:17–20 and Mark 14:12–18 (the disciples asked Jesus *where* to prepare the Passover). In Luke 22:7–14, Jesus *instructs* the disciples to go and prepare the Passover. Note in Mark 14:12 and Luke 22:7, we see that *the Passover lamb* was slain the *same day* that Jesus celebrated the Last Supper with His disciples. It is so important to read the Bible with *fresh eyes*. As I noted previously in chapter 7, when we come to the Last Supper passage, we're thinking *the Lord's Supper*, but when the disciples were gathered there with Jesus, they were thinking *Passover*. After all, that's what He instructed them to prepare. Jesus had told them on three separate occasions that He was going to be killed at the hands of evil men, but only in a few somewhat cryptic sayings did He hint at *why* He was going to be killed. They are noted below:

> Even as the Son of man came not to be ministered unto, but to minister, and to *give his life a ransom for many*. (Matthew 20:28)

> Then Jesus said unto them, Verily, verily, I say unto you, *Except ye eat the flesh of the Son of man, and drink his blood, ye have no life in you*. Whoso *eateth my flesh*, and *drinketh my blood, hath eternal life;* and I will raise him up at the last day. (John 6:53–54)

> I am the good shepherd: *the good shepherd giveth his life for the sheep*. (John 10:11)

> Greater love hath no man than this, *that a man lay down his life for his friends*. (John 15:13)

In each of these scriptures, we, looking back, rightly understand Jesus to be talking about His atoning death on the cross, but it's doubtful the disciples comprehended this. This point is further strengthened by the fact that human sacrifice was forbidden by God. So can you imagine what it was like when Jesus was gathered around the Passover table with them, and said the following:

> And he said unto them, With desire *I have desired to eat this passover with you before I suffer:* For I say unto you, I will not any more eat thereof, until it be fulfilled in the kingdom of God. And he took the cup, and gave thanks, and said, Take this, and divide it among yourselves: For I say unto you, I will not drink of the fruit of the vine, until the kingdom of God shall come. And *he took bread*, and gave thanks, and *brake it*, and *gave unto them*, saying, *This is my body which is given for you:* this do in remembrance of me. Likewise also the cup after supper, saying, *This cup is the new testament in my blood, which is shed for you*. (Luke 22:15–20)

I'm sure their jaws must have dropped when He said this. They must have been totally shocked—can you imagine being a disciple in that room when He said that? Jesus told them, and by extension us, to "do this in remembrance of Me." What a blessed ordinance in the Christian church! The apostle Paul wrote the following in his letter to the Corinthian church.

> For as often as ye eat this bread, and drink this cup, ye do shew the Lord's death till he come. (1 Corinthians 11:26)

So every time we partake of the Lord's Supper, we're looking backward and forward—backward at what our salvation cost Jesus, and forward because He's coming again!

5. Pillar of Fire and Cloud (Theophany)

After the Passover in chapter 12, we are told in Exodus 13 that the Lord was leading Moses and the Israelites in a pillar of cloud by day and a pillar of fire by night. Here we see an Old Testament snapshot of Immanuel, which means "God with us"—see Isaiah 7:14 and Matthew 1:18–25.

> But *God led the people about, through the way of the wilderness of the Red Sea:* and the children of Israel went up harnessed out of the land of Egypt. And Moses took the bones of Joseph with him: for he had straitly sworn the children of Israel, saying, God will surely visit you; and ye shall carry up my bones away hence with you. And they took their journey from Succoth, and encamped in Etham, in the edge of the wilderness. And *the LORD went before them by day in a pillar of a cloud*, to lead them the way; *and by night in a pillar of fire, to give them light; to go by day and night: He took not away the pillar of the cloud by day, nor the pillar of fire by night, from before the people.* (Exodus 30:18–22)

6. Crossing of the Red Sea (Type/Shadow)

Exodus 14:13–31

> And *Moses stretched out his hand over the sea*; and *the LORD caused the sea to go back by a strong east wind all that night,* and made the sea dry land, and the waters were divided. And *the children of Israel went into the midst of the sea upon the dry ground: and the waters were a wall unto them on their right hand, and on their left.* (Exodus 14:21–22)

> And *the LORD said unto Moses, Stretch out thine hand over the sea*, that the waters may come again upon the Egyptians, upon their chariots, and upon their horsemen. And Moses stretched forth his hand over the sea, and *the sea returned to his strength when the morning appeared*; and the Egyptians fled against it; and *the LORD overthrew the Egyptians in the midst of the sea.* And the waters returned, and covered the chariots, and the horsemen, and *all the host of Pharaoh that came into the sea after them; there remained not so much as one of them.* (Exodus 14:26–28)

The crossing of the Red Sea by Israel is a picture of New Testament baptism. Baptism symbolizes the believer's being united with Christ in His death, in order that he can be united with Christ in His resurrection (Romans 6:1–14). As baptism symbolizes a believer's turning from his old life of sin to a new life of faith in Christ (John 10:10), so the crossing of the Red Sea was God's supernatural enabling of Israel to leave behind their bondage to Egypt (symbolizing the bondage of sin) on their way to the new life God promised them in Canaan (symbolizing the new life in Christ—see 2 Corinthians 5:17). However, there is another body of water that Israel will supernaturally cross before they enter Canaan. This crossing will take place in the book of Joshua.

7. **Manna** (Type/Shadow)

> And the whole congregation of the children of Israel murmured against Moses and Aaron in the wilderness: And the children of Israel said unto them, Would to God we had died by the hand of the LORD in the land of Egypt, when we sat by the flesh pots, and when we did eat bread to the full; for ye have brought us forth into this wilderness, to kill this whole assembly with hunger. Then *said the LORD unto Moses, Behold, I will rain bread from heaven for you; and the people shall go out and gather a certain rate every day*, that I may prove them, whether they will walk in my law, or no. (Exodus 16:2–4)

> And the LORD spake unto Moses, saying, I have heard the murmurings of the children of Israel: speak unto them, saying, *At even ye shall eat flesh, and in the morning ye shall be filled with bread;* and ye shall know that I am the LORD your God. And it came to pass, that *at even the quails came up, and covered the camp*: and *in the morning the dew lay round about the host. And when the dew that lay was gone up, behold, upon the face of the wilderness there lay a small round thing, as small as the hoar frost on the ground.* And when the children of Israel saw it, *they said one to another, It is manna*: for they wist not what it was. And Moses said unto them, *This is the bread which the LORD hath given you to eat.* (Exodus 16:11–15)

> And *the house of Israel called the name thereof Manna*: and it was like coriander seed, white; and the taste of it was like wafers made with honey. (Exodus 16:31)

In this account, we see Israel grumbling and complaining that they would've been better off back in Egypt. In response to their complaint, God tells Moses that He will supernaturally provide food for them—quail in the evening and manna in the morning. However, we're only looking at manna as a *type* of Christ. The name *manna* is the Hebrew word for Israel's question when they saw it on that first morning, "What is it?" Over 1,400 years later, Jesus was speaking to the Pharisees, who challenged him to show them a sign, citing to Him the Old Testament sign of manna as an example. In His answer, Jesus presented Himself as the Bread of Life (John 6:31–35), one of His seven *I Am* statements recorded in John's gospel that we looked at earlier in this chapter. So we see that this supernatural *what-is-it* bread called *manna* is a *type* of Christ, a picture of Him as the Bread of Life. This *type* is further strengthened by the ordinance of the Lord's Supper, in which the two elements of *bread* and grape juice are used to symbolize *the body* and blood of Jesus in which He took our sin upon Himself on the cross. The Last Supper of Jesus with His disciples (Luke 22:14–20) was the inaugural event that the Lord's Supper is based on. It is also recorded in Matthew and Mark's gospels (Matthew 26:26–30 and Mark 14:22–26).

8. Water from the Rock (Type/Shadow)

> And all the congregation of the children of Israel journeyed from the wilderness of Sin, after their journeys, according to the commandment of the LORD, and pitched in Rephidim: and *there was no water for the people to drink.* Wherefore the people did chide with Moses, and said, Give us water that we may drink. And Moses said unto them, Why chide ye with me? wherefore do ye tempt the LORD? And the people thirsted there for water; and the people murmured against Moses, and said, Wherefore is this that thou hast brought us up out of Egypt, to kill us and our children and our cattle with thirst? And *Moses cried unto the LORD, saying, What shall I do unto this people? they be almost ready to stone me. And the LORD said unto Moses, Go on before the people, and take with thee of the elders of Israel; and thy rod,* wherewith thou smotest the river, take in thine hand, and go. Behold, *I will stand before thee there upon the rock in Horeb; and thou shalt smite the rock,* and *there shall come water out of it, that the people may drink. And Moses did so in the sight of the elders of Israel.* And he called the name of the place Massah, and Meribah, because of the chiding of the children of Israel, and because they tempted the LORD, saying, Is the LORD among us, or not? (Exodus 17:1–7)

In this passage, both the *water* and the *rock* are *types* of Christ. Although this passage doesn't record the water coming from the rock, it can be inferred from the passage. We will see the scene of water coming forth from a rock again in the book of Numbers, although with a much different result! In fact, the second account is what cost Moses the privilege of crossing into the Promised Land of Canaan. The two passages taken together form an even stronger *type* of Christ, as we will see when we look at that passage. Alluding to this type, Paul wrote to the Corinthian church:

The Rock as a Type

> Moreover, brethren, I would not that ye should be ignorant, how that all our fathers were under the cloud, and all passed through the sea; And were all baptized unto Moses in the cloud and in the sea; And did all eat the same spiritual meat; And *did all drink the same spiritual drink: for they drank of that*

spiritual Rock that followed them: and *that Rock was Christ*. (1 Corinthians 10:1–4)

Jesus is also referred to prophetically as "the *stone* which the builders rejected," which became "the chief corner *stone*" (Psalm 118:22). Also, Jesus said that He would build His church *upon this rock*, believed by many to be referring either *directly to Himself* or to *Peter's confession of Him as the Christ* (Matthew 16:18).

Water as a Type

You may recall Jesus's conversation with the Samaritan woman at the well, in which He offered her a special kind of water.

> Jesus answered and said unto her, *If thou knewest the gift of God, and who it is that saith to thee, Give me to drink; thou wouldest have asked of him, and he would have given thee living water*. The woman saith unto him, Sir, thou hast nothing to draw with, and the well is deep: from whence then hast thou that living water? Art thou greater than our father Jacob, which gave us the well, and drank thereof himself, and his children, and his cattle? Jesus answered and said unto her, Whosoever drinketh of this water shall thirst again: But *whosoever drinketh of the water that I shall give him shall never thirst; but the water that I shall give him shall be in him a well of water springing up into everlasting life*. (John 4:10–14)

In another instance, Jesus publicly gave a similar invitation using the water metaphor of Himself:

> In the last day, that great day of the feast, *Jesus stood and cried*, saying, *If any man thirst, let him come unto me, and drink. He that believeth on me, as the scripture hath said, out of his belly shall flow rivers of living water*. (But this spake he of the Spirit, which they that believe on him should receive: for the Holy Ghost was not yet given; because that Jesus was not yet glorified.) (John 7:37–39)

Jesus may here be referencing Psalm 1:3, Isaiah 44:3, 55:1, and 58:11.

9. Not Just Any Altar (Type/Shadow)

> An *altar of earth* thou shalt make unto me, and shalt sacrifice thereon thy burnt offerings, and thy peace offerings, thy sheep, and thine oxen: in all places where I record my name I will come unto thee, and I will bless thee. And if thou wilt make me an *altar of stone*, thou shalt *not build it of hewn stone*: for *if thou lift up thy tool upon it, thou hast polluted it. Neither shalt thou go up by steps unto mine altar, that thy nakedness be not discovered thereon*. (Exodus 20:24–26)

153

Uncut Stones

The Lord here instructed that a worshipper building an altar to Him must build it of earth or uncut stones, and that it should not be accessible by steps. The strong language here is intriguing—that a tool would pollute or *profane* (NASB) it. Some see this prohibition as a means of inhibiting idolatry that might be inherent with an elaborate altar, that men might be enticed to worship the altar rather than the God for whom the altar is erected. Others see the prohibition as a *type* that salvation is by grace and not by works, which is how I see it. The altar being either of *dirt* or *uncut stones* is a *type* of salvation by grace alone and not of man's works, works here being represented by a cutting tool and the labor of man. May I add that these two views are not mutually exclusive, so it doesn't have to be one or the other; it could be both.

Note that the provision for this altar precedes the instructions for the tabernacle and its furnishings. Someone might ask, "Why would the Lord here command an altar of uncut stones but later command the elaborate altars for the tabernacle worship?" In the tabernacle, there is the bronze altar near the entrance and the golden altar of incense in the Holy Place before the veil. There is also the golden mercy seat atop the Ark of the Covenant that serves as an altar on the Day of Atonement. Is there ambivalence on God's part? As the apostle Paul would say, "May it never be!" You see, the Mosaic Law *is* based on works. However, the problem with the law is that no one can be saved by it (Romans 3:20), for two simple reasons: (1) no one can keep it (Galatians 3:10), and (2) there is not a single law which is able to impart life (Galatians 3:21). In another sense, the law is based on *one* work, because it points to the finished work of the sinless Christ, who perfectly fulfilled it. We will see later in the passages on the tabernacle worship and the Day of Atonement how they portray Christ and His finished work.

No Steps

Because men wore skirts, ascending steps would reveal their physical nakedness. Physical nakedness is also a *metaphor* for our spiritual depravity before a holy God, which was precisely the reason an offering was needed. An example of this is when the apostle Paul speaks of the tension we have here on earth as contrasted with our blissful and secure state in heaven.

> For we know that if our earthly house of this tabernacle were dissolved, we have a building of God, an house not made with hands, eternal in the heavens. For *in this we groan, earnestly desiring to be clothed* upon with our house which is from heaven: If so be *that being clothed we shall not be found naked.* (1 Corinthians 5:1–3)

Similarly, Jesus uses the same metaphor of nakedness in His message to the lukewarm Laodicean church as recorded by John. In this case, the wealthy Laodiceans had plenty of clothing, but Jesus is here telling them that they are *spiritually* naked.

Because thou sayest, I am rich, and increased with goods, and have need of nothing; and *knowest not that thou art wretched, and miserable, and poor, and blind, and naked*: I counsel thee to buy of me gold tried in the fire, that thou mayest be rich; and white raiment, *that thou mayest be clothed*, and *that the shame of thy nakedness do not appear*; and anoint thine eyes with eyesalve, that thou mayest see. (Revelation 3:17–18)

10. God Appears to Moses on Mount Sinai, Sprinkling of Blood (Theophany, Type/Shadow)

And he said unto Moses, *Come up unto the LORD*, thou, and Aaron, Nadab, and Abihu, and seventy of the elders of Israel; and worship ye afar off. And *Moses alone shall come near the LORD*: but they shall not come nigh; neither shall the people go up with him (Exodus 24:1–2)

And *Moses took the blood, and sprinkled it on the people*, and said, *Behold the blood of the covenant*, which the LORD hath made with you concerning all these words. *Then went up Moses, and Aaron, Nadab, and Abihu, and seventy of the elders of Israel: And they saw the God of Israel: and there was under his feet as it were a paved work of a sapphire stone, and as it were the body of heaven in his clearness*. And upon the nobles of the children of Israel he laid not his hand: also they saw God, and did eat and drink. And *the LORD said unto Moses, Come up to me into the mount*, and be there: and I will give thee tables of stone, and a law, and commandments which I have written; that thou mayest teach them. (Exodus 24:8–12)

And *Moses went into the midst of the cloud*, and gat him up into the mount: and *Moses was in the mount forty days and forty nights*. (Exodus 24:18)

In this passage, we see that God manifested Himself to Moses, Aaron, Nadab, Abihu, and the seventy elders. He appears to them in *bodily form* because He is said to be standing on *sapphire stone pavement*. Note in verse 8 that Moses took the sacrificial blood and sprinkled it on the people, stating, "Behold the blood of the covenant which the Lord hath made with you …" The sprinkling of the blood upon the people is a *type* of Jesus's cleansing blood of the New Covenant, which is commemorated in the ordinance of the Lord's Supper.

11. The Tabernacle as a Pattern for Worship (Type/Shadow)

In the epistle of Hebrews, a key theme of the book and, I believe, the primary theme is showing the superiority of the New Covenant in Christ over the Old Covenant of the Mosaic Law. We saw this in chapter 8, "Mechanics of OT Messianic Prophecy"—that the author of Hebrews *sees* in the Mosaic Law a clear picture of New Testament doctrine founded and sustained by Christ in His atoning death and in His present position of eternal high priest in heaven, at the right hand of God the Father. Below are passages from that chapter brought forward that clearly point to this.

> Now if He were on earth, He would not be a priest at all, since there are those who offer the gifts according to the Law; who serve a *copy* and *shadow* of the heavenly things, just as Moses was warned *by God* when he was about to erect the tabernacle; for, "SEE," He says, "THAT YOU MAKE all things ACCORDING TO THE PATTERN WHICH WAS SHOWN YOU ON THE MOUNTAIN." (Hebrews 8:4–5)

> The Holy Spirit is signifying this, that the way into the holy place has not yet been disclosed while the outer tabernacle is still standing … Therefore it was necessary for the *copies* of the things in the heavens to be cleansed with these, but the heavenly things themselves with better sacrifices than these. For Christ did not enter a holy place made with hands, *a mere copy* of the true one, but into heaven itself, now to appear in the presence of God for us; (Hebrews 9:8, 9:23–24)

> For the Law, since it has only *a shadow* of the good things to come and not the very form of things, can never, by the same sacrifices which they offer continually year by year, make perfect those who draw near. (Hebrews 10:1)

> By faith Abraham, when he was tested, offered up Isaac, and he who had received the promises was offering up his only begotten *son*; *it was he* to whom it was said, "IN ISAAC YOUR DESCENDANTS SHALL BE CALLED." He considered that God is able to raise *people* even from the dead, from which he also received him back *as a type*. (Hebrews 11:17–19)

Since the tabernacle is introduced in Exodus and expounded upon in Leviticus, Numbers, and Deuteronomy, we will look at it here—focusing on *elements of the tabernacle* and *the clothing of the high priest*. Later, as we go through the remaining three books of the Pentateuch in subsequent chapters, we will look at pertinent passages that are *types* in them. This study will show how Mosaic Law worship was a foreshadowing of Christ and His atonement. We will look at each of the following elements of the tabernacle worship:

Bronze Altar
Bronze Laver
Holy Place
Golden Lampstand
Table of Showbread
Altar of Incense
Holy of Holies
Ark of the Covenant

Garments of the High Priest

Bronze Altar (Exodus 27:1–8)

The bronze altar was made of acacia wood and overlaid with bronze. It measured 5 cubits square by 3 cubits high (7.5' × 7.5' × 4.5') and had a horn on each of its four corners. It had a bronze grating at the mid-height of the altar, and pails, shovels, forks, and fire pans for utensils.

Bronze Laver (Exodus 30:18–21)

The bronze laver was made with a base and was placed between the tent of meeting and the altar. It is noteworthy that the priests were instructed to wash their hands "so that they would not die."

Holy Place (Exodus 26:33)

The Holy Place was the larger room where the priests would minister daily. This room was adjacent to the Holy of Holies. The high priest, when entering the Holy of Holies, would pass through the Holy Place prior to entering the Holy of Holies. The veil functioned as the doorway separating the Holy of Holies from the Holy Place.

Golden Lampstand (Exodus 25:31–40)

The golden lampstand, as its name suggests, was made of pure gold and was kept in the Holy Place. It had seven lamps, which were to be kept burning at all times while the tabernacle was stationary.

Table of Showbread (Exodus 25:23–30)

The table of showbread was made of acacia wood and was overlaid with pure gold, measuring 2.0 cubits long × 1.0 cubit wide × 1.5 cubits high (3.00' × 1.50' × 2.25'). It was kept in the Holy Place. On this table, the *bread of the presence* was to be kept at all times while the tabernacle was stationary.

Altar of Incense (Exodus 30:1–16)

The altar of incense was made of acacia wood and overlaid with pure gold, measuring 1 cubit square × 2 cubits high (1.5' × 1.5' × 3.0'). It was located in the Holy Place outside the veil separating the Holy of Holies from the Holy Place. Incense was to be kept burning on it at all times while the tabernacle was stationary.

Holy of Holies (Exodus 26:31–34)

The Holy of Holies (aka the Most Holy Place, KJV) was the inner sanctuary of the tabernacle, the room where the Ark of the Covenant was kept. This room was so sacred that only the high priest could enter it, and only once a year on the Day of Atonement, which we will look at later when we go through Leviticus. The penalty for improper entry was instant death.

Ark of the Covenant (Exodus 25:10–22)

The Ark of the Covenant was a box 2.5 cubits long × 1.5 cubits wide × 1.5 cubits high (3.75' × 2.25' × 2.25'). It was constructed out of acacia wood and overlaid with gold. Atop the ark was the *mercy seat*, which extended its full length and width. There were two golden cherubs (angels) projecting above the mercy seat, one at each end, with their faces toward the mercy seat and their wings projecting upward over the mercy seat. The wing tips of each met and touched each other above the center of the mercy seat. This was the most sacred place in the tabernacle and was the very seat of God's presence! *God's presence, manifested as a pillar of cloud by day and a pillar of fire by night, hovered over the mercy seat* of the Ark whenever the tabernacle was stationary. When the pillar of cloud/fire would move, Israel would break camp, pack up the tabernacle, and follow the pillar of cloud/fire until it stopped at the next encampment.

See figure 10.1, *The Tabernacle*, on the adjacent page, showing the eight elements of the tabernacle. So let's examine how they are prophetic *types* of Christ.

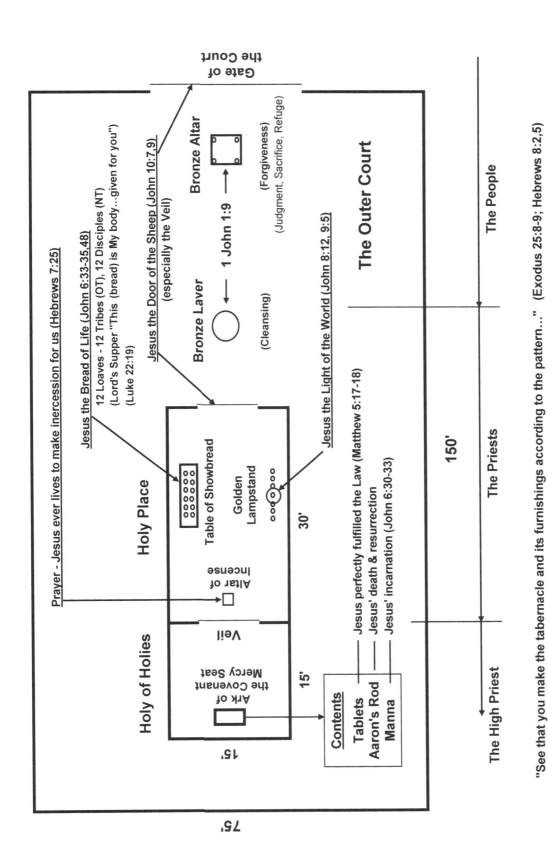

Prayer - Jesus ever lives to make intercession for us (Hebrews 7:25)

Jesus the Bread of Life (John 6:33-35,48)
12 Loaves - 12 Tribes (OT), 12 Disciples (NT)
(Lord's Supper "This (bread) is My body...given for you")
(Luke 22:19)

Jesus the Door of the Sheep (John 10:7,9)
(especially the Veil)

Bronze Altar

1 John 1:9

(Forgiveness)
(Judgment, Sacrifice, Refuge)

Bronze Laver

(Cleansing)

Jesus the Light of the World (John 8:12, 9:5)

Gate of
the Court

The Outer Court

Holy Place

Table of Showbread

Golden
Lampstand

30'

Altar of
Incense

Veil

Holy of Holies

Ark of
the Covenant
Mercy Seat

15'

Contents
Tablets
Aaron's Rod
Manna

Jesus perfectly fulfilled the Law (Matthew 5:17-18)
Jesus' death & resurrection
Jesus' incarnation (John 6:30-33)

150'

The High Priest

The Priests

The People

75'

15'

"See that you make the tabernacle and its furnishings according to the pattern..." (Exodus 25:8-9; Hebrews 8:2,5)

Tabercacle Dimensions: Outer Court (Ex 27:9-13); Tabernacle Proper (Ex 26:15-18,22)

Figure 10.1 - The Tabernacle

159

The *first element* you encounter as you enter the outer court of the tabernacle is the *bronze altar*. This represents *sacrifice*. Notice three things about the bronze altar:

1) A *fire* was to be kept burning continually on it (Leviticus 6:9, 6:12–13), which reminds us of God's presence—the burning bush, pillar of fire, the consuming of Elijah's offering, God's judgment, and the eternal lake of fire (Revelation 20:7–10, 20:12–15).

2) *Sacrifices* were offered on it. Hebrews 9:22 reads, "And almost all things are by the law purged with blood; and *without shedding of blood is no remission.*" This verse ties back to Leviticus 17:11, which reads, "For *the life of the flesh is in the blood*: and *I have given it to you upon the altar* to make an *atonement* for your souls: for it is the blood that maketh an *atonement* for the soul."

3) The *four horns* on the corners of the altar were a place of refuge. A person fleeing from death could grab hold of the horns of the altar to escape death—Adonijah is an example (1 Kings 1:50–53).

So the altar is a *type* of Christ's atoning sacrifice on the cross. Jesus's atoning death protects us from the eternal *fire* of God's wrath against sinners. Jesus's *sacrifice* of Himself on the cross became the full payment of our sin debt, which purchased our *forgiveness* from God, making Him our *refuge*. So we have this glorious threefold picture of the cross—the place of God's judgment against sinners, the perfect substitutionary sacrifice of His Son, and our glorious place of refuge!

The *second element* that we encounter is the *bronze laver*. The priests were instructed to wash their hands so that they would not die, so obviously, more is going on here than just handwashing—the external washing here is symbolic of the *spiritual cleansing* we have through the blood of Christ! Second Corinthians 5:21 reads, "For he hath made him to be sin for us, who knew no sin; that we might be made the righteousness of God in him." Christ took our sin upon Himself on the cross in order that we might be clothed in *His righteousness*!

After the bronze laver, we come to the tabernacle entrance. The tabernacle has two rooms, the Holy Place and the Holy of Holies. So the *third element* we encounter is the *Holy Place*. Once we place our faith in Jesus, we become *children* of God as we are told in John 1:12, and are baptized into the *body of Christ*. Only the *priests* could enter the Holy Place. The apostle Peter writes the following concerning Christians: "But ye are a chosen generation, *a royal priesthood*, an holy nation, a peculiar people; that ye should shew forth the praises of him who hath called you out of darkness into his marvellous light; Which in time past were not a people, but are now the people of God: which had not obtained mercy, but now have obtained mercy" (1 Peter 1:9–10).

The *fourth* and *fifth* elements we encounter upon entering the Holy Place are the *golden lampstand* and the *table of showbread*. Jesus, in two of His "I Am" statements, said, "I am the *Light of the World*" (John 8:12, 9:5) and "I am the *Bread of Life*" (John 6:33–35, 6:48). Therefore, we have the golden lampstand on the left and the table of showbread on the right. These were perpetually kept in the Holy Place and are symbolic of *Christ's abiding presence*—enlightening and guiding us, symbolized by His *light*, and sustaining us, symbolized by Him being *the bread*. Also, as we know, the bread that we partake of in the Lord's Supper symbolizes His body, which was broken for us.

The *sixth element* we encounter is the *altar of incense*. Incense in the Bible symbolizes *prayer*. We are told that Jesus Christ "is able also to save them to the uttermost that come unto God by him, seeing *he ever liveth to make intercession* for them" (Hebrews 7:25). So the altar of incense symbolizes the perpetual prayer of Christ on our behalf.

The *seventh element* we encounter is the *Holy of Holies*. This represents the very *presence* of God! As the altar of incense symbolizes Christ's prayer for us, the Holy of Holies symbolizes *our ability to approach God in prayer* during our lives here on earth and to live eternally in His presence after we die! In Hebrews 4:16, we read, "Let us therefore *come boldly* unto *the throne of grace*, that *we may obtain mercy*, and find *grace to help* in time of need."

The *eighth element* we encounter is the *Ark of the Covenant*. On top of the Ark is the *mercy seat*. Just as we saw above in Hebrews 4:16, we can come to God and *obtain mercy*! The ultimate mercy God gives us is forgiveness and cleansing and the privilege of being His child, but He grants us innumerable mercies throughout our life's journey as well.

So we see in this brief explanation how the tabernacle worship is a picture of our *redemption* in Christ. Next, we will see how the high priest is a *picture* of Jesus Christ, and how the *garments* of the Old Testament high priest picture Christ, who is our ultimate and eternal high priest.

12. The High Priest, a Picture of Christ, Who Is Our Eternal High Priest (Type/Shadow)

In the Old Testament worship system, the priests were the central figures in the tabernacle worship. Duties of the priests included teaching the people God's Law (Leviticus 10:11), offering sacrifices, burning incense, and taking care of the altar (Leviticus 6:12–13), maintaining the lamps and the showbread (Leviticus 24:1–9). In general, the people brought their sacrifices to the priest, who would offer them on the brazen altar. In this sacrificial role, the priest acted as the mediator between God and man – that is, the priest would approach God through the sacrificial rite on behalf of the person he was representing. So the people, one by one, would bring their sacrifices to the priest, who would in turn offer them to God according to the Law.

The high priest was the leader of the other priests. The ultimate expression of the Old Testament priesthood occurred on the Day of Atonement, which we will see in Leviticus. On this special day, which occurred only once a year, the high priest would enter the Holy of Holies to offer sacrifices in the very presence of God. This was the only time he could enter, and he was the only one who could enter.

Exodus 28 describes the garments of the high priest. In these garments, we see some *types* that point to Christ.

1) The garments were made for *glory* and for *beauty* (v. 2), representing *the glory of Christ!*

2) The garments were *holy* (v. 4), symbolizing the *sinless, perfect Christ!*

3) Two onyx stones (v. 9), one for each shoulder, were used to support the linen ephod. On each stone were engraved six tribes of Israel so that *all twelve tribes* were *carried on the high priest's shoulders.* So the high priest approached God on behalf of the nation of Israel—as *Christ approaches God on behalf of every soul who believes in Him!*

4) The Breastpiece of *Judgment* (vv. 15–21, 30), which contains four rows of three stones each, again *representing the twelve tribes of Israel.* The Breastpiece of *Judgment* was to be *worn over the heart* of the high priest (Aaron) when he would go in before the Lord. What a picture of Christ! When He is seated at the right hand of God, *we are on His heart!*

5) The turban worn on the head of the high priest had a golden plate attached to the front of it with the inscribed words "Holy to the Lord." This, of course, represents *Christ's perfect holiness!*

The key thought in all of this is that the priests in general, and especially the high priest on the Day of Atonement, served as the mediators between a holy God and sinful people. The priests offered sacrifices first for their own sin, then on behalf of the people. Jesus, on the other hand, offered Himself as a human sacrifice for the people's sin. So in this case, a sacrifice on the part of the priest had to be offered—the Old Testament priests offered sacrifices in order to be made holy to God, and Jesus, who was already holy to God, made the sacrifice of Himself for the propitiation of our sins! In this way, He became the "great high priest who has passed into the heavens, Jesus the Son of God" (Hebrews 4:14).

13. Moses's Face Shone (Type/Shadow)

And it came to pass, when Moses came down from mount Sinai with the two tables of testimony in Moses' hand, when he came down from the mount, that Moses wist not *that the skin of his face shone while he talked with him.* And when Aaron and *all the children of Israel saw Moses, behold, the skin of his face shone; and they were afraid to come nigh him.* And Moses called unto them; and Aaron and all the rulers of the congregation returned unto him: and Moses talked with them. And afterward all the children of Israel came nigh: and he gave them in commandment all that the LORD had spoken with him in mount Sinai. *And till Moses had done speaking with them, he put a vail on his face.* But *when Moses went in before the LORD to speak with him, he took the vail off,* until he came out. And he came out, and spake unto the children of Israel that which he was commanded. And *the children of Israel saw the face of Moses, that the skin of Moses' face shone*: and *Moses put the vail upon his face again, until he went in to speak with him.* (Exodus 34:29–35)

What an interesting *type* of Christ! Can you recall any instance in Jesus's life where his face shone supernaturally? You guessed it—*the transfiguration.* The account of the transfiguration is recorded in all three of the synoptic Gospels—Matthew 17:1–8; Mark 9:2–8; and Luke 9:28–36. The Matthew account is shown below.

And after six days *Jesus taketh Peter, James, and John his brother, and bringeth them up into an high mountain apart, And was transfigured before them: and his face did shine as the sun, and his raiment was white as the light.* And, behold, *there appeared unto them Moses and Elias talking with him.* Then answered Peter, and said unto Jesus, Lord, it is good for us to be here: if thou wilt, let us make here three tabernacles; one for thee, and one for Moses, and one for Elias. While he yet spake, behold, *a bright cloud overshadowed them: and behold a voice out of the cloud, which said, This is my beloved Son, in whom I am well pleased; hear ye him.* And when the disciples heard it, they fell on their face, and were sore afraid. And Jesus came and touched them, and said, Arise, and be not afraid. And *when they had lifted up their eyes, they saw no man, save Jesus only.* (Matthew 17:1–8)

Interestingly, John's gospel does not record the transfiguration, but does that mean that John did not record Jesus's face shining? Absolutely not, for we read the following in his encounter with the risen Christ:

And in the midst of the seven candlesticks one like unto the Son of man, clothed with a garment down to the foot, and girt about the paps with a golden girdle. His head and his hairs were white like wool, as white as snow; and his eyes were as a flame of fire; And his feet like unto fine brass, as if they burned in a furnace; and his voice as the sound of many waters. And he had in his right hand seven stars: and out of his mouth went a sharp twoedged sword: and *his countenance was as the sun shineth in his strength.* And when I saw him, I fell at his feet as dead. And he laid his right hand upon me, saying unto me, Fear not; I am the first and the last: I am he that liveth, and was dead; and, behold, I am alive for evermore, Amen; and have the keys of hell and of death. (Revelation 1:13–18)

What an interesting *type* and what an interesting fulfillment! And *who* showed up at Jesus's transfiguration? Moses, *the type of Christ,* was Jesus's guest, along with Elijah, at Jesus's transfiguration, and Jesus spoke to both of them! One thing that is so cool about this is the fact that Moses, because of his disobedient act of striking the rock (which we will see in the book of Numbers), was prevented from crossing over into the Promised Land. However, even though Moses died in the wilderness and was buried by God (Deuteronomy 34:4–6), Moses did get to visit the Promised Land during the brief transfiguration!

14. The Sabbath (Type/Shadow)

> And Moses gathered all the congregation of the children of Israel together, and said unto them, *These are the words which the LORD hath commanded*, that ye should do them. Six days shall work be done, but *on the seventh day there shall be to you an holy day, a sabbath of rest to the LORD:* whosoever doeth work therein shall be put to death. Ye shall kindle no fire throughout your habitations upon the sabbath day. (Exodus 35:1–3)

The writer of the book of Hebrews explains to us how the Sabbath day is a *type* of the rest that the believer has in salvation—because as children of God, we have the righteousness of Christ imputed to our account. We no longer feel the need to try to earn God's acceptance by good works. In fact, the Bible is quite clear that no one can be saved by good works or by keeping God's law (the Mosaic Law).

Imputed Righteousness

What shall we say then that Abraham our father, as pertaining to the flesh, hath found? For if Abraham were justified by works, he hath whereof to glory; but not before God. For what saith the scripture? *Abraham believed God, and it was counted unto him for righteousness.* Now to him that worketh is the reward not reckoned of grace, but of debt. But *to him that worketh not, but believeth on him that justifieth the ungodly, his faith is counted for righteousness.* Even as *David also describeth the blessedness of the man, unto whom God imputeth righteousness without works,* Saying, *Blessed are they whose iniquities are forgiven, and whose sins are covered. Blessed is the man to whom the Lord will not impute sin.* (Romans 4:1–8)

The Sabbath Rest of the Believer

Let us therefore fear, lest, a promise being left us of *entering into his rest*, any of you should seem to come short of it. For unto us was the gospel preached, as well as unto them: but the word preached did not profit them, not being mixed with faith in them that heard it. *For we which have believed do enter into rest,* as he said, As I have sworn in my wrath, THEY SHALL NOT ENTER MY REST, (NASB) although the works were finished from the foundation of the world. *For he spake in a certain place of the seventh day on this wise, And God did rest the seventh day from all his works.* And in this place again, THEY SHALL NOT ENTER MY REST. (NASB) Seeing therefore it remaineth that some must enter therein, and they to whom it was first preached entered not in because of unbelief: Again, he limiteth a certain day, saying in David, To day, after so long a time; as it is said, To day if ye will hear his voice, harden not your hearts. For if Joshua (NASB) had given them rest, then would he not afterward have spoken of another day. *There remaineth therefore a rest to the people of God. For he that is entered into his rest, he also hath ceased from his own works, as God did from his.* Let us labour therefore to enter into that rest, lest any man fall after the same example of unbelief. (Hebrews 4:1–11)

In the Hebrews passage above, the writer is reminding us of Israel's disobedience in the wilderness, which resulted in their not being allowed to enter the Promised Land rest that had been promised them. All the adults who refused to trust God when the initial time came to enter the Promised Land ended up dying in the wilderness. Only Joshua and Caleb, who did believe God, ended up crossing over, as well as the children who grew up in the wilderness. Just as those who heard God's Word and refused to believe it in Moses's day did not enter Canaan, so people who hear the gospel of Christ and refuse to believe it today will not enter the promised rest of heaven. However, in the latter case, *the rest begins here in this life*—as we increasingly place our faith in Christ, we are increasingly able to rest in His love and grace. You see, "the fear of the Lord is the beginning of wisdom …" (Proverbs 9:10), but "perfect love casteth out fear" (1 John 4:18). As it was then for the Israelites in Moses's day, so it is now for us today—faith is the mechanism for entering into God's rest, and Jesus, the object of our faith, is the enabler to those who trust Him to give us that rest. His invitation today is the same as it was 2,000 years ago: *"Come unto me, all ye that labour and are heavy laden, and I will give you rest.* Take my yoke upon you, and learn of me; for I am meek and lowly in heart: and *ye shall find rest unto your souls.* For *my yoke is easy, and my burden is light"* (Matthew 11:28–30).

Summary of Messianic Prophetic Elements in Exodus

1.	Moses as a Type	(Type/Shadow)
2.	Moses's Deliverance from Death as Baby	(Type/Shadow)
3.	The Burning Bush	(Theophany, Prophesy)
4.	The Passover	(Type/Shadow)
5.	Pillar of Fire and Cloud	(Theophany)
6.	Crossing of the Red Sea	(Type/Shadow)
7.	Manna	(Type/Shadow)
8.	Water from the Rock	(Type/Shadow)
9.	Not Just Any Altar	(Type/Shadow)
10.	God Appears to Moses on Mt Sinai, Sprinkling of Blood	(Theophany, Type/Shadow)

11.	The Tabernacle as a Pattern for Worship	(Type/Shadow)
12.	The High Priest, Picture of Christ	(Type/Shadow)
13.	Moses's Face Shone	(Type/Shadow)
14.	The Sabbath	(Type/Shadow)

11

JESUS IN LEVITICUS

WE WILL NOW EXAMINE THE BOOK OF LEVITICUS. THE ENTIRE PENTATEUCH (GENESIS through Deuteronomy) was written by Moses around 1400 BC. Genesis records the creation and the beginning of human life, God's covenants with Adam, Noah, the patriarchs (Abraham, Isaac, Jacob, and Joseph), and the early history of mankind from Adam to Joseph. Exodus records the story and calling of Moses and the exodus from Egypt, the Mosaic Law given on Mt. Sinai, the wilderness wanderings, and the plans for and construction of the tabernacle.

The book of Leviticus, perhaps as much as any book of the Old Testament, portrays the huge chasm between God's holiness and mankind's sinfulness. The Levites were the priestly tribe responsible for the maintenance and movement of the tabernacle and for sacrificial offerings. Aaron was the first high priest, and his sons assisted him as priests. Not any Levite could become high priest; only Aaron's descendants could succeed him as high priest. The Lord struck down Aaron's sons Nadab and Abihu for their irreverent worship (Leviticus 10:1–2). After Aaron's death, his son Eleazar became high priest (Numbers 3:2–4; 20:25–28). Leviticus includes the regulations concerning the sacrificial offerings and the priesthood in general. It also includes dietary laws, treatment of and quarantine for leprosy and other medical regulations, laws concerning morality, idolatry, religious festivals and holy days, the law of redemption, and various other laws. The priests, especially the high priest, were the principal agents responsible for teaching and administering these various laws. So the content of Leviticus established the daily regulations for tabernacle worship as well as the domestic life of the Israelites.

1. The Sacrificial System and Priesthood (Type/Shadow)

Sacrificial System: The sacrificial system was a daily reminder of the holiness of God and the people's sinfulness. The sacrificial system included both animal and grain sacrifices. So the animal sacrificial system is a rich *type* of Christ. The sacrificial animal was *a male without defect*. However, one exception to the requirement that the animal be a male (Leviticus 5:6) was that the sacrifice for an unintentional or careless sin was to be a female animal, but in all others, a male was required. The requirement of a male without defect is laid out in detail in Leviticus 22:17–25. You might recall Malachi's rebuke of the people for bringing *damaged goods* as sacrifices. God said,

> A son honoureth his father, and a servant his master: if then I be a father, where is mine honour? and if I be a master, where is my fear? saith the LORD of hosts unto you, *O priests, that despise my name.* And ye say, Wherein have we despised thy name? *Ye offer polluted bread upon mine altar*; and ye say, Wherein have we polluted thee? In that ye say, The table of the LORD is contemptible. And *if ye offer the blind for sacrifice, is it not evil? and if ye offer the lame and sick, is it not evil? offer it now unto thy governor; will he be pleased with thee, or accept thy person?* saith the LORD of hosts. (Malachi 1:6–8)

So we see that the requirement that the sacrificial animal be a male without defect pictures Christ who was sinless. In John 8:46, Jesus asks, "*Which of you convinceth me of sin? And if I say the truth, why do ye not believe me?*" The animal was typically a bull, a sheep, or a goat, although pigeons or doves were allowed for some offerings for those too poor to afford a large animal. The animal was slain adjacent to the bronze altar, and his blood sprinkled on the altar.

The animal sacrifices were blood sacrifices. These sacrifices pointed forward to the perfect blood sacrifice, where Jesus Christ offered Himself as a *sinless* human sacrifice to pay the full debt for all or our sins!

> For the life of the flesh is in the blood: and I have given it to you upon the altar to make an atonement for your souls: for it is the blood that maketh an atonement for the soul. (Leviticus 17:11)

> And *almost all things are by the law purged with blood; and without shedding of blood is no remission.* (Hebrews 9:22)

Priesthood: Also, the priesthood, especially the high priest, is a *type* of Christ. We saw in Exodus how even the high priest's garments pictured various aspects of Christ and His role as our high priest. So in this sacrificial system, both the *sacrifice* and the *priest* are rich *types* of Christ, our perfect sacrifice and our eternal high priest at the right hand of God, who is able to save us "to the uttermost" because he "ever lives to make intercession" for us (Hebrews 7:25)!

Note, in the larger Hebrews passage below, the comparison between the priests and Christ.

> so much the more also Jesus has become the guarantee of a better covenant.

> The *former* priests, on the one hand, existed in greater numbers because they were prevented by death from continuing, but Jesus, on the other hand, *because He continues forever, holds His priesthood permanently.* Therefore *He is able also to save forever* those who draw near to God through Him, since *He always lives to make intercession for them.*

> For it was fitting for us to have such a high priest, *holy, innocent, undefiled, separated from sinners and exalted above the heavens;* who does not need daily,

like those high priests, to offer up sacrifices, first for His own sins and then for the *sins of the people, because this He did once for all when He offered up Himself.* For the Law appoints men as high priests who are weak, but *the word of the oath, which came after the Law, appoints a Son, made perfect forever.*

Now the main point in what has been said *is this: we have such a high priest, who has taken His seat at the right hand of the throne of the Majesty in the heavens, a minister in the sanctuary and in the true tabernacle, which the Lord pitched, not man.* (Hebrews 7:22–8:2 NASB)

We see from this passage the *type* of the priests and the *fulfillment* of the *prophetic type* in Christ. It's no wonder that the writer of Hebrews uses the word *shadow* as another word for *type*! Because just like a *shadow* pales in significance to the *object* from which it is cast, so the *type* of Christ pales in significance to *Christ Himself*! We can make the following comparisons between the shadow of Christ and Christ.

Shadow

Many priests because of death
Earthly priests, no lasting intercession
Priests could only "save" temporally
Priests were fallible, sinful
Priests offered sacrifice for their own sins first
Priests were weak
Priests ministered in a temporal sanctuary

Christ

Christ—eternal high priest because of life
Christ—eternally able to intercede
Christ saves eternally
Christ—holy, innocent, undefiled
Christ offered Himself as sacrifice for others
Christ is perfect forever
Christ ministers in God's eternal presence

Below is a table summarizing the various offerings specified in Leviticus.

General Offering Types in Leviticus

		Type	Category	Chapter	Purpose	Reference
Type	1	Burnt	Animal	Lev. 1	Repentance, Forgiveness, and Cleansing	Lev. 1:4
	2	Grain	Vegetative	Lev. 2	Devotion and Thanksgiving	Lev. 2:12
Purpose	3	Peace	Animal	Lev. 3	Devotion and Thanksgiving	Lev. 3:12, 3:16
	4	Sin	Animal	Lev. 4	Repentance, Forgiveness, and Cleansing	Lev. 4:2–3, 4:13, 4:22, 4:27
	5	Guilt	Animal	Lev. 5–6	Repentance, Forgiveness, and Cleansing	Lev. 5:1–5, 6:2–3, 6:4–5

Table 11.1

2. Identification with the Sacrifice (Type/Shadow)

One prominent feature of the animal sacrificial system was the person's identification with the sacrifice. This was true both for the person bringing the animal sacrifice to the priest, as well as for the priest who had previously offered sacrifice for himself to serve in his mediatorial role. Below are references concerning the person bringing the sacrifice.

Identification of the person with the sacrifice

Speak unto the children of Israel, and say unto them, If any man of you bring an offering unto the LORD, ye shall bring your offering of the cattle, even of the herd, and of the flock. If his offering be a burnt sacrifice of the herd, let him offer *a male without blemish*: he shall offer it of his own voluntary will at the door of the tabernacle of the congregation before the LORD. And *he shall put his hand upon the head of the burnt offering*; and *it shall be accepted for him to make atonement for him.* And *he shall kill the bullock before the LORD*: and the priests, Aaron's sons, shall bring the blood, and sprinkle the blood round about upon the altar that is by the door of the tabernacle of the congregation. And he shall flay the burnt offering, and cut it into his pieces. (Leviticus 1:2–6)

Additional references include Leviticus 3:2, 3:8, 3:13; 4:4, 4:15, 4:24, 4:29, 4:33; and 8:14, 8:18, 8:22, 8:30. The placement of the person's hand upon the head of the animal was a continual reminder that the animal's shed blood and consumption by fire was payment for that person's sin. That is, the animal was a substitute for the person offering him.

Identification of the priests with the sacrifice

Below are references concerning the priests' identification with the sacrifice.

And thou shalt cause a *bullock to be brought before the tabernacle* of the congregation: and *Aaron and his sons shall put their hands upon the head of the bullock.* And *thou shalt kill the bullock* before the LORD, by the door of the tabernacle of the congregation. And thou shalt take of the blood of the bullock, and put it upon the horns of the altar with thy finger, and pour all the blood beside the bottom of the altar. (Exodus 29:10–12)

Thou *shalt also take one ram*; and *Aaron and his sons shall put their hands upon the head of the ram.* And *thou shalt slay the ram*, and thou shalt take his blood, and sprinkle it round about upon the altar. (Exodus 29:15–16)

And thou shalt *take the other ram*; and *Aaron and his sons shall put their hands upon the head of the ram.* Then shalt thou *kill the ram*, and *take of his blood*, and *put it upon the tip of the right ear of Aaron*, and upon the tip of the right ear of *his sons*, and upon *the thumb of their right hand*, and upon the *great toe of their right foot*, and sprinkle the blood upon the altar round about. And thou shalt *take of the blood that is upon the altar*, and of the anointing oil, and *sprinkle it upon Aaron*, and *upon his garments*, and *upon his sons*, and *upon the garments of his sons* with him: and he shall be hallowed, and his garments, and his sons, and his sons' garments with him. (Exodus 29:19–21)

So we see that the priests were identified with the dead animals that were slain on their behalf, even as the lay offerors were identified with their dead animals.

Paul notes a similar identification that we have with Christ, who is our perfect sacrifice!

What shall we say then? Shall we continue in sin, that grace may abound? God forbid. How shall we, that are dead to sin, live any longer therein? Know ye not, that *so many of us as were baptized into Jesus Christ were baptized into his death*? Therefore *we are buried with him by baptism into death*: that like *as Christ was raised up from the dead by the glory of the Father, even so we also should walk in newness of life*. For if we have been planted together in the likeness of his death, we shall be also in the likeness of his resurrection: Knowing this, that *our old man is crucified with him*, that the body of sin might be destroyed, that henceforth we should not serve sin. For he that is dead is freed from sin. Now *if we be dead with Christ, we believe that we shall also live with him*. (Romans 6:1–8)

Therefore *if any man be in Christ*, he is a new creature: old things are passed away; behold, all things are become new. And all things are of God, who hath reconciled us to himself by Jesus Christ, and hath given to us the ministry of reconciliation; To wit, that God was in Christ, reconciling the world unto himself, not imputing their trespasses unto them; and hath committed unto us the word of reconciliation. Now then *we are ambassadors for Christ, as though God did beseech you by us*: we pray you in Christ's stead, be ye reconciled to God. For *he hath made him to be sin for us,* who knew no sin; *that we might be made the righteousness of God in him*. (2 Corinthians 5:17–21)

I am crucified with Christ: nevertheless I live; yet not I, but Christ liveth in me: and the life which I now live in the flesh I live by the faith of the Son of God, who loved me, and gave himself for me. (Galatians 2:20)

My little children, of whom I travail in birth again *until Christ be formed in you*. (Galatians 4:19)

For we are his workmanship, created in Christ Jesus unto good works, which God hath before ordained that we should walk in them. (Ephesians 2:10)

3. Laws on Leprosy and Uncleanness (Type/Shadow)

One thing that is so fascinating in the study of *types* and *shadows* is their pervasiveness in the Old Testament, which makes it practically impossible for anyone to discover every one of them. They are found even in some of the mundane provisions of the law as we will see in this present case. When we look at the constraints on those with physical defects in chapter 21, we will again see something similar. It has been noted that there are certain things that were discovered in the medical community centuries after their mention in the Bible—two of which are mentioned in connection with our passage on leprosy—quarantine and cleansing (washing of hands in medicine).

Laws on Leprosy

Leviticus 13 addresses the problem of leprosy and how to deal with it. First, it covers how to recognize it, not only on a person, but also on objects, including the walls of a house. Next, it covers what to do when leprosy is found—quarantine of the person, house or objects for seven days, then either extending or ending the quarantine depending on the result of the reinspection. The priest was the responsible party enforcing these regulations.

Leviticus 14, however, addresses the action taken once the leprosy is eradicated. This is where we see the *type*. Once the leper was cleansed, as determined by the priest's inspection, he then was instructed to report to the priest at the sanctuary. Something quite fascinating ensues. Stop and think—does a person's contracting the disease of leprosy constitute a sin? I think we would all agree that the answer to that question is no. So why was the person instructed to come to the sanctuary to offer sacrifices? In Leviticus 14:4–20, the cleansed person was instructed to bring the following with him to the sanctuary, and the following action ensued:

1) The leper *brought two live clean birds,* cedarwood, scarlet (possibly scarlet string), and hyssop.
2) The priest *killed one of the birds* in an earthen vessel over running water.
3) The priest then *took the living bird,* the *cedarwood,* and the *scarlet* and *hyssop* and *dipped them in the blood of the dead bird* and *sprinkled the blood upon the cleansed leper* seven times.
4) The priest then *let the live bird go loose* in the open field.
5) The cleansed leper then washed himself and his clothes and shaved off all his hair and had to live outside his tent for seven days.
6) On the eighth day, the cleansed leper *brought two male lambs without blemish and one yearling ewe lamb without blemish* along with flour and oil.
7) The priest would then *slay the lamb* and offer him for *a trespass offering.*
8) The priest would then *take some of the blood* of the trespass offering and *put it on the top of the right ear, thumb and toe of the cleansed leper,* then …

9) The priest would *offer the other two lambs for a sin offering and a burnt offering to make atonement for the cleansed leper.*

The remainder of the chapter provides for a lesser offering for the poor. Also, atonement was even required for a cleansed house (v. 53). So what is this all about? Why would a person diseased by leprosy have to bring these offerings to receive *atonement*? Atonement is something we would have expected for a person who sinned, but why was it required for a person who innocently contracted leprosy? Again, this is a picture of God's holiness! Animals without blemish were *pictures* of Christ, who would become a sinless sacrifice, and leprosy was a *picture* of sin—it was a result of man's original sin. God had warned Adam that in the day that he ate of the tree of the knowledge of good and evil that he would die (Genesis 2:17), and Adam and Eve began dying that very day. I learned in science class at an early age that we begin to die the day we're born. Sin separates us from God and *taints* us with all sorts of things—leprosy being just one. So this *taintedness* makes us unfit to be in God's presence. The leprosy here is a *picture* of sin and its deadly effects, and so we have this built-in reminder in the Mosaic Law of God's holiness, our sinful inadequacy, and our need for a Savior! God said, "*You shall be holy for I am holy*" (Exodus 19:6, Leviticus 21:8).

Laws on Uncleanness

In Leviticus 15, we see the laws on uncleanness. As was the case for leprosy, so for uncleanness, the priest was the regulatory authority. In this case, uncleanness was involved if a person had a runny sore or a man had a seminal emission, or if a woman were in her menstrual cycle or if she had a flow of blood outside that cycle or beyond that cycle. The uncleanness included both the person and objects that they touched, so if another person touched those objects, they were unclean as well. In each case, the person was regarded as unclean by the law and was required to bathe and wash his/her clothes and be unclean until evening. In the case of the seminal emission, the man, and the woman if applicable, as well as a person touching any unclean object, the person would be unclean until evening, and no further action was required. In the other cases, however, a runny sore, a menstrual cycle, or a flow of blood outside or beyond the menstrual cycle, the person directly involved remained in the unclean condition for seven days. On the eighth day, the person was required to bring two turtledoves or two young pigeons to the priest. The priest would offer one for a sin offering and the other for a burnt offering. Thus, the priest would make *atonement* for the person.

So again we see how uncleanness in the Mosaic Law is simply a *picture* of our sinful condition that required *atonement* before a person could enter the tabernacle to worship God. Similarly, our sinful carnal nature separates us from God, and we need the imputed righteousness of Christ, to enable us to be at peace with God. Paul reminds us of our carnal condition in his letters, speaking of his own struggle in Romans 7, wherein he fails to do what he knows is right and he fails to not do what he knows is wrong. He states in 2 Corinthians 5:2–3 that "we *groan,* earnestly desiring to be clothed upon with our house which is from heaven: If so be that being clothed we shall not be found naked."

4. Day of Atonement (Type/Shadow)

In Leviticus 16, we have one of the most amazing *types* of Christ in the Old Testament. On this day, which happened only one day in the year, an amazing feat was accomplished. The first six chapters of Leviticus cover the various types of offerings and the particular types of sin that each one atoned for. It is noted that the sin offering alone covered unintentional sins that the sinner would later become aware of. Obviously, for this type of sin, an Israelite could logically ask the question "What if I committed a sin against God, and I'm not even aware of it?" Also, he could ask another question, "What if I committed a sin that I meant to bring an offering for, but because of some emergency, I failed to follow through?" That could certainly create some tension in his heart. The Day of Atonement would cover that. It was a very special day on so many levels. The chapter begins with a reminder of what happened to Aaron's two sons when they offered strange fire to God in Leviticus 10 and God slew them. This day was very special for all the people, and it was very special for the high priest.

Only the high priest could enter the Holy of Holies because it was the very seat of God's presence as manifested by the pillar of cloud by day and the pillar of fire by night. In fact, it was so sacred that even he could only enter it on this holy day once a year. The most sacred place in the Holy of Holies was the mercy seat atop the Ark of the Covenant. The mercy seat was the sacred altar for the Day of Atonement. On this day, the high priest would enter the very presence of God to offer his offerings. First, he offered offerings for himself to make him acceptable as high priest, and then he offered offerings on behalf of the people.

The High Priest—the high priest had to do several things on this day.

1) He had to enter the Holy Place with a bull for a sin offering and a ram for a burnt offering.
2) He had to bathe and put on the priestly garments—the tunic, the undergarments, the linen sash, and the linen turban with the plate engraved with "Holy to the Lord."
3) He brought one bull for a sin offering and one ram for a burnt offering for himself.
4) He brought two male goats for a sin offering and one ram for a burnt offering for the congregation.
5) He presented the two goats before the Lord at the tabernacle door and cast lots for the goats—one for the Lord (the sacrificial goat) and one for the scapegoat.
6) He killed the bull for the sin offering to make atonement for himself and his household.
7) He took a censer of burning coals and two handfuls of incense into the veil so that the cloud of incense would cover the mercy seat.
8) *He sprinkled the blood of the bull on the mercy seat* and in front of it seven times.
9) *He killed the sacrificial goat for the sin offering for the congregation.*

10) *He sprinkled the blood of the goat on the mercy seat* and in front of it seven times.

11) He made atonement for the altar with the blood of the bull and the goat seven times.

12) *He laid his hands on the live goat (the scapegoat) and confessed over him all the sins of the children of Israel and sent him into the wilderness by an appointed man.*

13) No other person was allowed anywhere in the tabernacle during all this time.

14) He came back into the tabernacle, removed his clothes, and bathed.

15) He then put on his clothes and offered the burnt offerings, one for himself and one for the people.

16) The assisting priest who released the scapegoat in the wilderness then had to bathe.

17) The bullock's and goat's hide and refuse were carried outside the camp to be burned, and the assisting priest who disposed of them bathed and washed his clothes.

So after this arduous process, full atonement was accomplished for the high priest, all the other priests, the holy sanctuary, the tabernacle, the altar, and all the people so that *all* their sins were now forgiven and cleansed on this one special day each year! So each year in the seventh month, on the tenth day of the month, the Day of Atonement was observed. All the people had a perfectly clean slate on this one day of the year!

All this tedium and slaying of animals on this special day was a yearly reminder of the need for forgiveness and cleansing. It pointed forward to the Savior Jesus Christ, who would one day become both the high priest and the perfect atoning sacrifice. What an extraordinary *picture* of Christ!

HOW THE DAY OF ATONEMENT IS A PICTURE OF CHRIST AND SALVATION

1. **High Priest, Only:** The high priest was the *only one* who could make atonement. He was the one exclusively designated by God for this purpose (Leviticus 16:2, 16:29–33). None of the other priests had any part in this; in fact, they had to remain outside the tabernacle with the rest of the people.

    Similarly, Jesus is the only one who can make atonement for us! In fact, this was God's plan from before creation!

    Forasmuch as ye know that ye were not redeemed with corruptible things, as silver and gold, from your vain conversation received by tradition from your fathers; But *with the precious blood of Christ*, as of *a lamb without blemish and without spot*: Who verily *was foreordained before the foundation of the world*, but was manifest in these last times for you. (1 Peter 1:18–20)

Jesus saith unto him, I am the way, the truth, and the life: *no man cometh unto the Father, but by me.* (John 14:6)

Neither is there salvation in any other: for there is *none other name under heaven given among men, whereby we must be saved.* (Acts 4:12)

2. **High Priest, Holy:** The high priest was made holy by God—in the Lord's instructions to the priests, He says, "I am the Lord who sanctifies you" (Leviticus 22:32, see also 21:15, 23 and 22:9). This sanctification by God was accomplished through the high priest's original anointing, by the priestly garments he wore, and by the sacrifices that he made for himself. You may recall from Exodus that the high priest wore a turban with a plate in which the words "Holy to the Lord" were engraved (Exodus 28:36–37). Also, you see above in the description of his Day of Atonement duties that he was required to sacrifice a bull and a ram as sacrifices for his own sins.

Similarly, Jesus is holy but with a huge distinction. The high priest's holiness was *imputed* and *temporal*, whereas Jesus's holiness is *intrinsic* and *eternal*! As God the Son, He has been holy from all eternity! The writer of Hebrews gives us glorious insight into Jesus's holy nature, which was profoundly on full display in His passion:

His Nature (God)
For unto which of the angels said he at any time, Thou art my Son, this day have I begotten thee? And again, *I will be to him a Father, and he shall be to me a Son*? And again, when he bringeth in the first begotten into the world, he saith, And *let all the angels of God worship him.* And of the angels he saith, Who maketh his angels spirits, and his ministers a flame of fire. But *unto the Son he saith, Thy throne, O God, is for ever and ever*: a sceptre of righteousness is the sceptre of thy kingdom. (Hebrews 1:5–8)

His Passion (Learned Obedience, Made Perfect)
Who *in the days of his flesh*, when he had *offered up prayers and supplications with strong crying and tears* unto him that was able to save him from death, and was heard in that he feared; *Though he were a Son, yet learned he obedience by the things which he suffered*; And *being made perfect, he became the author of eternal salvation* unto all them that obey him; *Called of God an high priest* after the order of Melchisedec. (Hebrews 5:7–10)

3. **High Priest, in God's Presence:** The high priest on this one day a year enters through the veil into the Holy of Holies and stands in the very presence of God! The Ark of the Covenant with the mercy seat on top is the center of God's presence. The pillar of cloud by day and the pillar of fire by night touch the mercy seat and extend upward to

heaven, so the high priest would literally stand before the pillar of cloud as he offered the atoning sacrifices.

Similarly, Jesus, forty days after His resurrection (Acts 1:3, 1:9–11), ascended back to heaven, where He has been in God's presence ever since.

Stephen's testimony as he was being stoned to death
But he, being full of the Holy Ghost, *looked up stedfastly into heaven, and saw the glory of God*, and *Jesus standing on the right hand of God, And said, Behold, I see the heavens opened, and the Son of man standing on the right hand of God.* (Acts 7:55–56)

For Christ is *not entered into the holy places made with hands*, which are the figures of the true; *but into heaven itself, now to appear in the presence of God for us*: (Hebrews 9:24)

Having therefore, brethren, *boldness* to *enter into the holiest by the blood of Jesus*, By *a new and living way*, which he hath consecrated for us, *through the veil, that is to say, his flesh*. (Hebrews 10:19–20)

4. **High Priest, People's Representative:** The high priest entered the Holy of Holies as the *representative* of the people—everyone else had to remain outside the tabernacle! You may recall two articles of his priestly garment that indicate this—the *breastpiece* of the linen ephod, which had twelve stones in four rows of three, each engraved with the name of a tribe of Israel thereon (Exodus 28:15–21), and the *two onyx stones*, which had the names of the twelve tribes engraved on them, six on each stone (Exodus 28:9–10). The onyx stones were used to fasten the linen ephod and breastpiece to the shoulders of the priest's robe. Note that the breastpiece was referred to as *the breastpiece of judgment* (v. 15), indicating that the high priest was, in effect, bringing the people into God's presence *for judgment*.

Similarly, Jesus is our representative and our advocate before God. In fact, He is our righteousness before God!

My little children, these things write I unto you, that ye sin not. And if any man sin, *we have an advocate with the Father, Jesus Christ the righteous*: And *he is the propitiation for our sins*: and not for ours only, but also for the sins of the whole world. (1 John 2:1–2)

For he hath made him to be sin for us, who knew no sin; *that we might be made the righteousness of God in him*. (2 Corinthians 5:21)

Forasmuch then as the children are partakers of flesh and blood, he also himself likewise took part of the same; that through death he might destroy him that had the power of death, that is, the devil; And deliver them who through fear of death were all their lifetime subject to bondage. For verily he took not on him the nature of angels; *but he took on him the seed of Abraham.* Wherefore in all things *it behoved him to be made like unto his brethren, that he might be a merciful and faithful high priest* in things pertaining to God, to make reconciliation for the sins of the people. For *in that he himself hath suffered being tempted, he is able to succour them that are tempted.* (Hebrews 2:14–18)

For we have not an high priest which cannot be touched with the feeling of our infirmities; but *was in all points tempted like as we are, yet without sin. Let us therefore come boldly unto the throne of grace, that we may obtain mercy, and find grace to help in time of need.* (Hebrews 4:15–16)

5. **High Priest, Offered Incense:** The high priest took burning coals and offered incense in the Holy of Holies. In the Day of Atonement account, we read the following:

And he shall take *a censer full of burning coals* of fire from off the altar before the LORD, and *his hands full of sweet incense* beaten small, and *bring it within the vail:* And *he shall put the incense upon the fire before the LORD, that the cloud of the incense may cover the mercy seat* that is upon the testimony, that he die not: (Leviticus 16:12–13)

Incense, in the Bible, is symbolic of prayer. So the high priest was required to bring incense into the Holy of Holies. Notice also that incense was burnt in enough quantity so that its cloud *covered* the mercy seat. Wow! What a picture of Christ!

Similarly, Jesus, our eternal high priest, prays for us in heaven. Not only was His life characterized by prayer on earth, as He would daily rise early and pray and, at times, would pray through the night (Luke 6:12–13), but we are told that He prays for us in heaven also.

But this man, because he continueth ever, *hath an unchangeable priesthood. Wherefore he is able also to save them to the uttermost that come unto God by him, seeing he ever liveth to make intercession for them.* (Hebrews 7:24–25)

6. **High Priest, Offered Sacrifice:** The high priest offered blood sacrifice in the presence of God within the Holy of Holies. He offered the bull for himself and his household and the sacrificial goat for the people. He then took the blood of the bull and of the goat and sprinkled it on the mercy seat to make atonement for himself, the other priests, the

Holy Place, the tabernacle, and all the people. The two rams, one for himself and his household, and the other for all the people were offered on the bronze altar as burnt offerings, consumed in their entirety.

Similarly, Jesus, our eternal high priest offered a blood sacrifice, which was accomplished on Calvary's hill on a cruel Roman cross, and presented His offering to God in the tabernacle of heaven itself!

But Christ being come *an high priest of good things to come, by a greater and more perfect tabernacle, not made with hands,* that is to say, not of this building; Neither by the blood of goats and calves, *but by his own blood he entered in once into the holy place, having obtained eternal redemption for us.* For if the blood of bulls and of goats, and the ashes of an heifer sprinkling the unclean, sanctifieth to the purifying of the flesh: *How much more shall the blood of Christ, who through the eternal Spirit offered himself without spot to God, purge your conscience from dead works to serve the living God?* (Hebrews 9:11–14)

7. **The People Remained Outside:** This too is a picture of salvation. There was nothing whatsoever the people could *do* to accomplish their atonement. Their atonement was accomplished solely by the high priest. As they waited outside the tabernacle, all they could do was *trust* that what the high priest was doing would provide for their atonement.

And *there shall be no man in the tabernacle of the congregation when he goeth in to make an atonement in the holy place, until he come out,* and have made an atonement for himself, and for his household, and for all the congregation of Israel. (Leviticus 16:17)

What a picture of salvation! This can be seen in the words of Jesus and Paul.

Then said they unto him, *What shall we do, that we might work the works of God?* Jesus answered and said unto them, *This is the work of God, that ye believe on him whom he hath sent.* (John 6:28–29)

For by grace are ye saved through faith; and that not of yourselves: it is the gift of God: *Not of works, lest any man should boast. For we are his workmanship, created in Christ Jesus* unto good works, which God hath before ordained that we should walk in them. (Ephesians 2:8–10)

8. **The Two Goats:** The two goats are an extraordinary *type* of Christ! They were used to atone for the people. They cast lots to determine the role of each goat. One lot was for the Lord and the other for the scapegoat. The goat upon which the Lord's lot fell was a

sacrificial offering for sin. He was slain, and his blood was sprinkled on the mercy seat. The goat upon which the lot fell to be the scapegoat was presented alive before the Lord to make atonement. Aaron was to lay both his hands upon the head of the live goat and confess over him all the sins of the children of Israel, putting them upon the head of the goat. The goat was then sent away by the hand of a fit man into the wilderness, where the goat would bear upon himself all their sins unto an uninhabited land.

Similarly, Jesus, who accomplished our atonement, is *pictured* in these two goats, as He became both the sacrifice for our sins as well as the scapegoat, by taking the blame and punishment for our sins upon Himself!

9. **The Mercy Seat:** On the Day of Atonement only, the altar used was the mercy seat atop the lid of the Ark of the Covenant. On all other days, the bronze altar was used for sacrifices. Two cherubim, one at each end of the mercy seat, extended over it, facing down toward it, representing the loving gaze of our Heavenly Father. What a name for this special altar!

Similarly, Jesus became our means of mercy! No wonder the writer of Hebrews proclaimed, "Therefore, *let us draw near with confidence* to the throne of grace, so *that we may receive mercy* and find grace to help in time of need!" (Hebrews 4:16).

10. **All Sins Forgiven:** On this one day of the year, the tenth day of the seventh month (Leviticus 23:27–32) *all* the people's sins were forgiven! Every person's slate was wiped clean! On every other day of the year, offerings were brought by the people to receive atonement for *specific* sins. A sacrifice was required every time a sin was committed, both for intentional sins and for unintentional or careless sins. Can you imagine the angst the people felt, questioning whether they had fulfilled their sacrificial quota to cover every sin they had committed during the year. What a blessing it must have been for them to know that on this one day of the year, they were fully cleansed and forgiven! No more sin debt hung over their heads!

Similarly, Jesus accomplished our forgiveness and cleansing! However, His forgiveness and cleansing are not only for past sins, but also cover future sins! John the apostle tells us this in his first epistle.

If we confess our sins, he is faithful and just to *forgive us our sins*, and to *cleanse us from all unrighteousness*. (1 John 1:9)

So we see in these ten pictures a beautiful portrait of the finished work of Christ that paid for our salvation. This is the gospel message!

5. **Regulations for the Priests** (Type/Shadow)

Leviticus 21 and 22 provided regulations that the priests had to follow. These regulations also prohibited certain people from becoming priests. The priests were to be physically perfect, without defect. The following guidelines are found in Leviticus 21 and 22 and fall into two general categories—defilement and physical defect as noted below. Falling into the categories below resulted in either a suspension of priestly duties or a permanent prohibition:

Defilement

1) Defilement from touching a dead person (except for mother, father, son, daughter, brother, or virgin sister) (21:1–4)
2) Making baldness on his head, shaving off the edges of his beard, or cutting his skin (21:5)
3) Taking a woman profaned by harlotry or marrying a divorced woman (21:6–7)
4) The anointed priest (on duty) shall not uncover his head or tear his clothes nor even defile himself by touching his dead father or mother, nor leave the sanctuary (21:10–12)
5) Could not marry anyone other than a virgin from his own relatives (tribe of Levi) (21:13–15)
6) One who touches any teeming thing (unclean insect or bird, reptiles, and other animals) (22:5–7)
7) One who touches an animal that died naturally or was killed by another animal (22:8)

Physical Defect

1) blind or lame man (21:18)
2) man with a disfigured face or deformed limb (21:18)
3) man with a broken foot or hand (21:19)
4) hunchback or dwarf (21:20)
5) eye defect, eczema, scabs, crushed testicles (21:20)
6) leper or one with a discharge (22:4)

All these prohibitions against defilement and physical defect regarding the priesthood are *types* that symbolically point to Christ, our perfect high priest, in the same way that only animals without defect were to be brought for sacrifices, which point to Christ as our perfect sacrifice!

6. The Lamp and the Bread of the Sanctuary (Type/Shadow)

The Lamp (Leviticus 24:1–4)

The priests were required to keep the seven lamps on the lampstand burning all night (from evening until morning). This is a *type* of Christ, who proclaimed that He is the light of the world.

Then spake Jesus again unto them, saying, *I am the light of the world*: he that followeth me shall not walk in darkness, but shall have the light of life. (John 8:12)

The Bread of the Sanctuary (Leviticus 24:5–9)

Every Sabbath, the priests were required to bake twelve cakes (of bread, v. 7) and set them on the table of bread in two rows of six, placing frankincense on them. It is interesting that the bread was laid out in twelve cakes—one for each of the twelve tribes, thus a *picture* of Israel's identification with the bread. At this time, the priests would remove the previous Sabbath's bread and replace it with the freshly baked bread. They were permitted to feed their families with the week-old sanctified bread. The bread is a *type* of Christ, and the eating of the bread is a *type* of the bread portion of the Lord's Supper. Note below Jesus's proclamation that He is the Bread of Life, which He made after the miraculous feeding of the 5,000. The excerpted verses below are part of Jesus's response to the Jews who requested a sign like the manna that Moses gave. Jesus explained that it was God, not Moses, who gave the manna. He then contrasted Himself as the Bread of Life, which gives eternal life, with manna, which only temporarily sustains life.

> For the bread of God is he which cometh down from heaven, and giveth life unto the world. Then said they unto him, Lord, evermore give us this bread. And *Jesus said unto them, I am the bread of life*: he that cometh to me shall never hunger; and he that believeth on me shall never thirst. (John 6:33–35)

> Verily, verily, I say unto you, *He that believeth on me hath everlasting life. I am that bread of life.* Your fathers did eat manna in the wilderness, and are dead. This is the bread which cometh down from heaven, that a man may eat thereof, and not die. *I am the living bread which came down from heaven: if any man eat of this bread, he shall live for ever*: and *the bread that I will give is my flesh, which I will give for the life of the world.* (John 6:47–51)

7. Sabbatical Year, Year of Jubilee (Type/Shadow)

Sabbatical Year (Leviticus 25:1–7)

In the Jewish calendar, there is the weekly Sabbath, the sabbatical year, and the year of Jubilee. The Sabbath principle was first introduced in Genesis 2:1–3, wherein God rested from His work of creation on the seventh day, and He blessed and sanctified the seventh day. The fourth commandment is "Remember the Sabbath day, to keep it holy" (Exodus 20:8–11). In the Leviticus passage noted above, the idea is further expanded—every seventh year is a sabbatical year. In the sabbatical year, God instructed that the land was to have a sabbath rest—the people were not to sow their field, nor to prune their vineyard, nor to reap the aftergrowth. Thus, we have another example of the Sabbath principle in the Old Testament—that is, the principle of rest and devotion to God. The author of Hebrews makes the comparison between a believer's rest in Christ and God's rest from His work of creation on the seventh day. That is, the believer rests from the futility of his working to earn God's favor and trusts in Christ's finished work on the cross. This is found in Hebrews 4:9–10: "There remaineth therefore a rest to the people of God. For he that is entered into his rest, he also hath ceased from his own works, as God did from his."

Year of Jubilee (Leviticus 25:8–22)

Additionally, the Jews were instructed to count off seven sabbatical years, yielding forty-nine years. So on the Day of Atonement of the fiftieth year, they sounded a ram's horn to consecrate the fiftieth year as the year of Jubilee. So the year of Jubilee was celebrated every fiftieth year on Israel's calendar and was a very special year to them. During the year of Jubilee, the following things would happen:

1) The year of Jubilee was an additional sabbatical year (that is, year 49 and year 50 would be observed as consecutive sabbatical years). So God would so bless the sowing in the sixth year of the seventh sabbatical cycle that it would yield crops for three years, the third year being the year of Jubilee (Leviticus 25:11–12, 25:18–22).
2) Anyone who sold his land to another person would reclaim and return to his property (Leviticus 25:13–16, 25:23–28).
3) Anyone who sold a house in an unwalled city was allowed to reclaim and move back in it (Leviticus 25:31). It is noted that a house in a walled city that was sold could be redeemed up to a year after the sale but, if not redeemed within that period, became the permanent property of the buyer and did not revert in the year of Jubilee.
4) Any person who became an indentured servant to pay a debt was released from service on the year of Jubilee (Leviticus 25:10, 25:35–41)

So the year of Jubilee represented freedom—people were able to return to their property, all debts were forgiven, and all Israelite slaves were set free! The freedom of the year of Jubilee is a *picture* of the freedom we have in Christ, whose death on the cross purchased our forgiveness from our debt of sin that we had no means to pay. The return to the land is a picture of our entrance into the millennial kingdom and our eternal habitation in the new heavens and new earth. The imagery in Revelation 21 and 22 speaks of an existence similar to but better than the Garden of Eden. It is a *return* in the sense that our forefather Adam lost it, but we as believers will reclaim it.

> And I heard a great voice out of heaven saying, Behold, *the tabernacle of God is with men, and he will dwell with them,* and *they shall be his people, and God himself shall be with them, and be their God.* And *God shall wipe away all tears from their eyes; and there shall be no more death, neither sorrow, nor crying,*

neither shall there be any more pain: for the former things are passed away.
(Revelation 21:3–4)

And he shewed me *a pure river of water of life, clear as crystal, proceeding out of
the throne of God and of the Lamb.* In the midst of the street of it, *and on either
side of the river, was there the tree of life, which bare twelve manner of fruits,* and
yielded her fruit every month: and *the leaves of the tree were for the healing of
the nations.* And *there shall be no more curse:* but *the throne of God and of the
Lamb shall be in it; and his servants shall serve him:* And *they shall see his face;*
and his name shall be in their foreheads. (Revelation 22:1–4)

Jesus's death on the cross purchased our right to become children of God in lieu of slaves of
sin under God's wrath!

8. Law of Redemption and Kinsman Redeemer (Type/Shadow)

This provision of the Mosaic Law provided for the redemption of land or a house in a walled
city that was sold, and for the redemption of an indentured servant (Leviticus 25:23–56).

1) **Redemption of Land**: If an Israelite was forced to sell his property because of financial
   instability, this law allowed him to buy it back as soon as he had the means.

2) **Kinsman Redeemer**: If the landowner never obtained the necessary funds to buy
   back his land, his nearest kinsman could buy the land back for him. If neither he nor
   a relative was able to buy back the land, it would still revert to his ownership in the
   year of Jubilee.

3) **Redemption of a House in a Walled City**: If an Israelite were forced to sell his house in
   a walled city, he had a redemption right for one full year. If he obtained the necessary
   funds within that period, he could buy back his house. However, if he was unable to
   buy the house back within that time, it would remain permanently in the hands of
   the purchaser and not revert in the year of Jubilee. In America, the right of property
   redemption is patterned after the Mosaic Law; at least it is in Alabama. After our
   house flooded in Louisiana, we purchased a house in Alabama that was in foreclosure.
   The person whose house is in foreclosure has up to one year to pay the delinquent
   payments and interest to reclaim the house for himself. When we purchased our
   house on December 30, 2016, the previous owner had until June 2017 to pay their
   missed payments and interest. If that had happened, we would have had to vacate the
   house and our purchase price would have been refunded. After June 2017, the right of
   redemption expired, and the house was ours free and clear.

4) **Redemption of a House in an Unwalled City**: If an Israelite were forced to sell his
   house in an unwalled city, he had the right of redemption to buy it back himself,

or one of his kinsmen could buy it back for him. There was no time limit on this right. However, if he never found the means to buy it back, it would still revert to his ownership in the year of Jubilee.

5) **Redemption of a Poor Man**: If a poor man is forced to sell himself as an indentured servant, he would retain the right of redemption with no time limit. A near relative (kinsman redeemer) would have the right to purchase his freedom, or if the man himself obtained the necessary funds, he could purchase his own freedom. However, if neither he nor a near relative were able to purchase his freedom, he would become free in the year of Jubilee.

This idea of redemption was ingrained in the Mosaic Law. It was a reminder of God's ownership of everything, and it was another instance of a *type* of the redemption that we have in Christ! Additionally, the near kinsman is a *type* of Christ our Redeemer!

Summary of Prophetic Elements in Leviticus

1.	The Sacrificial System and Priesthood	(Type/Shadow)
2.	Identification with the Sacrifice	(Type/Shadow)
3.	Laws on Leprosy and Uncleanness	(Type/Shadow)
4.	Day of Atonement	(Type/Shadow)
5.	Regulations for the Priests (Imperfections)	(Type/Shadow)
6.	The Lamp and the Bread of the Sanctuary	(Type/Shadow)
7.	Sabbatical Year and the Year of Jubilee	(Type/Shadow)
8.	Law of Redemption and Kinsman Redeemer	(Type/Shadow)

12

JESUS IN NUMBERS

As we continue our journey through the Pentateuch, we will now turn our attention to the book of Numbers. Genesis is the book of beginnings, ending with Israel joining Joseph in Egypt to escape the famine. Exodus records the plight of Israel enslaved in Egypt, its birth as God's nation and His deliverance of them, and their wilderness wanderings. Leviticus is concerned with worship and ordinances governing civilian life. Now in Numbers we see the continuing story of Israel, God's numbering of the people, their continued wilderness wanderings, beginning with their departure from Mount Sinai.

As we go through this book, we will see some remarkable *types* of Christ. One of them is referenced in Jesus's conversation with Nicodemus in John 3.

1. **Ordination of the Levites** (OT Language and Culture)

Numbers 8:5–22

In this passage we have the ordination of the Levites. I see in this passage some *mini types* that I'd like for us to consider. Not all messianic prophecy and types in the Old Testament are about Christ specifically. Many are about Him, to be sure, but some relate to the new covenant in Him, some relate to the salvation of the Gentiles, some to redemption, forgiveness and cleansing from sin, and various other things. Perhaps the best way to start our trek through this passage is to begin with a simple outline of the scripture passages below:

Exodus 12	The first Passover, slaying of the firstborn males, and exodus from Egypt
Exodus 13:1–2, 13:10–15	All firstborn males belong to the Lord (purchased by Passover lamb's blood)
Exodus 28	Only Aaron's descendants could be priests, description of priestly garments
Exodus 29	Consecration of Aaron and his sons as priests

Numbers 8:5–13	Ordination of the Levites
Numbers 8:14–18	Levites substituted in place of all firstborn sons (see also Numbers 3:11–12)
Numbers 8:19–22	Non-Aaronic Levites given to assist Aaron and his descendants the priests

In Exodus 12, we read about the first Passover in preparation for Israel's exodus from Egypt. Each household was to obtain a one-year-old male lamb without defect, slay it on the fourteenth day, dip a bunch of hyssop into the blood, and spread it on the doorposts and lintel of the house. This they did, and when the death angel came to slay all the firstborn males of Egypt, both man and beast, he passed over all the Israelite houses because of the blood.

In Exodus 13, God required the consecration of all the firstborn males of Israel as belonging to Him, since He had purchased them for Himself with the Passover lamb's blood. The firstborn male beasts were required as animal sacrifices, with the exception that a donkey could be redeemed by sacrificing a lamb. All firstborn sons were to be redeemed with a lamb's blood. This was to commemorate annually God's deliverance of Israel's firstborn sons on the night of the Exodus.

Fast-forward to Numbers 3:11–12, and we see that God made a substitution—instead of sanctifying *every firstborn son from all the tribes* as belonging to him, He chose to substitute *every Levite son*. Therefore, the Levites belonged to God—they did not inherit any property as did the other tribes, but they were given cities to live in. Also, their food was an allotment obtained from the animals they sacrificed in their priestly service.

In Exodus 28:1–4, 40–43, we see that not every Levite man could serve as priest, but only Aaron and his sons (immediate and descendants) could serve in that capacity.

In Exodus 29:1–30, we read about the consecration of Aaron and his sons as priests prior to being placed into service.

This brings us to Numbers 8. The first four verses are about the golden lampstand. In Numbers 8:5–22, we are given the ordination of the non-priest Levites who were not descendants of Aaron. This included sprinkling purifying water over them, shaving their whole body, and washing their clothes. It also included the sacrificial part of their ordination, which included two bulls—one for a sin offering and the other for a burnt offering. Aaron also made atonement for them (v. 21). So, they were thus set apart from the children of Israel for God's service in assisting Aaron and his sons the priests. In the final verses (23–26) of the chapter, we are given the age of twenty-five when they could begin serving, and the mandatory retirement age of fifty.

In Numbers 8:5–13, we have the ordination of the non-Aaronic Levite men. It seems clear from verses 6 and 13 that this ordination was for the Levite men who were not descendants of Aaron.

In Numbers 8:14–18, the Lord again mentions the substitution of all Levite men as belonging to Him in place of the firstborn sons of every tribe, as he previously noted in Numbers 3:11–12.

In Numbers 8:19–22, we are told that the men so ordained were given by God to assist Aaron and his sons the priests. That is, they would not offer sacrifices as priests but were to assist them, so they were responsible for the maintenance and transport of the tabernacle, its furniture, holy vessels, and other implements.

So let's unpack all this and see the types that relate to the Messiah.

1) **God's Possession:** It was God's purpose to have the men from the Levitical tribe as His personal possession—God had *bought* all the firstborn of Israel, represented by the Levitical men, with the blood of the Passover lamb. Similarly, Jesus purchased the church and every believer with His own blood, so we are His possession! Peter made this proclamation of the church in his first letter: "But you are A CHOSEN RACE, A ROYAL PRIESTHOOD, A HOLY NATION, A PEOPLE FOR *God's* OWN POSSESSION, so that you may proclaim the excellencies of Him who has called you out of darkness into His marvelous light" (1 Peter 2:9).

2) **Redemption, Purchased by Blood:** The Levite men were redeemed. Initially, every firstborn son had to be redeemed with a lamb's blood, and later, in their stead, all Levite men had to be redeemed with the blood of a bull (Numbers 8:8). Similarly, Jesus redeemed us from our sin with His own blood (Romans 3:24; 1 Corinthians 6:20; Ephesians 1:7, 5:25; Colossians 1:13–14; Hebrews 9:12; 1 Peter 1:18–19, 1 John 1:7, Revelation 1:5). So as the Levites were the community of the redeemed under the Mosaic Law, the church is the community of the redeemed in the New Testament era. Paul stated, "In Him *we have redemption through His blood*, the forgiveness of our trespasses, according to the riches of His grace" (Ephesians 1:7).

3) **Sanctification:** The Levitical men were sanctified—set apart for God's service. Similarly, we as believers in the church are sanctified by the blood of Christ and by His sanctifying work in our lives (Acts 26:18; 1 Corinthians 1:2, 6:11; 2 Corinthians 5:21; Philippians 1:6, 2:13; Hebrews 10:14). Paul gave us this incredible truth in his second letter to the Corinthians: "He made Him who knew no sin *to be* sin on our behalf, so *that we might become the righteousness of God in Him*" (2 Corinthians 5:21). Christ took our sins upon Himself on the cross, and He sanctifies every believer, enabling him to live righteously.

4) **Purpose to Serve God:** All the Levites were set apart to serve God. They were sanctified for that purpose. In this sense, they are a picture of the church. Jesus told the disciples

"You are the salt of the earth … the light of the world" (Matthew 5:13–14), and He gave us the Great Commission. The apostle Paul said, "Whatever you do, do your work heartily, as for the Lord rather than for men, knowing that from the Lord you will receive the reward of the inheritance. It is the Lord Christ whom you serve" (Colossians 3:23). So we are set apart to serve God.

So we see in this ordination of the Levites various *types* of the church, in that we are God's possession; we're His redeemed, we're sanctified by Him, and our purpose is to serve Him, as we follow Him in obedience. So all these things point to Christ. In chapter 8, "Mechanics of Old Testament Messianic Prophecy," we saw that one of the prophetic devices found in the Old Testament was the language and culture surrounding the Mosaic Law. The law produced a language that looked forward to the New Testament fulfillment of various *types* and *shadows* embedded in the Old Testament law, so this rite of the ordination of the Levites is just another example.

2. Second Passover Observance (Type/Shadow)

> And the Lord spake unto Moses in the wilderness of Sinai, *in the first month of the second year after they were come out of the land of Egypt*, saying, Let the children of Israel also keep the passover at his appointed season. In the fourteenth day of this month, at even, ye shall keep it in his appointed season: according to all the rites of it, and according to all the ceremonies thereof, shall ye keep it. And Moses spake unto the children of Israel, that they should keep the passover. And *they kept the passover on the fourteenth day of the first month at even in the wilderness of Sinai*: according to all that the Lord commanded Moses, so did the children of Israel. (Numbers 9:1–5)

This was the Israelites' second observance of the Passover. The first observance had been in Egypt the night just before their exodus, and now they were celebrating it in the wilderness at Sinai, where they had received the law that included the Ten Commandments. It is further noted in this passage that if a person was made unclean by touching a dead person (a near relative) or if he were away on a far journey (Numbers 9:5–10), or if he were an alien (Numbers 9:14), he would still be allowed to celebrate the Passover.

As we noted before in Exodus, the Passover is a *picture* of the salvation we have in Christ. The one-year-old *male unblemished lamb* is a *picture* of Christ, the sinless Son of God. The slain lamb's blood was spread on the vertical doorposts and horizontal lintel (in Egypt), which is a picture of the wooden post and crossbeam forming the cross that Jesus shed His blood on for us. The extra detail in verses 5–10 and 14 allowing the ceremonially unclean, those far away, and the alien to participate further enhances the Passover as a *type* of salvation, in that *all* sinners who place their faith in Christ are saved. The aliens among them would be Gentiles, which is a *picture* of God's plan to include the Gentiles in salvation.

Below is a description of *how* the Passover is a *type* of Christ repeated from the Exodus chapter.

- An *unblemished* male lamb *one year* old—this points to Christ's *sinlessness* and His crucifixion *in the prime of His life.*
- Blood on *wooden* or stone *doorpost and lintel* (KJV "upper door post")—Jesus's blood on the *vertical* and *horizontal* members of a wooden cross (wood doorpost suggested by Exodus 21:5–6)
- Death angel *prevented* from harming household *with the blood*—those who trust in the *atoning blood* of Christ are *protected* from eternal death
- Passover lamb eaten with *unleavened* bread—leaven in the Bible represents *sin*; this also points to the *sinlessness* of Christ
- Passover lamb eaten with *bitter* herbs—a picture of the *bitter agony* of Jesus's passion
- Jesus gives new meaning to the Passover at the Last Supper

3. Pillar of Cloud and Fire (Theophany)

We first saw the pillar of cloud and fire in Exodus; the pillar of cloud and fire was God's continual abiding presence with the children of Israel. In this passage we are given more detail about the theophany—we are told how Israel would break camp, to set out on their next journey, then set up camp upon arrival at their next destination, all based on the movement or stopping of the pillar of cloud or fire. All theophanies in the Old Testament are *types* of Christ as Immanuel (God with us). Below are excerpts from the noted passage.

> And *on the day that the tabernacle was reared up the cloud covered the tabernacle,* namely, the tent of the testimony: and at even there was upon the tabernacle as it were the appearance of fire, until the morning. So it was alway: *the cloud covered it by day, and the appearance of fire by night.* And *when the cloud was taken up from the tabernacle, then after that the children of Israel journeyed: and in the place where the cloud abode, there the children of Israel pitched their tents* ...

> Or *whether it were two days, or a month, or a year, that the cloud tarried upon the tabernacle,* remaining thereon, *the children of Israel abode in their tents, and journeyed not: but when it was taken up, they journeyed.* At the commandment of the LORD they rested in the tents, and at the commandment of the LORD they journeyed: they kept the charge of the LORD, at the commandment of the LORD by the hand of Moses. (Numbers 9:15–23)

4. Aaron's Rod that Budded (Type/Shadow)

In Numbers 16, we are given the story of Korah's rebellion against Moses (and by extension, against God). To make an example of Korah, God caused him and his company to be swallowed alive when the ground opened up beneath their feet and then closed back over them. To avert future rebellions, the Lord had Moses assemble with leaders of the twelve tribes, with each one bringing a rod with his name inscribed thereon. This account is given in the passage below:

And the LORD spake unto Moses, saying, Speak unto the children of Israel, and *take of every one of them a rod according to the house of their fathers,* of all their princes *according to the house of their fathers twelve rods: write thou every man's name upon his rod.* And *thou shalt write Aaron's name upon the rod of Levi:* for one rod shall be for the head of the house of their fathers. And thou shalt lay them up in the tabernacle of the congregation before the testimony, where I will meet with you. And *it shall come to pass, that the man's rod, whom I shall choose, shall blossom:* and I will make to cease from me the murmurings of the children of Israel, whereby they murmur against you. And Moses spake unto the children of Israel, and every one of their princes gave him a rod apiece, for each prince one, according to their fathers' houses, even twelve rods: and the rod of Aaron was among their rods. And *Moses laid up the rods before the LORD in the tabernacle of witness.* And it came to pass, that *on the morrow Moses went into the tabernacle* of witness; *and, behold, the rod of Aaron for the house of Levi was budded, and brought forth buds, and bloomed blossoms, and yielded almonds.* And Moses brought out all the rods from before the LORD unto all the children of Israel: and they looked, and took every man his rod. And the LORD said unto Moses, *Bring Aaron's rod again before the testimony, to be kept for a token against the rebels*; and thou shalt quite take away their murmurings from me, that they die not. (Numbers 17:1–10)

So, what is the point of this story? A dead rod from the priestly tribe of Levi budded, blossomed, and even yielded almonds! You must admit, that doesn't happen every day! Have you ever seen an old person walking with a cane that had live leaves or blooms on it? Levi was the priestly tribe—they were the worship leaders, and the care and transport of the tabernacle was their responsibility, as noted earlier. So, we have in this dead rod that budded, a picture of the death and resurrection of the Lord Jesus Christ! Also, this rod identified Aaron as the one chosen by God to serve as the first high priest, who was temporal (as the dead rod would suggest). However, the rod's budding is a picture of our resurrected eternal high priest, Jesus Christ!

5. Ashes of a Red Heifer Used for Purification (Type/Shadow)

In Numbers 19:1–10, the ordinance of the red heifer is given. At God's command, Moses instructed the people to bring an unblemished red heifer with no defect, and on which a yoke was never placed. Eleazar, the high priest, was to witness the slaying of the animal outside the camp. Then Eleazar was to take some of the blood with his finger and sprinkle it toward the front of the tabernacle seven times. Then the heifer was to be burned in his sight. Then he was to take cedar wood, hyssop, and scarlet material and cast it into the fire of the burning animal. Then he and the others assisting in this were to cleanse themselves. In verse 9 below, we find the purpose for this ordinance.

> Now a man who is clean shall *gather up the ashes of the heifer and put them outside the camp in a clean place*, and the congregation of the sons of Israel shall *keep them for water to remove impurity; it is purification from sin.* (Numbers 19:9 NASB)

Here we have another instance of a sacrifice—in this case a red heifer. The ashes of the red heifer, cedar, hyssop, and scarlet material were stored in a clean place outside the camp, to be kept for purification from uncleanness. At the time of its use for that purpose, some ashes would be sprinkled in water and then applied to the unclean person.

We have noted previously that all of the sacrifices were pictures pointing to Christ's perfect sacrifice. So, what is the symbology of this *type*? It is interesting that a *red* heifer was chosen, and one without defect—pointing to our perfect sinless Savior. Could this red color be symbolic of blood? Also, it is interesting that cedar*wood*, hyssop, and scarlet material were chosen. Jesus was crucified on a wooden cross. Hyssop was used at Passover to paint the unblemished lamb's blood on the doorpost and lintel of the home. Scarlet material is again a picture of blood. Even though this purification was for uncleanness rather than moral sin, uncleanness is still a picture of our separation from God as a result of the fall. This cleansing ash-water, resulting from a sacrificed animal, is another picture of the spotless blood of Christ, which cleanses us from all sin!

6. Water from the Rock (Type/Shadow)

Numbers 20:8–13

We were introduced to the first instance of God providing water from a rock as we were journeying in our study through Exodus in chapter 17. Now, in Numbers 20, we see the second instance. Borrowing from the Exodus study, we saw that both the *rock* and the *water* are *types* of Christ.

The rock as a *type*

We also saw Paul's reference to a rock as being a *type* of Christ. Borrowing from that passage, Paul writes, "all our fathers were under the cloud, and all passed through the sea; and were baptized under Moses … and did all eat the same spiritual meat; and did all drink the same spiritual drink; for they drank of that spiritual Rock that followed them; and that Rock was Christ" (1 Corinthians 10:1–4).

In Psalm 118:22–24, which is clearly a messianic psalm, we have

> ²² The stone which the builders refused is become the head stone of the corner.
> ²³ This is the LORD's doing; it is marvellous in our eyes.

We see Jesus quote this verse as referring to Himself in Matthew 21:42, and it was quoted by the apostles in Acts 4:11, Ephesians 2:20, and 1 Peter 2:7.

I will add an additional reference. After Peter's great confession that Jesus was "the Christ, the Son of the Living God" (Matthew 16:16–18), Jesus said to him, "You are Peter, and upon *this rock* I will build My church." *This rock* is generally interpreted in one of three ways:

1) As referring to Peter (or Peter and the apostles)
2) As referring to Peter's confession of Christ
3) As referring to Jesus Himself

If the third interpretation is correct, we have another instance of Jesus being referenced as either a rock or a stone.

Water as a type

Jesus told the Samaritan woman that He would give her *living water* and that whoever drinks of that water shall never thirst again and that it would be in her a *well of water springing up into everlasting life* (John 4:10–14). We further saw at the feast that Jesus cried out, saying, "If any man thirst let him come to me in drink. *He that believeth on Me … out of his belly shall flow rivers of living water*" (John 7:37–39).

What is quite interesting, however, is the different instruction that God gave Moses in each instance. In the Exodus passage, God told Moses to "smite the rock," whereas in the captioned passage, God told Moses to "speak to the rock" (v. 8). In the Exodus account, Moses obeyed God's command and smote the rock, and water came forth. However, in our current passage in Numbers, Moses, because of his exasperation with his grumbling followers, failed to obey God's command, but reacted in anger.

> And Moses and Aaron gathered the congregation together before the rock, and he said unto them, *Hear now, ye rebels; must we fetch you water out of this rock? And Moses lifted up his hand, and with his rod he smote the rock twice: and the water came out abundantly,* and the congregation drank, and their beasts also. (Numbers 20:10–11)

As you may recall, this single act of disobedience kept Moses from entering the Promised Land.

> And the LORD spake unto Moses and Aaron, *Because ye believed me not, to sanctify me in the eyes of the children of Israel, therefore ye shall not bring this congregation into the land which I have given them.*

Some expositors have taught that since the rock is a *type* of Christ, the first incident where God instructed Moses to smite the rock (and he obeyed) is a picture of Christ's death by scourging and crucifixion, noting that Christ died *once*. Accordingly, when Moses struck the rock on this occasion, not only was he disobedient and irreverent ("must *we* fetch you water …") to God, but his disobedience diminished the *type*. So this interpretation further strengthens the *type* in that the rock should've only been struck once. That God commanded Moses to speak to the rock instead of striking it on this second occasion also fits the *type*.

7. **Fiery Serpents and the Bronze Serpent** (Type/Shadow)

> And they journeyed from mount Hor by the way of the Red sea, to compass the land of Edom: and the soul of the people was much discouraged because of the way. And the people spake against God, and against Moses, Wherefore have ye brought us up out of Egypt to die in the wilderness? for there is no bread, neither is there any water; and our soul loatheth this light bread. And *the Lord sent fiery serpents among the people, and they bit the people; and much people of Israel died. Therefore the people came to Moses, and said, We have sinned*, for we have spoken against the Lord, and against thee; *pray unto the Lord, that he take away the serpents from us*. And Moses prayed for the people. And *the Lord said unto Moses, Make thee a fiery serpent, and set it upon a pole*: and *it shall come to pass, that every one that is bitten, when he looketh upon it, shall live*. And *Moses made a serpent of brass, and put it upon a pole*, and *it came to pass, that if a serpent had bitten any man, when he beheld the serpent of brass, he lived*. (Numbers 21:4–9)

This is one of the more visible *types* of Christ in the Old Testament, and one that Jesus referred to in His conversation with Nicodemus, who came to Him one night.

> And no man hath ascended up to heaven, but he that came down from heaven, even the Son of man which is in heaven. And *as Moses lifted up the serpent in the wilderness, even so must the Son of man be lifted up: That whosoever believeth in him should not perish, but have eternal life. For God so loved the world, that he gave his only begotten Son, that whosoever believeth in him should not perish, but have everlasting life*. (John 3:13–16)

We see several chapters later in John's gospel Jesus's inner turmoil about His impending death and the manner of it.

> Now is *my soul troubled; and what shall I say? Father, save me from this hour: but for this cause came I unto this hour*. (John 12:27)

> And I, if I be *lifted up* from the earth, *will draw all men unto me*. This he said, *signifying what death he should die*. (John 12:32–33)

So let's unpack the symbolism within this remarkable *type*. We'll first look at the story in Numbers and then look at the parallels with Jesus.

1) The people sinned against Moses and God by grumbling.
2) God responded by sending fiery (i.e., poisonous) snakes that bit them, and they were dying.
3) The people repented and asked Moses to intercede to the Lord for them.
4) Moses interceded, and God commanded him to make a bronze snake and raise it on a pole.
5) Moses did, and whoever looked at the bronze snake lived.

Hopefully, it is obvious to you that this story is indeed a *type* (a veiled picture) of the crucifixion. Let's look at its parallels to the crucifixion.

1) We, like the Israelites, have all sinned against God (Romans 3:23).
2) God told Adam in the Garden (and by extension, all of us) that he was going to die (Genesis 3:19, Romans 6:23).
3) Repentance is a necessary part of salvation (Luke 13:3, 5) and brings us to Jesus (just as it led the people to Moses).
4) God ordained that Jesus die by crucifixion, in which He was nailed to a cross and raised above the earth. This cross is where Jesus paid the full penalty for *our* sin (2 Corinthians 5:21).
5) When a person looks to Jesus by faith for salvation, he will live for all eternity (John 3:16)! Praise the Lord! Any Israelites bitten by a poisonous snake who failed to look at the bronze snake died. Similarly, anyone who fails to look to Jesus by faith will be sentenced to eternal damnation.

I would like to make a point that may not be particularly obvious—the fact that fiery (poisonous) snakes were the punishment of death, and a bronze snake was the deliverance from death. You could say that the fiery snakes, in a sense, were a *representation* of the people's sin. In Romans 8, Paul makes a very intriguing point about Christ.

> For what the law could not do, in that it was weak through the flesh, *God sending his own Son in the likeness of sinful flesh*, and for sin, condemned sin in the flesh: (Romans 8:3)

This point is further supported in Hebrews.

> Wherefore in all things it behoved him *to be made like unto his brethren*, that he might be a merciful and faithful high priest in things pertaining to God, to make reconciliation for the sins of the people. For *in that he himself hath*

suffered being tempted, he is able to succour them that are tempted. (Hebrews 2:17–18)

For we have not an high priest which cannot be touched with the feeling of our infirmities; but *was in all points tempted like as we are, yet without sin.* (Hebrews 4:15)

8.   The Angel of the Lord and Balaam (Theophany or Christophany)

Setting: King Balak, ruler of Moab, saw what Israel had done to the Amorites and was concerned about his own kingdom. So, he concocted a scheme to pay a seer to curse his Israelite enemies and persuaded the elders of Midian to go along with him. They send a delegation to Balaam the seer. After their arrival, they give Balak's message to Balaam, who invites them to spend the night, and he will give them the Lord's answer the next morning. God speaks to Balaam the next morning and informs him not to go with them, so he gives them the Lord's message and sends them off.

Obviously, the king was not particularly happy with Balaam's response, so he determined to send a second, more numerous and more prestigious delegation back to Balaam. Upon their arrival, Balaam again invites them to spend the night. This time, the Lord tells him to go with the men, but to speak "only the word that I shall give you." So, Balaam departs with the men that morning, and along the way …

And God's anger was kindled because he went: and *the angel of the LORD stood in the way for an adversary against him.* Now he [Balaam] was riding upon his ass, and his two servants were with him. And the ass saw *the angel of the LORD standing in the way,* and *his sword drawn in his hand:* and the ass turned aside out of the way, and went into the field: and Balaam smote the ass, to turn her into the way. But *the angel of the LORD stood in a path of the vineyards,* a wall being on this side, and a wall on that side. And when the ass saw the angel of the LORD, she thrust herself unto the wall, and crushed Balaam's foot against the wall: and he smote her again. And *the angel of the LORD went further,* and *stood in a narrow place,* where was no way to turn either to the right hand or to the left. And when the ass saw the angel of the LORD, she fell down under Balaam: and Balaam's anger was kindled, and he smote the ass with a staff. *And the LORD opened the mouth of the ass, and she said unto Balaam,* What have I done unto thee, that thou hast smitten me these three times? And Balaam said unto the ass, Because thou hast mocked me: I would there were a sword in mine hand, for now would I kill thee. And the ass said unto Balaam, Am not I thine ass, upon which thou hast ridden ever since I was thine unto this day? was I ever wont to do so unto thee? and he said, Nay. Then *the LORD opened the eyes of Balaam,* and *he saw the angel of the LORD standing in the way, and his sword drawn in his hand:* and he bowed down his head, and fell flat on his face. And the angel of the LORD said unto him, Wherefore hast thou smitten thine ass these three times? behold, I went out to withstand thee, because thy way is perverse before me: And the ass saw me, and turned from me these three times: unless she had turned from me, surely now also I had slain thee, and saved her alive. And Balaam said unto the angel of the LORD, I have sinned; for I knew not that thou stoodest in the way against me: now therefore, if it displease thee, I will get me back again. And the angel of the LORD said unto Balaam, Go with the men: but only the word that I shall speak unto thee, that thou shalt speak. So Balaam went with the princes of Balak. (Numbers 22:22-35)

This is the beginning of a larger story which shows God's love for His people Israel. The moral of this portion of the story appears to be God's anger at Balaam's double-mindedness (or covetousness). You see, God had given Balaam a very clear answer when the first delegation came. Yet he decided to bid the second delegation to spend the night instead of sending them on their way. As Balaam is en route to King Balak, three times the angel of the Lord plants himself on the path in front of Balaam, with his sword drawn. It is quite interesting that all three times, the donkey sees the angel and Balaam doesn't. The first time, the donkey takes a wide path around the angel; the second, the donkey presses Balaam's foot against the wall to get around the angel; and the third, the donkey, seeing no way around, lies down under Balaam. Balaam strikes the donkey all three times, and on the third time, God enables the donkey to talk—and she and Balaam have this conversation, wherein the donkey is calm and rational, and Balaam is shouting out of control. The angel of the Lord then opens Balaam's eyes and informs him that his donkey saved his life.

Thus, we have another example of the angel of the Lord. Many believe *the angel of the Lord* to be a physical manifestation of God. Some believe Him to be a physical appearance of God the Father (theophany), and others believe Him to be an appearance of Christ specifically (Christophany). As such, these manifestations are *types* of Christ, who is called Immanuel, which means "God with us" (Isaiah 7:14, Matthew 1:21–23).

9. Balaam's Prophecies (Prophecy)

As we just saw, Balaam is now trying to fulfill King Balak's request to curse Israel, despite that it is God's clearly revealed will that Israel is to be blessed, not cursed. So, Balaam delivers four prophetic announcements, as we will see below:

1) First Prophecy

And he took up his parable, and said, Balak the king of Moab hath brought me from Aram, out of the mountains of the east, saying, Come, curse me Jacob, and come, defy Israel. *How shall I curse, whom God hath not cursed? or how shall I defy, whom the* LORD *hath not defied?* For from the top of the rocks I see him, and from the hills I behold him: lo, the people shall dwell alone, *and shall not be reckoned among the nations.* Who can count the dust of Jacob, and the number of the fourth part of Israel? *Let me die the death of the righteous, and let my last end be like his!* (Numbers 23:7–12)

Balaam positioned himself, so that he is looking at a portion of the people (Numbers 22:41) as he prophesies, but he is unable to curse them, because they are God's chosen people, through whom, centuries later, He will bring the Messiah.

2) Second Prophecy

And he took up his parable, and said, Rise up, Balak, and hear; hearken unto me, thou son of Zippor: God is not a man, that he should lie; neither the son of man, that he should repent: hath he said, and shall he not do it? or hath he spoken, and shall he not make it good? Behold, *I have received commandment to bless: and he hath blessed;* and I cannot reverse it. *He hath not beheld iniquity in Jacob, neither hath he seen perverseness in Israel: the* LORD *his God is with him, and the shout of a king is among them.* God brought them out of Egypt; he hath as it were the strength of an unicorn. *Surely there is no enchantment against Jacob, neither is there any divination against Israel: according to this time it shall be said of Jacob and of Israel, What hath God wrought!* Behold, *the people shall rise up as a great lion, and lift up himself as a young lion: he shall not lie down until he eat of the prey, and drink the blood of the slain.* (Numbers 23:18–24)

Balaam again begins his prophecy from a vantage point of viewing a portion of Israel. We again see the Lord's favor on Israel. However, we see some additional information: "*the shout of a king is among them*" and "*the people shall rise up as a great lion*" and "*he shall ... eat of the prey ... drink the blood of the slain.*" This language is reminiscent of Jacob's prophecy over Judah in Genesis 49:8-12, which speaks of Judah's victory over his enemies, his rulership over his brothers (Israel), the imagery of a lion attacking his prey, etc. This "king among them" will begin with Saul (of Benjamin) approximately 400 years later. Then David (of Judah), the king by which all other kings would be measured, would arise, and the promise that God would establish his throne forever, which of course, points to Jesus Christ, who will one day return to rule this earth forever!

3) Third Prophecy

And he took up his parable, and said, Balaam the son of Beor hath said, and the man whose eyes are open hath said: He hath said, which heard the words of God, which saw the vision of the Almighty, falling into a trance, but having his eyes open: *How goodly are thy tents, O Jacob, and thy tabernacles, O Israel!* As the valleys are they spread forth, as gardens by the river's side, as the trees of lign aloes which the LORD hath planted, and as cedar trees beside the waters. He shall pour the water out of his buckets, and his seed shall be in many waters, and *his king shall be higher than Agag, and his kingdom shall be exalted.* God brought him forth out of Egypt; he hath as it were the strength of an unicorn: *he shall eat up the nations his enemies,* and shall *break their bones,* and *pierce them through with his arrows. He couched, he lay down as a lion,* and *as a great lion: who shall stir him up?* Blessed is he that blesseth thee, and cursed is he that curseth thee. (Numbers 24:3–9)

Balaam once again positions himself so that he sees Israel camping tribe by tribe, and he takes up his discourse. Again, we see God's favor on Israel, an allusion to Israel's king "being higher than Agag" and "his kingdom shall be exalted." We see the king's superiority over his enemies, and once again, the imagery of a lion, which points back to Jacob's prophesy as noted above, which ultimately points to Christ.

4) **Fourth Prophecy**

And he took up his parable, and said, Balaam the son of Beor hath said, and the man whose eyes are open hath said: He hath said, which heard the words of God, and knew the knowledge of the most High, which saw the vision of the Almighty, falling into a trance, but having his eyes open: *I shall see him, but not now: I shall behold him, but not nigh: there shall come a Star out of Jacob, and a Sceptre shall rise out of Israel, and shall smite the corners of Moab, and destroy all the children of Sheth.* And Edom shall be a possession, Seir also shall be a possession for his enemies; and Israel shall do valiantly. *Out of Jacob shall come he that shall have dominion,* and shall destroy him that remaineth of the city. (Numbers 24:15–19)

Here, Balaam takes up his final discourse, advising King Balak of what the nation of Israel will do to his people in the days to come. He says, "I see him, but not now: I behold him, but not nigh." Balaam is here describing a monumental event that will happen in the distant future ("not now," "not nigh"). There shall come a "Star out of Jacob," and a "Sceptre shall rise out of Israel." Most commentators see this prophecy as messianic, which is my view. Some commentators see both Star and Sceptre as references to Jesus's end-time rulership. This correlates well with Jacob's prophecy over Judah that designated his descendants as the royal line.

The scepter shall not depart from Judah,
Nor the ruler's staff from between his feet,

> Until Shiloh comes, [Shiloh refers to Messiah]
> *And to him shall be the obedience of the peoples* (Genesis 49:10 NASB)

Some see the star as possibly referring to the supernatural star that the wise men followed first to Jerusalem where they inquired "Where is He who has been born King of the Jews?" (Matthew 2:2), and afterward, it then led then to the house where Jesus lived, probably two or more years after His birth in the manger (Matthew 2:16).

Notice in v. 19 the phrase "Out of Jacob shall come he that shall have dominion …" I believe this is also a reference to Jesus Christ, the King of kings and Lord of lords who will one day return to this earth and destroy the wicked and set up His righteous kingdom!

Balaam's final three prophecies are about other nations and don't appear to have any messianic implications.

10. Joshua a Type of Christ (Type/Shadow)

You may recall that from Exodus after the twelve spies brought back their report on Canaan, there was an uprising among the people because ten of the twelve spies brought back a bad report that the people of the land were so formidable that Israel had no chance. Only Joshua and Caleb urged the people to trust God and cross over into the land to conquer it. The people's refusal to listen to these two brave men caused them to wander in the wilderness for forty years and to die there.

In the passage below, Moses is nearing his death and asks God to appoint a leader to succeed him. That leader was Joshua.

> And Moses spake unto the LORD, saying, Let the LORD, the God of the spirits of all flesh, *set a man over the congregation*, Which may go out before them, and which may go in before them, and which may lead them out, and which may bring them in; that the congregation of the LORD be not as sheep which have no shepherd. And *the LORD said unto Moses, Take thee Joshua the son of Nun, a man in whom is the spirit*, and lay thine hand upon him; And set him before Eleazar the priest, and before all the congregation; and give him a charge in their sight. (Numbers 27:15–19)

> And *Moses did as the LORD commanded him: and he took Joshua, and set him before Eleazar the priest*, and before all the congregation: And *he laid his hands upon him, and gave him a charge, as the LORD commanded by the hand of Moses.* (Numbers 27:22–23)

Joshua is a type of Christ in the sense that he led the people over the Jordan and into Canaan, the Promised Land. Canaan is often seen as a type of heaven. Recall the hymn "On Jordan's

Stormy Banks," first verse and chorus shown below. Obviously, when we sing this song, we're not singing about someday moving to the Middle East, but rather, we're singing about heaven.

> On Jordan's stormy banks I stand,
> And cast a wishful eye
> To Canaan's fair and happy land,
> Where my possessions lie.
>
> I am bound for the promised land,
> I am bound for the promised land;
> Oh, who will come and go with me?
> I am bound for the promised land.

In that Joshua led the people into Canaan which involved conquering the inhabitants there, he is a *type* of Christ who conquered death on the cross and led the way as an atoning sacrifice and as the first fruits of the resurrection—paving the way for our resurrection and entrance into heaven!

Joshua is a *type* of Christ in another sense—his name. The name Joshua translates the Hebrew name Yehowshua (Yeh-ho-shoo'-ah). The name Jesus is translated from the Greek name Iesous (Ee-ay-sooce'). This Greek name is derived from the Hebrew name Yehowshua. So Jesus and Joshua have the same Hebrew name, which means "Jehovah saved"!

11. Cities of Refuge (Type/Shadow)

These cities are first introduced in Numbers 35:6–34. Their purpose, as the name suggests, was to provide a place of refuge for those whose lives were in a particular kind of danger. One of the provisions of the Mosaic Law was the kinsman redeemer. The kinsman redeemer in scripture was the nearest male relative of the person who needed "redeeming." The kinsman redeemer had several responsibilities in scripture as noted below:

1) Levirate marriage (Deuteronomy 25:5–10)
2) Redemption of a poor relative from slavery (Leviticus 25)
3) Redemption of a poor relative's property (Leviticus 25)
4) Avenger (aka Blood Avenger, Avenger of Blood) (Numbers 35)

The best illustration of the kinsman redeemer in scripture is the beloved story of Ruth in the book named after her, where Boaz performed the duty of the levirate marriage by marrying Ruth to raise up a son (Obed) to carry on the lineage of Ruth's deceased husband Mahlon.

Under the Mosaic Law, killing was a capital offense (Exodus 21:12). If a killing took place in a city, the elders of that city were to hand the killer over to the avenger. So, the killer would be handed over to the kinsman redeemer who was charged with executing him. However, what if the killing was accidental (Deuteronomy 19:4–5)? It would hardly seem fair to execute him. So, to resolve this dilemma, the manslayer could flee to a city of refuge to escape the avenger. When the avenger would come to the city of refuge, looking for the killer, the congregation would judge between the manslayer and the avenger (Numbers 35:12, Deuteronomy 35:24–30), and depending on the evidence, or lack thereof, would either allow the manslayer to remain in the city of refuge or turn him over to the avenger for execution.

God instructed Moses that six cities of refuge were to be provided for the Promised Land—three on each side of the Jordan River. You may recall that Reuben, Gad, and the half-tribe of Manasseh lived on the wilderness side of the Jordan and the remaining tribes lived on the Canaan side. The locations of each of these cities were designated by Joshua (Joshua 20:7–9).

So, what is the point in all of this? In what way does this portray Christ? Actually, both the cities of refuge and the avenger (kinsman redeemer) are *types* of Christ. You may recall from our study of Leviticus that there were offerings for both intentional sins and unintentional sins. As believers, our refuge is in Christ, whose blood cleanses us from all sin, saving us from the wrath of God. The good news of the gospel is that people can flee to Christ for refuge from the wrath of God. On the other hand, God will avenge the blood of every Christian who has been wounded or injured by the cruelty of others, unless the offender repents and turns to Him as *their* refuge. Perhaps the clearest example of this truth is found in Revelation 6 in the breaking of the sixth seal, where the martyred souls cried out to God, longing for their vindication, the avenging of their blood on those responsible (Revelation 6:9–11).

Summary of Prophetic Elements in Numbers

1.	Ordination of the Levites	(OT Language and Culture)
2.	Second Passover Observance	(Type/Shadow)
3.	Pillar of Cloud and Fire	(Theophany)
4.	Aaron's Rod that Budded	(Type/Shadow)
5.	Ashes of a Red Heifer Used for Purification	(Type/Shadow)
6.	Water from the Rock	(Type/Shadow)
7.	Fiery Serpents and the Bronze Serpent	(Type/Shadow)
8.	The Angel of the Lord and Balaam	(Theophany or Christophany)
9.	Balaam's Prophecies	(Prophecy)
10.	Joshua a Type of Christ	(Type/Shadow)
11.	Cities of Refuge	(Type/Shadow)

13

JESUS IN DEUTERONOMY

As we continue our journey through the Pentateuch, we will now turn our attention to the book of Deuteronomy. Genesis is the book of beginnings, ending with Israel joining Joseph in Egypt to escape the famine. Exodus records the plight of Israel enslaved in Egypt, its birth as God's nation and His deliverance of them in the exodus, and the beginning of their wilderness wanderings. Leviticus is concerned with worship and ordinances governing civilian life. In Numbers, we see the continuing story of Israel, God's numbering of the people, their continued wilderness wanderings, beginning with their departure from Mount Sinai. Now in Deuteronomy, also known as the Second Giving of the Law, we see Moses giving his final instructions to Israel. In chapter 5, we see the Ten Commandments repeated. The book is almost entirely Moses's words to the people except for brief sections at the end of the book.

As we go through this book, we will see primarily *types* of Christ; some of them will be repeated from previous books. Several of them will be quite subtle, but significant nonetheless.

1. Cities of Refuge (OT Language and Culture)

As we saw in Numbers 35:6–34, these special cities provided a place of refuge for a person who had accidentally killed a person, what would be called negligent homicide today. In the Numbers passage, God had instructed that six of these cities be provided when the Israelites settled in the Promised Land. In the passage below, these six cities are listed by name and their locations given.

> **Three Cities on the Wilderness Side of the Jordan River**
> Then Moses set apart three cities across the Jordan to the east, that a manslayer might flee there, who unintentionally slew his neighbor without having enmity toward him in time past; and by fleeing to one of these cities he might live: *Bezer* in the wilderness on the plateau for the Reubenites, and *Ramoth* in Gilead for the Gadites, and *Golan* in Bashan for the Manassites. Deuteronomy 4:41-43 NASB)

So, in this passage, we are given the three cities east of the Jordan River, on the wilderness side of the river. This land was inhabited by the tribes of Reuben, Gad, and the half-tribe of Manasseh. The cities of Bezer, Ramoth, and Golan were located within the three tribes of Reuben Gad, and the half-tribe of Manasseh, respectively.

Explanation of the Purpose of the Six Cities of Refuge

When the LORD your God cuts off the nations, whose land the LORD your God gives you, and you dispossess them and settle in their cities and in their houses, you shall set aside three cities for yourself in the midst of your land, which the LORD your God gives you to possess. You shall prepare the roads for yourself, and divide into three parts the territory of your land which the LORD your God will give you as a possession, *so that any manslayer may flee there.*

Now this is the case of *the manslayer who may flee there and live: when he kills his friend unintentionally*, not hating him previously—as when *a man* goes into the forest with his friend to cut wood, and his hand swings the axe to cut down the tree, and the iron *head* slips off the handle and strikes his friend so that he dies—he may flee to one of these cities and live; otherwise the avenger of blood might pursue the manslayer in the heat of his anger, and overtake him, because the way is long, and take his life, though he was not deserving of death, since he had not hated him previously. Therefore, I command you, saying, "You shall set aside three cities for yourself."

If the LORD your God enlarges your territory, just as He has sworn to your fathers, and gives you all the land which He promised to give your fathers—if you carefully observe all this commandment which I command you today, to love the LORD your God, and to walk in His ways always—then *you shall add three more cities for yourself, besides these three. So innocent blood will not be shed in the midst of your land* which the LORD your God gives you as an inheritance, and bloodguiltiness be on you.

But if there is a man who hates his neighbor and lies in wait for him and rises up against him and strikes him so that he dies, and he flees to one of these cities, then the elders of his city shall send and take him from there and deliver him into the hand of the avenger of blood, that he may die. You shall not pity him, but you shall purge the blood of the innocent from Israel, that it may go well with you. (Deuteronomy 19:1-13 NASB)

Three Cities on the Canaan Side of the Jordan River

So they set apart *Kedesh* in Galilee in the hill country of Naphtali and *Shechem* in the hill country of Ephraim, and *Kiriath-arba* (that is, *Hebron*) in the hill country of Judah. Beyond the Jordan east of Jericho, they designated Bezer in the wilderness on the plain from the tribe of Reuben, and Ramoth in Gilead from the tribe of Gad, and Golan in Bashan from the tribe of Manasseh. These were the appointed cities for all the sons of Israel and *for the stranger who sojourns among them, that whoever kills any person unintentionally may flee there*, and not die by the hand of the avenger of blood until he stands before the congregation. (Joshua 20:7-9 NASB)

So in this passage, we are given the three cities west of the Jordan River, on the Canaan side of the river. The cities of Kedesh, Shechem, and Kiriath-Arba (aka Hebron) were located within the tribes of Naphtali, Ephraim, and Judah, respectively. Although this volume ends with Deuteronomy and does not cover the book of Joshua, this passage is included for the names and locations of the three cities on the Canaan side of the Jordan.

As was pointed out in this same topic in Numbers, these cities were a place to flee for the person who committed a negligent homicide. As such, it is a picture of Christ, who is our place to flee for refuge for all sins, intentional and unintentional, whereas the cities of refuge were only for unintentional homicides. Jesus is our *city of refuge* to protect us from the wrath of God.

2. **Sabbatical Year, Bondslaves** (Type/Shadow)

In the Bible, our very first introduction to the Sabbath was in Genesis 2:1–3:

> Thus the heavens and the earth were finished, and all the host of them. And *on the seventh day God ended his work* which he had made; *and he rested on the seventh day* from all his work which he had made. And *God blessed the seventh day, and sanctified it:* because that in it he had rested from all his work which God created and made.

So God blessed the seventh day and sanctified it, because He rested on the seventh day. Later, in Exodus 35:1–3, God commanded that the seventh day be set aside as a holy day, a Sabbath of complete rest. In Leviticus 25, the sabbatical year is introduced, with the stipulation that the land shall have a sabbath to the Lord in which no planting shall be done on the seventh year. Then after seven sabbatical years (forty-nine years), the fiftieth year shall be celebrated as a year of Jubilee.

This brings us to our current passage in Deuteronomy 15:

> *At the end of every seven years thou shalt make a release.* And this is the manner of the release: *Every creditor that lendeth ought unto his neighbour shall release it;* he shall not exact it of his neighbour, or of his brother; because *it is called the LORD's release.* Of a foreigner thou mayest exact it again: but that which is thine with thy brother thine hand shall release. (Deuteronomy 15:1–3)

And *if thy brother, an Hebrew man*, or an *Hebrew woman, be sold unto thee*, and serve thee six years; then *in the seventh year thou shalt let him go free from thee.* And when thou sendest him out free from thee, *thou shalt not let him go away empty: Thou shalt furnish him liberally* out of *thy flock*, and out of *thy floor*, and out of *thy winepress*: of that wherewith the LORD thy God hath blessed thee thou shalt give unto him. (Deuteronomy 15:12–14)

In this passage, we again have this principle of the sabbatical year as a type of Christ. In this case, the law provides for the forgiveness of debt of fellow Israelites. The law did not apply to the debts of foreigners; their debts were still owed back to the borrower. Second, we see that in the case of an Israelite man or woman who becomes an indentured slave to pay off a debt, he or she must be released in the seventh year. Notice that this forgiveness is unmerited—the debtor still legitimately owes his creditor, but the creditor completely forgives the debtor. In like manner, the indentured slave still owes service to his master, but his enslavement is canceled.

What a picture of God's forgiveness this is! Not only does He forgive us and set us free, but then He makes us His children! Once again, we see this *type* of Christ as a vivid picture of God's forgiveness of us and our forgiveness of others as an expression of our thankfulness to Him for His forgiveness.

The Bondslave

And it shall be, *if he say unto thee, I will not go* away from thee; *because he loveth thee and thine house*, because he is well with thee; Then *thou shalt take an aul, and thrust it through his ear unto the door, and he shall be thy servant for ever.* And also unto thy maidservant thou shalt do likewise. (Deuteronomy 15:16–17)

We see from verses 16 and 17 that the bondslave is a special case. This is the case of a slave who loves his master so much that he wants to continue as a slave! This speaks well of both the slave and the master, who was the kind of person that the slave would want to continue serving! What a picture of Christ this is! We see this beautiful passage in Philippians that many regard as an early Christian hymn.

Let this mind be in you, which was also in Christ Jesus: Who, *being in the form of God*, thought it not robbery to be equal with God: But *made himself of no reputation, and took upon him the form of a servant*, and was *made in the likeness of men*: And *being found in fashion as a man*, he *humbled himself, and became obedient unto death, even the death of the cross*. Wherefore God also hath highly exalted him, and given him a name which is above every name: That at the name of Jesus every knee should bow, of things in heaven, and things in earth, and things under the earth; And that every tongue should confess that Jesus Christ is Lord, to the glory of God the Father. (Philippians 2:5–11)

What a bondslave! Not in the sense of a released slave who chose to remain a slave, but one who is equal with God yet chose to become a bondslave! God the Son was equal with God the Father, but became a man, who gave His life in full-time service during His entire three-year ministry. Finally, He was faithful to become a human sacrifice for our sins, enduring grief in the garden where He sweated drops of blood from agony, betrayed by one disciple and forsaken by the others, enduring an illegal trial, Roman scourging, and six hours on a cross!

Also, some of the New Testament writers used the title of bondservant for themselves and for other believers—Paul (Romans 1:1; 2 Corinthians 4:5; Galatians 1:10; Philippians 1:1, Colossians 1:7, 4:7; 2 Timothy 2:24; Titus 1:1), James (James 1:1), Peter (2 Peter 1:1), Jude (Jude 1:1), and John (Revelation 1:1 NASB). So we see that the bondslave is both a *type* of Christ and also of His followers who are conformed to His image (Romans 8:29).

3. Passover and Other Feasts (Type/Shadow)

Passover and Feast of Unleavened Bread

The Passover is a *type* of Christ, as we have previously seen. The inaugural Passover, recorded in Exodus 12, was held in Egypt just prior to the plague of the death of the firstborn, in which the firstborn males of every Egyptian household were slain by the death angel. This included the firstborn son of every Egyptian household and the firstborn male animals as well. The Passover lamb was slain by the Israelites and its blood painted on the doorposts and lintel of the entrance to the house. As the death angel would see the blood, he would pass over the house and not slay the firstborn of the Israelites whose homes were so protected. Of course, this last plague finally brought Pharaoh to his proverbial knees, and the exodus occurred thereafter.

It should be noted here that Passover was to be celebrated as an annual feast on the fourteenth day of the first month Nisan (Exodus 12:1–22). So, one year after the inaugural celebration, they celebrated the first memorial Passover in the wilderness (Numbers 9:1–5).

However, because of Israel's disobedience after the return of the twelve who were sent to spy out the land (Numbers 13; 14:1–33), we read where ten of the spies brought back a negative report, and only Joshua and Caleb urged the people to proceed into Canaan. However, the people listened to the ten spies and refused to go, so the Lord punished their disobedience by making them wander in the wilderness for forty years. Only Joshua and Caleb would be allowed to cross into the Promised Land. The dissenters would all die in the wilderness and not cross over; however, their children would cross over. We find later in Numbers 20:8–12 that Moses's angry and irreverent outburst in the second miracle of bringing water from the rock cost him the privilege of crossing over into the Promised Land.

Because of the wilderness wanderings, Passover observance was held in abeyance for the remainder of the forty years. Given Moses's plight, he gives instructions for the annual observance of Passover to recommence once the Israelites are settled in the Promised Land at the place designated by the Lord. We see in Joshua 5:9–11 that this first Passover in the Promised Land was celebrated in Gilgal on the desert plains of Jericho. Below are Moses's instructions on this in Deuteronomy 16.

> Observe the *month of Abib*, and *keep the passover* unto the LORD thy God: for in the month of Abib *the LORD thy God brought thee forth out of Egypt by night.* Thou shalt therefore *sacrifice the passover unto the LORD thy God*, of the flock and the herd, in the place which the LORD shall choose to place his name there. Thou shalt eat *no leavened bread* with it; *seven days shalt thou eat unleavened bread therewith*, even the bread of affliction; for thou camest forth out of the land of Egypt in haste: that thou mayest remember the day when thou camest forth out of the land of Egypt all the days of thy life. And there shall be no leavened bread seen with thee in all thy coast seven days; *neither shall there any thing of the flesh, which thou sacrificedst the first day at even, remain all night until the morning.* Thou mayest not sacrifice the passover within any of thy gates, which the LORD thy God giveth thee: But at the place which the LORD thy God shall choose to place his name in, there thou shalt sacrifice the passover at even, at the going down of the sun, at the season that thou camest forth out of Egypt. And *thou shalt roast and eat it in the place which the LORD thy God shall choose*: and thou shalt turn in the morning, and go unto thy tents. *Six days thou shalt eat unleavened bread*: and on *the seventh day shall be a solemn assembly to the LORD thy God: thou shalt do no work therein.* (Deuteronomy 16:1–8)

Below is a description of *how* the Passover is a *type* of Christ repeated from the Exodus chapter.

- An *unblemished* male lamb *one year* old—this points to Christ's *sinlessness* and His crucifixion *in the prime of His life.*
- Blood on *wooden* or stone *doorpost and lintel* (KJV "upper door post")—Jesus's blood on the *vertical* and *horizontal* members of a wooden cross (wood doorpost suggested by Exodus 21:5–6)
- Death angel *prevented* from harming household *with the blood*—those who trust in the *atoning blood* of Christ are *protected* from eternal death.
- Passover lamb eaten with *unleavened* bread—leaven in the Bible represents *sin*; this also points to the *sinlessness* of Christ.
- Passover lamb eaten with *bitter* herbs—a picture of the *bitter agony* of Jesus's passion
- Jesus gives new meaning to the Passover at the Last Supper—as noted previously.

Other Feasts

There are a total of seven Jewish feasts in the Old Testament, all of which point to Christ. They are listed in their order of occurrence below, showing how they portray Christ:

Feast	Time and Length	Portrayal of Christ
1) Passover	Nisan 14 (1 day)	Christ, the Lamb of God
2) Feast of Unleavened Bread*	Nisan 15 (7 days)	Sinlessness of Christ
3) Feast of First Fruits	Nisan 16 (1 day)	Resurrection of Christ
4) Feast of Weeks (Harvest, Pentecost)*	Sivan 6 (2 days)	Birth of His Church
5) Feast of Trumpets	Tishri 1 (1 day)	Second Coming of Christ
6) Day of Atonement	Tishri 10 (1 day)	Christ our High Priest
7) Feast of Tabernacles*	Tishri 15 (7 days)	Eternal Dwelling with Christ

The dates above were obtained from *The Jewish Holidays*, a publication of Zola Levitt Ministries.[1]

Note that the month of Abib, noted in our Deuteronomy passage and the Exodus passage below, is the same month as Nisan shown in the table above, the first month of the year on the Jewish calendar. The three pilgrimage feasts, which all males were required to attend, are noted above with asterisks, as stated in the passages below.

Feast of Unleavened Bread

Three times a year you shall celebrate a feast to Me. You shall observe the *Feast of Unleavened Bread*; for seven days you are to eat unleavened bread, as I commanded you, at the appointed time in the month Abib, for in it you came out of Egypt. And none shall appear before Me empty-handed. Also *you shall observe* the *Feast of the Harvest of the first fruits* of your labors *from* what you sow in the field; also the *Feast of the Ingathering* at the end of the year when you gather in *the fruit of* your labors from the field. *Three times a year all your males shall appear before the Lord God*. (Exodus 23:14-17 NASB)

Speak to the sons of Israel and say to them, "When you enter the land which I am going to give to you and reap its harvest, *then you shall bring in the sheaf* of the *first fruits of your harvest* to the priest. He shall wave the sheaf before the Lord for you to be accepted; on the day after the sabbath the priest shall wave it." (Leviticus 23:10-11 NASB)

Three times in a year shall all thy males appear before the Lord thy God in the place which he shall choose; in the *feast of unleavened bread*, and in the *feast of weeks*, and in the *feast of tabernacles*: and they shall not appear before the Lord empty: Every man shall give as he is able, according to the blessing of the Lord thy God which he hath given thee. (Deuteronomy 16:16–17)

Clarification: For me, this was very confusing, because the Exodus passage lists the three pilgrimage feasts as Unleavened Bread, Harvest of First Fruits, and Ingathering (Tabernacles), while the Deuteronomy passage lists them as Unleavened Bread, Weeks, and Tabernacles. This raised two questions for me: (1) Is the second feast the Feast of First Fruits or the Feast of Weeks? (2) Is the Feast of the Harvest the same as the *Feast of First Fruits* or the *Feast of Weeks*? For me, the Leviticus passage provides the needed clarity when it speaks of *the sheaf of the first fruits of your harvest*. So the *sheaf* of the *first fruits* is not the *harvest* of the first fruits, but only the first sheaf of that harvest, with the actual harvest coming later. The *harvest of first fruits* in Exodus is not the same as *bringing the first fruits of the harvest*, which is observed in the Feast of First Fruits. Therefore, the *Feast of the Harvest* is synonymous with the *Feast of Weeks*, rather than the Feast of First Fruits. Accordingly, the three feasts noted in the table above with asterisks are the pilgrimage feasts.

Of the feasts listed above, we previously covered the Passover Feast and the Feast of Unleavened Bread. In the passage below, we see two other feasts mentioned—the Feast of Weeks (or Harvest or Pentecost) and the Feast of Tabernacles (or Booths or Ingathering). In addition to the feasts of Passover, Unleavened Bread, Weeks, and Tabernacles listed in Deuteronomy 16, we will add the Feast of First Fruits mentioned in Exodus and Leviticus in this section, since the Feast of Pentecost is celebrated fifty days after the Feast of First Fruits.

Feast of First Fruits

Also *you shall observe the Feast of the Harvest of the first fruits* of your labors *from* what you sow in the field; also the *Feast of the Ingathering* at the end of the year when you gather in *the fruit of* your labors from the field. (Exodus 23:16 NASB)

Then the Lord spoke to Moses, saying, "Speak to the sons of Israel and say to them, 'When you enter the land which I am going to give to you and reap its harvest, then *you shall bring in the sheaf of the first fruits of your harvest to the priest. He shall wave the sheaf before the Lord for you to be accepted; on the day after the sabbath the priest shall wave it.* Now on the day when you wave the sheaf, you shall offer a male lamb one year old without defect for a burnt offering to the Lord. Its grain offering shall then be two-tenths *of an ephah* of fine flour mixed with oil, an offering by fire to the Lord *for* a soothing aroma, with its drink offering, a fourth of a hin of wine. Until this same day, until you have brought in the offering of your God, you shall eat neither bread nor roasted grain nor new growth. It is to be a perpetual statute throughout your generations in all your dwelling places.'" (Leviticus 23:9-14 NASB)

So, after the Israelites entered the Promised Land, immediately after the Feast of Unleavened Bread, they were to observe the Feast of First Fruits. This feast, as all the feasts, was to be celebrated annually.

Feast of Weeks (Harvest, Pentecost)

You *shall also count for yourselves from the day after the sabbath,* from the day when you brought in the sheaf of the wave offering; there shall be *seven complete sabbaths. You shall count fifty days to the day after the seventh sabbath;* then you shall present a new grain offering to the LORD. (Leviticus 23:15-16 NASB)

Seven weeks shalt thou number unto thee: *begin to number the seven weeks from such time as thou beginnest to put the sickle to the corn.* And *thou shalt keep the feast of weeks unto the LORD thy God* with a tribute of a freewill offering of thine hand, which thou shalt give unto the LORD thy God, according as the LORD thy God hath blessed thee. (Deuteronomy 16:9–10)

This feast was the celebration of the spring harvest and was a feast of thanksgiving to the Lord.

Feast of Booths (Tabernacles, Ingathering)

And thou shalt rejoice before the LORD thy God, thou, and thy son, and thy daughter, and thy manservant, and thy maidservant, and the Levite that is within thy gates, and the stranger, and the fatherless, and the widow, that are among you, in the place which the LORD thy God hath chosen to place his name there. *And thou shalt remember that thou wast a bondman in Egypt: and thou shalt observe and do these statutes. Thou shalt observe the feast of tabernacles seven days, after that thou hast gathered in thy corn and thy wine: And thou shalt rejoice in thy feast, thou, and thy son, and thy daughter, and thy manservant, and thy maidservant, and the Levite, the stranger, and the fatherless, and the widow, that are within thy gates.* Seven days shalt thou keep a solemn feast unto the LORD thy God in the place which the LORD shall choose: because the LORD thy God shall bless thee in all thine increase, and in all the works of thine hands, therefore thou shalt surely rejoice. (Deuteronomy 16:11–15)

This feast was celebrated at the time of the fall harvest and commemorated God's provision for Israel as He dwelt with them during the wilderness wandering.

Summarizing from these feasts, we see the following types of Christ:

Passover—Jesus is the Lamb of God who was crucified during Passover for our sins!

Unleavened Bread—leaven is symbolic of sin in scripture, and Jesus was sinless, and as believers, we are to put away sin.

Regarding these two feasts, Paul in addressing the Corinthian Church for failing to deal with immorality in its midst, wrote in 1 Corinthians 5:7–8:

Clean out the old leaven so that you may be a new lump, just as you are in fact unleavened. For *Christ our Passover also has been sacrificed. Therefore let us celebrate the feast,* not with old leaven, nor with the leaven of malice and wickedness, but *with the unleavened bread of sincerity and truth.* (NASB)

Feast of Firstfruits—this is a picture of Christ's resurrection, Paul, in his comprehensive treatise on the resurrection, penned the following in 1 Corinthians 15:20, 15:22–23:

But now *Christ has been raised from the dead, the first fruits* of those who are asleep … For as in Adam all die, so also *in Christ all will be made alive.* But each in his own order: Christ the first fruits, after that those who are Christ's at His coming. (NASB)

Feast of Weeks—this agricultural harvest is a picture of the soul harvest that Jesus gathered at Pentecost during the celebration of this feast. Also, since it was a pilgrimage feast, people came from all over to attend it, which greatly contributed to the magnitude of the harvest—3,000 souls, and the geographical area which they were able to cover. This helped to kick-start the spread of the gospel! Luke records this in his history of the early church in Acts 2:37–38, 41.

Now when they heard *this,* they were pierced to the heart, and said to Peter and the rest of the apostles, "Brethren, what shall we do?" Peter *said* to them, *"Repent, and each of you be baptized in the name of Jesus Christ for the forgiveness of your sins*; and you will receive the gift of the Holy Spirit …" So then, those who had received his word were baptized; *and that day there were added about three thousand souls.* (NASB)

Feast of Tabernacles—this feast commemorated God's dwelling in a tabernacle with Israel during their wilderness wanderings. The tabernacles constructed and lived in by the Israelites during this feast reminded them of God's abiding presence during the wilderness wanderings. Also, they are a *picture* of our eternal dwelling place with Christ in heaven!

In My Father's house are many dwelling places; if it were not so, I would have told you; for *I go to prepare a place for you* … I will come again and receive you to Myself, that where I am, *there* you may be also. (John 14:2-3 NASB)

And I heard a loud voice from the throne, saying, "Behold, *the tabernacle of God is among men, and He will dwell among them,* and they shall be His people, and God Himself will be among them. (Revelation 21:3 NASB)

4. **Prophecy of Kings** (Prophecy, Type/Shadow)

When thou art come unto the land which the LORD thy God giveth thee, and shalt possess it, and shalt dwell therein, *and shalt say, I will set a king over me,* like as all the nations that are about me; Thou shalt in any wise *set him king over thee, whom the* LORD *thy God shall choose: one from among thy brethren shalt thou set king over thee*: thou mayest not set a stranger over thee, which is not thy brother. But he shall not multiply horses to himself, nor cause the people to return to Egypt, to the end that he should multiply horses: forasmuch as the LORD hath said unto you, Ye shall henceforth return no more that way. *Neither shall he multiply wives to himself, that his heart turn not away: neither shall he greatly multiply to himself silver and gold.* And it shall be, *when he sitteth upon the throne of his kingdom, that he shall write him a copy of this law in a book out of that which is before the priests the Levites: And it shall be with him, and he shall read therein all the days of his life:* that he may learn to fear the LORD his God, to keep all the words of this law and these statutes, to do them: That his heart be not lifted up above his brethren, and that he turn not aside from the commandment, to the right hand, or to the left: to the end *that he may prolong his days in his kingdom*, he, and his children, in the midst of Israel. (Deuteronomy 17:14–20)

Students of the Old Testament reading verse 17, shown in italics, will be immediately reminded of Solomon, who began his reign so well but ended it so poorly. The unfolding story of the kings *and the King in* the Bible is a fascinating one! The history of Israel's kings begins in 1 Samuel 8, where the people ask Samuel for a king. He is greatly displeased, and prays to the Lord, who tells him, "Listen to their voice (but) solemnly warn them" of the consequences of this decision. Just reading this story, one might have the impression that God would somehow now have to resort to some plan B, now that the people have rejected Him as their leader. However, that would be far from the truth. We see from the above passage that He is simply fulfilling His original plan. Christ (the King of kings) was slain from the foundation of the world (1 Peter 1:20), and centuries before this story, we see that it was God's plan from the beginning that Israel have kings. So in addition to the above passage in Moses's parting instructions to the people, we also see God's promise to Abraham and Jacob in the Genesis passages below.

And I will make thee exceeding fruitful, and I will make nations of thee, and *kings shall come out of thee.* (Genesis 17:6)

And God said unto him, I am God Almighty: be fruitful and multiply; a nation and a company of nations shall be of thee, and *kings shall come out of thy loins*; (Genesis 35:11)

It was God's plan for Israel to have kings from all eternity! This was the framework from which He chose to reveal Christ. Centuries after the above passage and after the abysmal failure of Israel's first king, Saul, God instructs Samuel to anoint a new king—David, the son of Jesse. This king had the distinction of being "a man after God's own heart" (1 Samuel 13:14) and was the *prototype* of Jesus Christ, the eternal King of kings! David went on to be the king that all the other kings succeeding him would be compared to. God used David's journey to becoming king in fleeing from paranoid Saul to build in him a godly character. God would later tell David, "Your house and your kingdom shall endure before Me forever; your throne shall be established forever" (2 Samuel 7:16-17 NASB). Of course, God was speaking of David only as a *type* of the real king, Jesus, the eternal King of kings and Lord of lords, who would fulfill this prophecy! Yet King David's unparalleled character took a precipitous fall in the matter of Bathsheba and Uriah the Hittite (2 Samuel 11–12).

So in this sense, the above passage and the history of Israel and Judah's kings is part of the foretelling of Christ. Of course, David the *prototype* was from Judah's line, as is the eternal king Jesus, aka the Lion of the tribe of Judah, the Root of David (Revelation 5:5), which harkens back to Jacob's blessing of Judah back in Genesis 49:8–12.

5. **A Prophet Like Moses** (Prophecy, Type/Shadow)

> *The LORD your God will raise up for you a prophet like me from among you,* from your countrymen, you shall listen to him. This is according to all that you asked of the LORD your God in Horeb on the day of the assembly, saying, "Let me not hear again the voice of the LORD my God, let me not see this great fire anymore, or I will die." The LORD said to me, "They have spoken well. *I will raise up a prophet from among their countrymen like you,* and *I will put My words in his mouth, and he shall speak to them all that I command him.* It shall come about that *whoever will not listen to My words which he shall speak in My name, I Myself will require it of him.*" (Deuteronomy 18:15-19 NASB)

This passage is speaking of Jesus! He is the prophet like Moses. Moses had the distinction of speaking with God face to face (Exodus 33:11). During his life, Moses was the sole spokesman for God. He performed miraculous signs by the hand of God. So we see this passage is both a prophecy in the sense that the prophetic promise is speaking of Christ, but it is also a *type* in the sense that Moses was an Old Testament *prefigure* of Christ as noted in chapter 10 on Exodus under the first entry—*Moses as a type.*

6. **Expiation of a Crime Sacrifice** (OT Language and Culture)

> *If one be found slain* in the land which the LORD thy God giveth thee to possess it, lying in the field, *and it be not known who hath slain him*: Then *thy elders and thy judges shall come forth, and they shall measure unto the cities which are round about him that is slain*: And it shall be, that *the city which is next unto the slain man, even the elders* of that city *shall take an heifer*, which hath not been wrought with, and *which hath not drawn in the yoke*; And *the elders of that city shall bring down the heifer unto a rough valley*, which is neither eared

nor sown, *and shall strike off the heifer's neck there in the valley:* And *the priests the sons of Levi shall come near;* for them the LORD thy God hath chosen to minister unto him, *and to bless in the name of the LORD;* and by their word shall every controversy and every stroke be tried: And all *the elders of that city, that are next unto the slain man, shall wash their hands over the heifer that is beheaded in the valley:* And they shall answer *and say, Our hands have not shed this blood, neither have our eyes seen it.* Be merciful, O LORD, unto thy people Israel, whom thou hast redeemed, and *lay not innocent blood unto thy people of Israel's charge. And the blood shall be forgiven them.* So shalt thou put away the guilt of innocent blood from among you, when thou shalt do that which is right in the sight of the LORD. (Deuteronomy 21:1–9)

All the animal sacrifices of the Mosaic Law are *types* of Christ the perfect sacrifice. This sacrifice covered the unusual situation of a dead person being found in a rural area with no one, other than the murderer, knowing who committed the crime. So the city closest to the dead person's remains would have the elders and priests slay a heifer and confess over it their innocence. This observance would absolve the city of wrongdoing. This provision is one further indication of the comprehensiveness of the Mosaic Law, in that it covered every sin situation imaginable. This pictures the comprehensive nature of Christ's forgiveness of our sins by His death on the cross.

7. Don't Mix Seeds, Threads, Animals (OT Language and Culture)

Thou shalt not sow thy vineyard with divers seeds: lest the fruit of thy seed which thou hast sown, and the fruit of thy vineyard, be defiled. Thou shalt not plow with an ox and an ass together. Thou shalt not wear a garment of divers sorts, as of woollen and linen together. (Deuteronomy 22:9–11)

This interesting provision of the Mosaic Law is a picture of purity. The people were not to mix seeds in planting, animals in plowing, or threads (or pieces of cloth) in garments. In each of these cases, the purity of only one type of seed, animal, or fabric depicts the perfect sinlessness of Christ. Isaiah stated, "But we are all as an unclean thing, and all our righteousnesses are as filthy rags; and we all do fade as a leaf; and our iniquities, like the wind, have taken us away" (Isaiah 64:6), but Jesus is the unblemished Lamb of God, who takes away the sin of the world.

8. Duty of a Brother, Levirate Marriage (Type/Shadow)

If brethren dwell together, and one of them die, and have no child, the wife of the dead shall not marry without unto a stranger: *her husband's brother shall go in unto her, and take her to him to wife, and perform the duty of an husband's brother unto her. And it shall be, that the firstborn which she beareth shall succeed in the name of his brother which is dead, that his name be not put out of Israel. And if the man like not to take his brother's wife, then let his brother's wife go up to the gate unto the elders, and say, My husband's brother refuseth to raise up unto his brother a name in Israel,* he will not perform the duty of my husband's brother. Then *the elders of his city shall call him, and speak unto him:* and if he stand to it, and say, I like not to take her; *Then shall his brother's wife come unto him in the presence of the elders,* and *loose his shoe from off his foot,* and *spit in his face,* and shall answer *and say, So shall it be done unto that man that will not build up his brother's house.* And *his name shall be called* in Israel, *The house of him that hath his shoe loosed.* (Deuteronomy 25:5–10)

This was the law of the levirate marriage. If a man died, it was the duty of his unmarried brother to marry the wife of the deceased. The first child born of that union would be the legal descendant of the deceased brother to carry on his name. This duty fell under the umbrella of the kinsman redeemer's responsibilities. The most well-known biblical account of a kinsman redeemer and a levirate marriage is in the book of Ruth. In the above passage, the levirate marriage is the responsibility of the unmarried brother. However, we see from the story of Ruth that it had a broader application than just the brother, perhaps this developed over time in cases where there was no living unmarried brother, as was the case for Ruth's first husband Mahlon (Ruth 1:3–5; 4:10), nor, apparently, for Naomi's husband Elimelech (Ruth 3:12). Accordingly, as the story developed, we find that there were two near kinsmen—Boaz and an unnamed man, the latter being the closer relative. In the story of Ruth, Boaz confronts the closer relative at the city gate in the presence of the elders, because he had first right of refusal (Ruth 4:1–12). When the unnamed man declined, he removed his sandal in accordance with the custom outlined in the passage above, and Boaz immediately took possession of the land of Elimelech, Mahlon, and Chilion, and acquired Ruth to become his wife! The story of Ruth is one of the most beloved stories in the Bible, and a favorite of mine as well. This story is the best-known illustration of the role of the kinsman redeemer and levirate marriage found in the Bible.

In this capacity, the kinsman redeemer provided for the financial needs and physical protection of the widow. This is a beautiful picture of our kinsman redeemer, Jesus, who provides for our justification before God, and our abundant life in Him (John 10:10).

9. Offering of First Fruits (OT Language and Culture)

And it shall be, *when thou art come in unto the land which the LORD thy God giveth thee* for an inheritance, *and possessest it, and dwellest therein;* That *thou shalt take of the first of all the fruit of the earth, which thou shalt bring of thy land* that the LORD thy God giveth thee, *and shalt put it in a basket,* and shalt *go unto the place which the LORD thy God shall choose to place his name there.* And thou shalt *go unto the priest* that shall be in those days, and *say unto him,* I profess this day unto the LORD thy God, that I am come unto the country which the LORD sware unto our fathers for to give us. And *the priest shall take the basket out of thine hand, and set it down before the altar of the LORD thy God.* And thou shalt speak and say before the LORD thy God, A Syrian ready to perish was my father, and he went down into Egypt, and sojourned there with a few, and became there a nation, great, mighty, and populous: And the Egyptians evil entreated us, and afflicted us, and laid upon us hard bondage: And *when we cried unto the LORD God of our fathers, the LORD heard our voice,* and looked on our affliction, and our labour, and our oppression: And *the LORD brought us forth out of Egypt with a mighty hand,* and with an outstretched arm, and with great terribleness, and *with signs, and with wonders: And he hath brought us into this place, and hath given us this land,* even a land that floweth with milk and honey. And now, behold, *I have brought the firstfruits of the land, which thou, O LORD, hast given me.* And *thou shalt set it before the LORD thy God, and worship before the LORD thy God.* (Deuteronomy 26:1–10)

As Moses continues his final instructions to the Lord's people, he charges them, once they enter Canaan, to divide and settle in the land, to bring the offering of first fruits to the Lord. You may recall that when they crossed the Jordan, the land was not simply handed to them on a silver platter as it were, but they had to conquer the Canaanite cities therein. This was recorded afterward in the book of Joshua. So once the land was apportioned to the tribes, they were to plant crops and gather a harvest. Moses said that the first order of business was to gather the *first fruits* of the first crop and bring it to the priest for a thanksgiving and memorial offering. This was yet another reminder to the people of the Lord's goodness in delivering them from Egyptian slavery and persecution, bringing them through the forty-year-long wilderness wandering, and leading them to victory over the Canaanites. The Lord displayed many miraculous signs during the deliverance from Egypt and the forty years in the wilderness, and this offering was to honor and worship Him for His faithfulness.

So you may be asking, "How does this foreshadow Christ or Christianity?" That is certainly a fair question—the answer is that the New Testament writers, specifically James (the brother of Jesus), Paul, and the apostle John used this term, *first fruits,* in their writing, knowing that the Jews in their audience would connect their meaning back to this provision of the Mosaic Law. In the New Testament, the term is used in four ways as you will see in the examples below: (1) to refer to believers' internal evidence of salvation, (2) to refer to Christ specifically or early believers as first fruits in the order of the resurrection, 3) to refer to specific believers as the first historically or in a particular area to come to Christ, and (4) to refer to the 144,000 in Revelation.

1) First fruits as internal evidence of salvation:

And not only this, but also we ourselves, having the *first fruits* of the Spirit, even we ourselves groan within ourselves, waiting eagerly for our adoption as sons, the redemption of our body. (Romans 8:23 NASB)

2) First fruits referring to Christ or early believers in the order of the Resurrection

But now Christ has been raised from the dead, the *first fruits* of those who are asleep. (1 Corinthians 15:20 NASB)

For as in Adam all die, so also in Christ all will be made alive. But each in his own order: Christ the *first fruits*, after that those who are Christ's at His coming, then *comes* the end, when He hands over the kingdom to the God and Father, when He has abolished all rule and all authority and power. (1 Corinthians 15:22-24 NASB)

3) First fruits referring to the first believers to come to Christ historically or in a particular area

Now I urge you, brethren (you know the *household of Stephanas*, that they were the *first fruits* of *Achaia*, and that they have devoted themselves for ministry to the saints). (1 Corinthians 16:15 NASB)

In the exercise of His will *He brought us forth* by the word of truth, so that we would be a kind of *first fruits* among His creatures. (James 1:18 NASB)

4) The 144,000 in Revelation

And they *sang a new song before the throne and before the four living creatures and the elders; and no one could learn the song except the *one hundred and forty-four thousand* who had been *purchased from the earth*. These are the ones who have not been defiled with women, for they have kept themselves chaste. These *are* the ones who *follow the Lamb wherever He goes*. These have been purchased from among men as *first fruits* to God and to the Lamb. And no lie was found in their mouth; they are blameless. (Revelation 14:3-5 NASB)

So, in this offering of the first fruits, we see yet another *type* of Christ and of Christianity. I will concede that this is one of the more subtle Old Testament types of Christ.

10. Altar of Uncut Stones Coated with Lime (Type/Shadow)

And it shall be on the day *when ye shall pass over Jordan unto the land which the* Lord *thy God giveth thee, that thou shalt set thee up great stones, and plaister them with plaister:* And *thou shalt write upon them all the words of this law,* when thou art passed over, that thou mayest go in unto the land which the Lord thy God giveth thee, a land that floweth with milk and honey; as the Lord God of thy fathers hath promised thee. Therefore it shall be when ye be gone over Jordan, that *ye shall set up these stones,* which I command you this day, *in mount Ebal*, and thou shalt *plaister them* with plaister. And there shalt thou *build an altar unto the* LORD *thy God*, an altar of stones: *thou shalt not lift up any iron tool upon them.* Thou shalt build the altar of the LORD thy God of whole stones: and thou shalt offer *burnt offerings* thereon unto the LORD thy God: And thou shalt offer *peace offerings,* and shalt eat there, and rejoice before the LORD thy God. And *thou shalt write upon the stones all the words of this law very plainly.* (Deuteronomy 27:2–8)

As Moses continues his final instructions to the people who are about to cross over to Canaan, he instructs them to build an altar on Mount Ebal. Moses was about to introduce them to the two mountains Ebal, the mountain of cursing, and Gerizim, the mountain of blessing. He commanded that the people be divided into two groups, six tribes for each group. One group would stand on Ebal, and the other group would stand on Gerizim. This is a very intriguing type. The altar was to be made of uncut stones. As we saw back in Exodus 20:4–6, the significance of uncut stones is that salvation is by grace alone, not of man's works, represented by a cutting tool and the labor of man. In this altar, we still see the requirement of uncut stones, but now we see an additional requirement—that they be coated with plaster, or lime in the NASB translation, and the words of the law be written therein. As I understand it, the law written on these stones would be the moral law, i.e., the Ten Commandments. The words of the law would be written in the soft plaster before it is set, then it would harden to yield a permanent record of the law on the memorial altar.

I find this to be a very intriguing *type* of Christ indeed. The uncut stones as already noted represent salvation by grace, but what about the coating of plaster with the law engraved therein? Jesus became a perfect sacrifice by perfectly fulfilling the law. You may recall Jesus's words from the Sermon on the Mount.

> *Think not that I am come to destroy the law, or the prophets: I am not come to destroy, but to fulfil.* For verily I say unto you, Till heaven and earth pass, one jot or one tittle shall in no wise pass from the law, till all be fulfilled. (Matthew 5:17–18)

Again, in Hebrews we see the following:

> Who *in the days of his flesh*, when he had offered up prayers and supplications with strong crying and tears unto him that was able to save him from death, and was heard in that he feared; *Though he were a Son, yet learned he obedience* by the things which he suffered; And *being made perfect, he became the author of eternal salvation unto all them that obey him*; (Hebrews 5:7–9)

So, you see that perfectly fulfilling the law made Jesus the perfect sacrifice that is able to eternally cleanse those who put their trust in Him. If I may add a third aspect of this type,

219

the fact that this lime coating *covered* the stone altar is a picture of the fact that our sins are covered by the atoning blood of Jesus. We see this in Paul's writing to the Romans.

> Saying, Blessed are they whose iniquities are forgiven, and *whose sins are covered*. Blessed is the man to whom the Lord will not impute sin. (Romans 4:7–8)

So, we see in this one *type* that

1) Salvation is not by works (uncut stones)
2) Jesus perfectly kept the law (the law engraved in lime)
3) Jesus's perfect sacrifice covers our sins (the lime coating with the law covering the altar of uncut stones).

11. God Will Circumcise Your Heart (Type/Shadow)

> And the LORD thy God will bring thee into the land which thy fathers possessed, and thou shalt possess it; and he will do thee good, and multiply thee above thy fathers. And *the LORD thy God will circumcise thine heart, and the heart of thy seed*, to love the LORD thy God with all thine heart, and with all thy soul, that thou mayest live. (Deuteronomy 30:5–6)

This is a picture of the New Covenant in Christ that God promised in the book of Jeremiah. Although it was promised to the house of Israel and the house of Judah, it is also available to all who put their trust in Christ for salvation.

> Behold, the days come, saith the LORD, that I will make *a new covenant* with the house of Israel, and with the house of Judah: Not according to the covenant that I made with their fathers in the day that I took them by the hand to bring them out of the land of Egypt; which my covenant they brake, although I was an husband unto them, saith the LORD: But *this shall be the covenant that I will make* with the house of Israel; After those days, saith the LORD, *I will put my law in their inward parts, and write it in their hearts; and will be their God*, and *they shall be my people. And they shall teach no more every man his neighbour, and every man his brother, saying, Know the LORD: for they shall all know me*, from the least of them unto the greatest of them, saith the LORD: for I will forgive their iniquity, and I will remember their sin no more. (Jeremiah 31:31–34)

In fact, it was inaugurated by Jesus at the Last Supper with His disciples.

> And when the hour was come, he sat down, and the twelve apostles with him. And he said unto them, *With desire I have desired to eat this passover with you*

before I suffer: For I say unto you, I will not any more eat thereof, until it be fulfilled in the kingdom of God. And he took the cup, and gave thanks, and said, Take this, and divide it among yourselves: For I say unto you, I will not drink of the fruit of the vine, until the kingdom of God shall come. And he *took bread, and gave thanks, and brake it,* and gave unto them, saying, *This is my body which is given for you: this do in remembrance of me.* Likewise *also the cup after supper, saying, This cup is the new testament in my blood, which is shed for you.* (Luke 22:14–20)

Although Jesus had told His disciples numerous times that He was going to be handed over to evil men to be killed, I'm of the opinion that His disciples did not understand *the reason* He was going to be turned over. In the three synoptic gospels, Matthew, Mark, and Luke, Jesus plainly told the disciples that He was going to die and, on the third day, rise from the dead (Matthew 16:21; 17:22–23; 20:17–19; Mark 8:31; 9:31–32; 10:32–34; Luke 9:22, 44–45; 18:31–34). However, in Mark 9:32 and Luke 9:45, we read that the disciples did not understand what Jesus meant and were afraid to ask Him. Also, in none of these passages does Jesus explain the reason that He will be handed over and killed. In Mark 10:45, Jesus says, "For even the Son of man came not to be ministered unto, but to minister, and *to give his life a ransom for many*," but you must admit, that's pretty cryptic. We know in John 14:1–6 that Jesus told His disciples that He was going to prepare a place for them and come again to take them to be with Him, and that "I am the way, the truth, and the life: no man cometh unto the Father, but by me," but did they understand how His death would bring life? I doubt it.

So, on that fateful night when they were gathered around the supper table, they were prepared to have a *Passover* meal with Jesus. In all three synoptic gospels, Jesus gave them instructions to prepare for the Passover meal. In Luke 22:15, Jesus says, "I have earnestly desired to eat this Passover with you before I suffer:" So there they were, somberly reclining around the table, eating the Passover meal, when Jesus broke bread and told them, "This is My body which is given for you …" and later He takes the cup and says, "This cup which is poured out for you is the *New Covenant* in My blood." What a monumental event! One moment they were eating a Passover meal with Jesus, and the next, they learn that Jesus Himself is the Passover! I can only imagine the looks on the disciples' faces as they heard these two sayings.

So back to the *type "The Lord Thy God will circumcise thine heart …"* The only way that God circumcises hearts today is through the new birth, which is through Christ. Paul noted in Romans 4 that the ordinance of circumcision predated the law and that it was the seal of Abraham's righteousness which he had before circumcision (v. 11). So God's proclamation that He would circumcise the hearts of the Israelites and Jeremiah's prophesy of the New Covenant pointed to the coming of Jesus Christ.

12. Song of Moses (Type/Shadow)

Deuteronomy 32

This song is Moses's song of praise to God in the hearing of the people. It praises God for His mighty acts and His lovingkindness toward His people. There are some interesting *types* of Christ in this song.

The Rock! (vv. 4, 13, 15, 18, 30–31, 37): We've encountered this rock before, which is used metaphorically to describe God and is also a *type* of Christ. The Rock was previously seen in Exodus 17 and in Numbers 20, and it is repeated in this song seven times! The rock as referring to Christ is also affirmed in Psalm 118:22–24, which speaks of Jesus as the cornerstone rejected by the builders. It is further seen in the second chapter of Daniel as the stone that was cut out without hands that struck the statue in Nebuchadnezzar's dream at its feet and destroyed it, which portrays the Second Coming of Christ! This is also affirmed in the New Testament in Acts 4:11, Ephesians 2:20, and 1 Peter 2:7 that Jesus is indeed the cornerstone, and in Matthew 21:42, Jesus quoted this psalm as referring to Himself. In 1 Corinthians 10:1–4, Paul speaks of "that spiritual rock which followed them; and that rock is Christ."

Is not He your Father who bought you? (v. 6): Recall, in Exodus, how God brought the ten plagues against Egypt and Pharaoh. So in what sense did God *buy* the Israelites? You recall the Passover lamb, which was slain, and his blood was brushed onto the doorpost and lintel of each Israelite home. Also recall the death angel, who brought the death of the firstborn male in every Egyptian household but passed over the Israelite houses that had the blood applied. We know that this pointed to the blood of Christ our Savior!

Of the blood of grapes you drank wine (v. 14): We see this phrase "the blood of grapes" here and in Genesis 49:11 in Jacob's prophecy concerning Judah. It is an interesting interplay of words *blood* and *grapes*. I see it as a prophetic allusion to the Lord's Supper, in which Jesus passed the cup to His disciples, stating that it signified the New Covenant in His blood.

The rock of his salvation (v. 15): This is one of the instances of "the Rock" noted above, which in each case refers to God. In this case, the Rock is the rock of *Israel's* Salvation. The word *salvation* appears over 119 times in the Old Testament, and this is yet another *type* of Christ as the Savior of the world. We are told in Isaiah 43:11 and 45:21 that there is no Savior besides God, so the phrase "rock of … salvation" is a reference both to Christ's deity and to Him as Savior.

The rock who begot you (v. 18): This reference to God as "the rock who begot you" points to the new birth that is only available through Jesus, God the Son, as later explained by Jesus to Nicodemus in John 3:1–8.

See now that I am He, and there is no god besides Me (v. 39): God makes it very clear that He is the only God. All others are simply inventions of mankind. In the gospel of John, Jesus used as a title God's name I Am in John 8:58 and in John 18:6, when the guards revealed that they were seeking Jesus, He responded "I am He," at which point they drew back and fell to the ground. Note in the latter reference that *He* is italicized, meaning that it was inserted by the translators, and not part of the original. You may recall in Exodus 3, when Moses asked God His name, God responded "I Am." In using that title, Jesus was proclaiming Himself as God. In Isaiah 45:21, we read, "Tell ye, and bring them near; yea, let them take counsel together: who hath declared this from ancient time? who hath told it from that time? have not I the LORD? and *there is no God* else *beside me*; a just God and a *Saviour; there is none beside me.*" So this is a *type* of Christ, in that it looks forward to Christ using the title of God for Himself.

So, this concludes our journey through Deuteronomy, concluding the Pentateuch, while exploring prophetic material pointing to Christ.

Summary of Prophetic Elements in Deuteronomy

1.	Cities of Refuge	(OT Language and Culture)
2.	Sabbatical Year, Bondslave	(Type/Shadow)
3.	Passover and Feast of Unleavened Bread	(Type/Shadow)
4.	Prophecy of Kings	(Prophecy, Type/Shadow)
5.	A Prophet Like Moses	(Prophecy, Type/Shadow)
6.	Expiation of a Crime Sacrifice	(OT Language and Culture)
7.	Don't Mix Seeds, Threads, Animals	(OT Language and Culture)
8.	Duty of a Brother, Levirate Marriage	(Type/Shadow)
9.	Offering of First Fruits	(OT Language and Culture)
10.	Altar of Uncut Stones Coated with Lime	(Type/Shadow)
11.	God Will Circumcise Your Heart	(Type/Shadow)
12.	Song of Moses	(Type/Shadow)

NOTES (CHAPTER 13)

[1] Mark Levitt, *The Jewish Holidays*, John Parsons, ed., Hebrew4Christians. Zola Levitt Ministries, hebrew4christians.com/Holidays/Introduction/introduction.html#:~:text=It%20was%20on%20Mount%20Sinai%20that%20God%20gave,Sivan%206-7%20Trumpets%20%28Yom%20Teru%27ah%29%20-%20Tishri%201 (accessed 09/26/24)

14

CONCLUSION

WELL, CONGRATULATIONS ON MAKING IT TO THE END OF THE BOOK. HOPEFULLY, YOU'VE learned some things along the way and have enjoyed the journey. Hopefully, you've gained a greater appreciation for the Bible—its uniqueness in the annals of literature and its glorious and compelling message of the gospel. You've also gotten an overview of the subject of Old Testament messianic prophecy—(1) its affirmation in the New Testament, (2) the covenantal nature of it, and (3) the various ways that it is conveyed. You have also seen examples of these various prophetic devices in our journey through the Pentateuch.

Hopefully, you've also gained a greater appreciation for the Old Testament in general, and for the book of Leviticus in particular—although it might seem boring to read, it contains some rich truth and is the backdrop for our understanding of Christ as our Eternal High Priest. Also, the spreadsheet in table1.1 is based on the rather boring-to-read genealogies in Genesis 5 and 11, but they connect the creation account to recorded history and facilitate the construction of timelines like the one in figure 1.1. The book of Hebrews is probably the most important book in the New Testament in understanding the Old Testament's purpose as a "tutor to lead us to Christ." (Galatians 3:23-24)

Concerning point 3 above in the first paragraph, consider the following introduction given by the author of the book of Hebrews.

> God, after He spoke long ago to the fathers in the prophets *in many portions and in many ways*, In these last days has spoken to us in His Son, whom He appointed heir of all things, through whom also He made the world. And He is the radiance of His glory and the exact representation of His nature, and upholds all things by the word of His power. (Hebrews 1:1-3)

Regarding point 2 in that paragraph, the covenantal nature of OT messianic prophecy informs us that the gospel is reliable because it stands on the very promises of God. The author of Hebrews is writing to the Jews to encourage them not to abandon their newfound Christian faith and return to the religion of their upbringing. He then proceeds to show them how the Old Testament points to Christ and the New Covenant as noted below.

Jesus Is God's Son

For to which of the angels did He ever say, "You are My Son, Today I have begotten You"? (Hebrews 1:5, Psalm 2:7 NASB)

But of the Son *He says*, "Your throne, O God, is forever and ever, And the righteous scepter is the scepter of His kingdom. (Hebrews 1:8, Psalm 45:6 NASB)

Jesus Is Superior to Angels

And when He again brings the firstborn into the world, He says, "And let all the angels of God worship Him." (Hebrews 1:6, Psalm 97:7 NASB)

Jesus Is Superior to Moses

For He has been counted worthy of more glory than Moses, by just so much as the builder of the house has more honor than the house. (Hebrews 3:3 NASB)

Jesus Is a Better High Priest

The *former* priests, on the one hand, existed in greater numbers because they were prevented by death from continuing, but Jesus, on the other hand, because He continues forever, holds His priesthood permanently. Therefore *He is able also to save forever those who draw near to God through Him, since He always lives to make intercession for them.* (Hebrews 7:23-25 NASB)

For we do not have a high priest who cannot sympathize with our weaknesses, but *One who has been tempted in all things as we are, yet without sin.* Therefore let us draw near with confidence to the throne of grace, so that we may receive mercy and find grace to help in time of need. (Hebrews 4:15-16 NASB)

Jesus is a Perfect High Priest

Although He was a Son, He learned obedience from the things which He suffered. *And having been made perfect,* He became to all those who obey Him the source of eternal salvation, being designated by God as a high priest according to the order of Melchizedek. (Hebrews 5:8-10 NASB)

Melchizedek is that enigmatic figure that we read about earlier in Genesis 14.

God Planned from the Beginning for the New Covenant in Christ

> For if that first *covenant* had been faultless, there would have been no occasion sought for a second. For finding fault with them, He says, "BEHOLD, DAYS ARE COMING, SAYS THE LORD, WHEN I WILL EFFECT A NEW COVENANT WITH THE HOUSE OF ISRAEL AND WITH THE HOUSE OF JUDAH; NOT LIKE THE COVENANT WHICH I MADE WITH THEIR FATHERS ON THE DAY WHEN I TOOK THEM BY THE HAND TO LEAD THEM OUT OF THE LAND OF EGYPT;... (Hebrews 8:7-9, Jeremiah 31:31-32 NASB)

The New Covenant in Christ Is Superior to the Old Covenant

> But when Christ appeared *as* a high priest of the good things to come, *He entered* through *the greater and more perfect tabernacle, not made with hands,* that is to say, not of this creation; and not through the blood of goats and calves, but through His own blood, *He entered the holy place once for all, having obtained eternal redemption.* For if the blood of goats and bulls and the ashes of a heifer sprinkling those who have been defiled sanctify for the cleansing of the flesh, *how much more will the blood of Christ, who through the eternal Spirit offered Himself without blemish to God, cleanse your conscience from dead works to serve the living God?* (Hebrews 9:11-14 NASB)

With this backdrop from the book of Hebrews, let us review the things we have seen in Genesis through Deuteronomy. Table 14.1—Summary of OT Messianic Prophetic Material is shown on the following pages. It summarizes the material in chapters 9–13 (Genesis—Deuteronomy) and serves as an index to those chapters.

Book	No.	Primary Passage(s)	Title	Prophetic Device	Messianic Prophetic Genealogy	How Prophetic of Christ
Genesis	1	1:1,26-27; 3:22; 11:5-9	The Holy Trinity	OT Language & Culture		Jesus, 2nd member of Trinity
	2	3:15	Protoevangelium	Prophecy	Eve	First Prophecy of Christ
	3	3:21	Garments of Skin	Type / Shadow		Blood Sacrifice > Christ
	4	4:4-5	Cain's & Abel's Offering	Type / Shadow		Blood Sacrifice > Christ
	5	See Figure 9.1	Genealogies	Covenantal Genealogy	All	Messianic Genealogy
	6	5:21-24	Enoch's Rapture	Type / Shadow		Rapture of Church
	7	5:32 - 9:17	Noah's Ark	Type / Shadow		Picture of Redemption
	8	12:1-3	Abraham	Prophecy, Prophetic Genealogy	Abraham	Prophetic Genealogy
	9	14:17-20	Melchizedek	Type/Shadow or Christophany		Type or Preincarnate Christ
	10	18:1-5	Visitation of Abraham by God	Theophany		Christ, Immanuel
	11a	21	Birth of Isaac	Type/Shadow, Prophetic Genealogy	Isaac	Type/Shadow, Prophetic Genealogy
	11b	15:2-4, 16:1-4,11-12, 17:1-22, 21:1?	Hagar / Sarah Allegory	Prophetic Allegory		The Law vs Grace
	12	22	Abraham & Isaac, Human Sacrifice	Type / Shadow		Picture of John 3:16
	13	25 - 47	Jacob; Israel - Father of Jewish nation	Prophetic Genealogy	Jacob	Prophetic Genealogy
	14	37 - 50	Joseph	Type / Shadow		Person Type of Christ
	15	49:8-12	Judah	Prophetic Genealogy, Type/Shadow	Judah	Prophesied tribe of Jesus
Exodus	1	Multiple (see Chapter 10)	Moses as a Type	Type / Shadow		Moses' life picture of Christ
	2	1:8,15-22;2:1-9	Moses' deliverance....as a baby	Type / Shadow		miracle birth, children slain
	3	3:1 - 4:7	The Burning Bush	Theophany, Prophecy		God appears, God's Name
	4	12:1-14	The Passover	Type / Shadow		Picture of Crucifixion, Atonement
	5	30:18-22	Pillar of Fire and Cloud	Theophany		Christ, Immanuel
	6	14:13-31	Crossing of the Red Sea	Type / Shadow		Picture of N T Baptism
	7	16:2-4,11-15,31	Manna	Type / Shadow		Picture of Christ the Bread of Life
	8	17:1-7	Water from a Rock	Type / Shadow		Water & Rock types of Christ
	9	20:24-26	Not Just Any Altar	Type / Shadow		Salvation not of works
	10	24:1-2,8-12,18	God Appears to Moses, Sprinkling Blood	Theophany, Type/Shadow		God with us, blood atonement
	11	25 - 30	Tabernacle as a Pattern of Worship	Type / Shadow		Tabernacle portrays Christ
	12	28	High Priest, picture of Christ	Type / Shadow		Jesus, our eternal High Priest
	13	34:29-35	Moses face shone	Type / Shadow		Picture of Transfiguration
	14	35:1-3	Sabbath	Type / Shadow		Picture of resting in Christ

Book	#	Reference	Description	Type	Fulfillment
Leviticus	1	1 - 5, 17:11	Sacrificial System & Priesthood	Type / Shadow	Picture of Blood Atonement
	2	1:2-6, 3:2-13, 4:4-33, 8:14-30	Identification with the sacrifice	Type / Shadow	Christ's substitutionary death
	3	13 - 15	Laws on Leprosy & Uncleaness	Type / Shadow	Christ's blood ceanses
	4	16	Day of Atonement	Type / Shadow	Christ our eternal High Priest
	5	21 - 22	Regulatons for the Priests	Type / Shadow	Pictures Christ's Sinlessness
	6	24:1-9	Lamp and Bread of Sanctuary	Type / Shadow	Light of the World, Bread of Life
	7	25	Sabbatical Year, Year of Jubilee	Type / Shadow	Christ's redemption
	8	25:23-56	Law of Redemption, Kinsman-Redeemer	Type / Shadow	Christ our Redeemer
Numbers	1	8:5-22	Ordination of the Levites	OT Language & Culture	Picture of the Church
	2	9:1-5	Second Passover Observance	Type / Shadow	Picture of Crucifixion, Atonement
	3	9:15-23	Pillar of Cloud and Fire	Theophany	Christ, Immanuel
	4	17:1-10	Aaron's Rod that Budded	Type / Shadow	Christ's Crucifixion, Resurrection
	5	19:1-10	Ashes of a Red Heifer for Purification	Type / Shadow	Christ' cleanses from sin
	6	20:8-13	Water from the Rock	Type / Shadow	Water & Rock types of Christ
	7	21:4-9	Fiery Serpents and Bronze Serpent	Type / Shadow	Picture of the Crucifixion
	8	22:22-35	Angel of the Lord & Balaam	Theophany or Christophany	Christ, Immanuel
	9	23:7-12,18-24; 24:3-9,15-19	Balaam's Prophecies	Prophecy	Israel progenitor of Christ & Christ
	10	27:15-19,22-23	Joshua a Type of Christ	Type / Shadow	Crossed Jordan, Same Name
	11	35:6-34	Cities of Refuge	Type / Shadow	Picture of Christ our Refuge
Deuteronomy	1	4:41-43, 19:1-3, Joshua 20:7-9	Cities of Refuge (locations)	OT Language & Culture	Picture of Christ our Refuge
	2	15:1-3,12-14,16-17	Sabbatical Year, Bondslaves	Type / Shadow	Freedom in Christ, Picture of Us
	3	16:1-8	Passover and Other Feasts	Type / Shadow	All Feasts portray Christ
	4	17:14-20	Prophecy of the Kings	Prophecy, Type/Shadow	Kings - Christ the King of Kings
	5	18:15-19	A Prophet Like Moses	Prophecy, Type/Shadow	Prophecy of Christ, Picture of Him
	6	21:1-9	Expiation of a Crime Sacrifice	OT Language & Culture	Christ's forgiveness Comprehensive
	7	22:9-11	Don't mix seeds, threads, animals	OT Language & Culture	Picture of Christ's sinlessness
	8	25:5-10	Duty of a Brother, Levirate Marriage	Type / Shadow	Pictures Christ as our Protector
	9	26:1-10	Offering of First Fruits	Type / Shadow	Salvation, Resurrection, Saints
	10	27:2-8	Altar of Uncut Stones Coated w/ Lime	OT Language & Culture	Saved by faith, Jesus' sinless life
	11	30:5-6	God will Circumcise Your Heart	Type / Shadow	Pictures New Covenant in Christ
	12	32	Song of Moses	Type / Shadow	Various Pictures of Christ
Total	**61**				

Table 14.1 - Summary of OT Messianic Prophetic Material

BIBLIOGRAPHY

1. Brand, Chad, Charles Draper, Archie England, Steve Bond, E. Ray Clendenen. Trent C. Butler, eds., Holman Illustrated Bible Dictionary (Nashville: Holman Bible Publishers, 2003)

2. Flexner, Stuart Berg, Eugene Ehrlich, Gorton Carruth, Joyce M Hawkins. Oxford American Dictionary, Heald College Edition, (New York, Avon, 1986)

3. Francis, James Allen. The Real Jesus and Other Sermons (Philadelphia: Judson Press, 1926, http://www. davidschrock.com/2013/12/16/one-solitary life/

4. Henry, Matthew. Matthew Henry's Commentary on the Whole Bible, Volume V – Matthew to John, (New Jersey: Fleming H. Revell Company), 1975)

5. Josephus, Flavius. The Works of Flavius Josephus / Translated by William Whiston, Antiquities, 18.3.3, (Nashville: Thomas Nelson, 1998)

6. Levitt, Mark *The Jewish Holidays*, John Parsons, ed., Hebrew4Christians. Zola Levitt Ministries, hebrew4christians.com/Holidays/Introduction/introduction. html#:~:text=It%20was%20on%20Mount%20Sinai%20that%20God%20gave,Sivan%20 6-7%20Trumpets%20%28Yom%20Teru%27ah%29%20-%20Tishri%201

7. Lewis, C. S. Mere Christianity (C. S. Lewis Pte. Ltd., 1952, Copyright renewed 1980 C.S. Lewis Pte. Ltd.)

8. McDowell, Josh. Evidence That Demands a Verdict (Campus Crusade for Christ, Inc., 1972)

9. Mulroy, Clare, "How Many Died in 9/11? A Look at the Tragic Attack 23 Years Ago," *USA Today*, September 11, 2024,http://www.usatoday.com/story/news/2024/09/10/how-many-people-died-in-911/75150354007/ (accessed 09/20/24)

10. *NASB Side-Column Reference Edition*, (Anaheim: The Lockman Foundation, 1996), footnote for Matthew 26:53, 48

11. Nijssen, Daan, Cyrus the Great, World History Encyclopedia, last modified February 21, 2018, https://www.worldhistory.org/Cyrus_the_Great/ (accessed 09/13/24)

12. Poole, Gary William. Flavius Josephus, Jewish Priest, Scholar, and Historian, last updated: 09/10/24, http:// www.britannica.com/biography/Flavius-Josephus

13. Religion by Country 2024. World Population Review, https://worldpopulationreview.com/ country-rankings/religion-by-country

14. Strong, James. The New Strong's Expanded Exhaustive Concordance of the Bible, Red Letter Edition (Nashville: Thomas Nelson, 2010)

15. Tenney, Merrill C. and J. D. Douglas. The Zondervan Pictorial Bible Dictionary, (Grand Rapids: Zondervan, 1999)

16. Walvoord, John F., and Roy B. Zuck, eds., The Bible Knowledge Commentary, New Testament (Colorado Springs: David C Cook, 1983)

17. Walvoord, John F., and Roy B. Zuck, eds., The Bible Knowledge Commentary, Old Testament, (Colorado Springs: David C Cook, 1985)